Far From the Reservation

The Transracial Adoption
of American Indian Children

A study conducted under the auspices of
The Child Welfare League of America,
New York, New York

by

DAVID FANSHEL

The Scarecrow Press, Inc.
Metuchen, N.J.   1972

362.734
Fan
c. 2

ISBN 0-8108-0454-9

Library of Congress Catalog Card Number 78-181701

This study was conducted under:
Research Grant R-151
Child Welfare Research and Demonstration Grants Program
Community Services Administration
Social and Rehabilitation Service
Department of Health, Education and Welfare

PREFACE

Membership in a minority racial group is often the sole factor which precludes the possibility of adoption for a child deprived of adequately functioning natural parents. The study reported here describes the experiences of 97 American Indian children who were adopted by white families. The children came from reservations in widely scattered parts of the country. They had been identified by social workers as being likely to spend their childhood years in indeterminate living arrangements; a succession of foster homes or boarding schools seemed to be their fate.

As described by Arnold Lyslo in Chapter II, the Indian Adoption Project was a cooperative undertaking of the Bureau of Indian Affairs of the Department of Interior and the Child Welfare League of America. From September, 1958 through December 31, 1967, there were 395 American Indian children placed through this joint effort. The placement of these children represents a significant effort to use the vehicle of adoption as a possible solution to the lifelong dilemma faced by minority group children whose parents have been defeated by life's circumstances.

The objectives of this research were twofold. One goal was to develop systematic knowledge about the characteristics of the couples who adopted the children. It was hoped thereby to gain increased understanding about the phenomenon of adoption across ethnic and racial lines. A second objective was to develop a picture of the experiences encountered by the families and children for a five-year period after the children were placed. If the placements proved viable and resulted in secure living situations for the children, with a minimum of developmental difficulties, agencies might thereby be encouraged to become increasingly venturesome in their placement policies.

The study was launched in 1960 and, because of the modest pace of the placement of the children it took five years to develop the full sample of adoptive families to receive the first of

iii

five annual interviews. Thus, the study stretches from 1960 to the end of the decade.

Many individuals contributed to this research enterprise. I am particularly appreciative of the cooperation of Arnold L. Lyslo who, as director of the Indian Adoption Project, made all of the necessary arrangements with the adoption agencies to make it possible for the families to participate in the research. As the director of the effort to secure adoptive homes for American Indian children, he provided invaluable assistance to me in a variety of ways.

I have very warm feelings of respect and friendship for Mary Davis who performed service beyond her energies in carrying the brunt of field interviewing in so many different states. Being "out on the road" can be stressful, but this did not interfere with her ability to develop positive working relationships with the adoptive families; so many of them have expressed appreciation for her considerateness and sensitivity in carrying out her interviewing tasks. I am also very indebted to my old friend and colleague, Rhoda Fishleder, who carried major interviewing responsibilities in the New York area. Her incisive clarity about human relations and her penetrating observations gave me many leads in pursuing this research. I am also appreciative of the efforts of Trude Bettelheim who picked up on interviewing tasks in the Midwest during the later stages of the project.

This project was financed by the Child Welfare Research and Demonstration Grants Program of the Children's Bureau, Social and Rehabilitation Service, Department of Health, Education and Welfare. The support I have received over the years from Dr. Charles P. Gershenson, now Director of Research and Evaluation, Office of Child Development, Department of Health, Education and Welfare, provides a model of the helping relationship between a research funding institution and scholars. The splendid development of child welfare research in the United States during the 1960's is a reflection of his careful nurturing of scholarship related to the welfare of children.

The research described here was initially developed on the basis of a grant from the Elizabeth McCormick Fund of Chicago. The executive of the Fund in the late 1950's, Donald Brieland, has remained an interested and helpful adviser on matters related to child welfare research. I also wish to note, with thanks, the firm support for independent scholarship received from Joseph H. Reid, Executive

Director of the Child Welfare League of America. Over the years, leading child welfare researchers have come to regard him as an understanding friend. I also wish to thank Ann W. Shyne, Research Director of the League for her helpful prodding when the final completion of the manuscript seemed so elusive.

I have been blessed with helpful assistance from most understanding and highly gifted secretaries. Elissa Queyquep provided stalwart help in the early years. In the final typing of the manuscript, Ann Gerlock patiently and skillfully made logic and order out of my scribbled notes and facilitated my work enormously.

I have received sound research advice over the years from Edgar F. Borgatta. I don't always listen to him, and when this happens, I usually learn to regret it. Jacob Cohen has also been very helpful in offering research consultation at various points in the research.

The coders who have worked for me from 1960 to 1968 are legion. I believe I was the major employer, for a time, of college students in the New York area. My appreciative thanks are offered to Susan Fanshel, Mallory Pepper, Marsha Goldman, Mike Phillips, Nora Fanshel, Marcia Kreitzer and Dora Lietz.

The agencies who cooperated in this endeavor are listed in the appendix. I thank them for being so helpful. Charles Rovin, Chief, Branch of Welfare of the Bureau of Indian Affairs was helpful in orienting me to some of the materials available about Indian affairs.

The families who participated in the study deserve special thanks. Their willingness to participate in annual research interviews made this study possible. I wish them and their adopted children lives rich in meaningful experiences and happiness.

To my wife, Florence, and my children, Ethan and Merrie, I give my love and appreciation for bearing up so well with the untidy computer output strewn around the house, my absorption in my data, and my irritability when my computer runs bombed out.

David Fanshel

New York
March, 1971

CONTENTS

FOREWORD

The Indian Adoption Project was initiated in 1958 by the Child Welfare League of America and the Bureau of Indian Affairs out of concern to open up the option of adoptive placement to the American Indian child whose own parents are unable to provide a home for him. Adoptive placement of the child in a family which could provide him with emotional support and meet his physical needs was assumed to be preferable to the more readily available options of transient placement in foster homes, life in an institution, or informal arrangements for care in homes which are often unable to meet the child's material or psychological needs. As few Indian families were to be found among adoptive applicants, who were, and continue to be, predominantly Caucasian, adoptive placements were sought for Indian children with Caucasian families.

That adoptive homes are available to Indian children was quickly attested to by the number of adoptive placements made. By 1968, when the Indian Adoption Project was incorporated in the Adoption Resource Exchange of North America (ARENA), a program designed to facilitate the adoption of all children who were seen as hard-to-place, 395 Indian children had already been placed for adoption, and it was beginning to be apparent that the Indian child was not "hard-to-place."

The early adoptive placements were far from the reservation geographically as well as culturally. In fact, well over half the 395 placements were made in the Eastern states. However, the receptivity of families in distant states led agencies in the children's home states to take a new look at the Indian child's adoptibility, with the result that more Indian children were adopted by Caucasian families in the states in which the Indian children had their origins. Even as the geographic distance is lessened, the cultural distance remains.

The research reported here was undertaken to explore the nature of the adoptions arranged through the Indian adoption project--the motives of the parents in adopting an Indian child, their backgrounds and social attitudes, the experiences of the children with their adoptive families, and their development and adjustment in their new families. Following the children for five years until they were, on the average, six years of age, David Fanshel found that the children had fared well physically, intellectually and emotionally and that the parents were highly satisfied with their experience in having adopted an Indian child. The adoptive parents were by no means a homogeneous group, coming as they did from a diversity of backgrounds and exhibiting a wide range of social attitudes. The writer has identified a number of characteristics in child and family that are associated to some degree with the success of the adoption, as indicated by the child's adjustment and the adoptive parents' satisfaction. As of the time when the children were about six years old, the weight of the evidence suggests that the placement of Indian children with Caucasian families had proved a desirable option.

This research does not, and could not, answer the question of the significance of the cultural distance the children have traveled from the reservation. Many of the families took a strong interest in the Indian backgrounds of their children and planned to encourage the children's interest in their heritage. The children were still too young to judge how well they had integrated the fact of their difference from their parents. Even if later follow-up were to show continued good adjustment on the part of the children and absence of problems of identity, there remains the issue that Dr. Fanshel discusses at the close of his report--is transracial adoption of Indian children sound? It is the position of the Child Welfare League of America that transracial adoption of American Indian children is a sound option until it is possible for all Indian children to be cared for by natural or adoptive Indian families. Justification for this position must be predicated on continuous support for efforts that help Indians improve their economic and social conditions and that expand and improve the health, educational and social services available to them toward this end.

Joseph H. Reid
Executive Director
Child Welfare League of America

Chapter I

INTRODUCTION TO THE RESEARCH

Prelude

The following letter was written in 1961 by a young
male social worker from a public welfare agency in the
southwestern part of the United States. He had just completed an unusual trip to a town over two thousand miles
away. Accompanying him on the first leg of this trip was a
six-year-old Indian girl. She did not return with him as the
letter will make clear. Names other than Mr. Lyslo's used
in the letter are fictitious; otherwise it is an exact replication of the original.

May 2, 1961

Mr. Arnold Lyslo, Director
Indian Adoption Project
Child Welfare League of America
44 East 23rd Street
New York 10, New York

Re: Anna Lovelace

Dear Mr. Lyslo:

It is a pleasure at this time to report on the
adoptive placement of Anna Lovelace. From the time I
picked Annie up at her foster home to the time I left her
with her new family in _____, the placement was surprisingly smooth. It was indeed a pleasure to work with
this very delightful child and it was gratifying to see her
placed in a good permanent home.

I had anticipated some problem at the time of departure from the foster home but there was none. Annie
was ready to go when I arrived and the good-bye's of the
foster parents was short and unemotional. It was easy
to see Annie's sorrow but she did not cry. When she got

into the car she sat in the back seat.   She took a book
out of her suitcase and sat for almost an hour looking at
the book.   There were tears in her eyes but never once
did she break down and cry.

It wasn't long before she began to look around and
talk and Annie mentioned with pride the fact that she
didn't cry when she left her parents.   From that point on,
the child was cheerful and happy throughout the trip and
the placement.   She brought out the pictures of the
Smiths which she had in her purse and stated, "Here is
my family."   She pointed out the picture that was her
favorite, one of her brother and sister.   This was quite
surprising to me as I had felt she paid little attention to
the pictures.   I was also surprised that she referred to
them as "my family."   She seemed at this point to have
accepted the idea that this was her family and that the
move was a permanent one.   She was not upset by this
and she apparently had confidence in the plan.

The long drive from the foster home to the munici-
pal airport in _____ was quite tiring for Annie and she
slept part of the way.   Once on the plane there was a
great deal to entertain her.   She clung hard to the arms
of the seat when the plane took off and she squealed with
delight when the plane rocked a little with the rough air.
I had colorbooks and clay for Annie to play with and these
two items occupied her time and entertained her very well
throughout her trip.   She also enjoyed reading to me from
the book which had been given to her by her first grade
teacher.

Upon arrival in New York Annie showed little sign
of fatigue.   She probably was tired but the excitement of
the day was keeping her going.   She delighted at the tall
buildings, which she compared with the tall pine trees we
had seen while traveling to the airport.   The escalator at
the airport was one of the highlights of the day, as was
the elevator ride in the hotel.

May I express again my appreciation for your help
in meeting us at the airport and getting us settled for the
night in New York.   Your assistance made that portion of
the trip much easier and more enjoyable for Annie and
myself.

It took Annie a little while to get to sleep that

night in New York but once asleep she slept well.   She
was very tired the next morning and it was hard for her
to wake up but, even so, she was cheerful and happy and
looking forward to the train ride to her "new family." She
asked several times during the trip how much longer before we get to "them."

    While riding the train from New York to _____ ,
I attempted to discuss the idea of meeting and staying
with her new family.   I asked Annie if she had thought
what she might say when she met her new mother. She
said she had not and it was obvious that she did not want
to talk about it.   She quickly changed the subject so I
did not push her to talk about the meeting.   Annie began
to draw a picture of all the things she had seen during
the trip.   This included the train on which we were riding, the river directly outside, the airplane we had rid-
den in and the mountains and trees we had come through
after we left the foster home.   She asked me to put it in
my briefcase to show to her "new family."

    At one time on the train Annie mentioned that if
she didn't like her new family she would be able to come
back.   I felt she was testing me to see if she might plan
on coming back.   I answered by saying we know she
would be happy and she interrupted my answer by saying,
"Oh, I know I'll be happy." At that point she seemed to
have accepted the permanence of the placement.   Her reactions after meeting the family indicated that she had fully accepted this as a permanent home.

    We were met in _____ by Mr. Roberts of
_____ Adoption Agency and taken to the hotel in
_____.   Annie was obviously tired and I asked her if
she would like to take a nap.   It was approximately
2:30 p.m.   Annie would not lie down so we had a quick
lunch and went out to meet her new family.   I had asked
Annie if she wanted to stay with her new family at their
home the first night or with me at the hotel.   She stated
that she preferred to stay at the hotel but later it was
found that her motive for wanting to stay in the hotel was
to ride the elevator.   When she found no elevator in the
hotel she was quite willing to stay with her family.

    The initial meeting was quite disappointing to me.
There was a great deal of confusion about the house and
there were so many people I could not tell who were

family members and who were not. I was sure the child
was confused also. Mrs. Smith moved too fast in getting
acquainted with Annie and the child was somewhat
frightened by her new mother. Jane Smith was quite
timid and her approach to the child was much slower.
It was just right for Annie, however, and she quickly
made a strong attachment to this ten year old girl. Had
it not been for Jane, I fear the whole experience would
have been very frightening for Annie. Mr. Smith was not
at home at the time we arrived. It was suggested that
Annie be told specifically who her family members were
as there were so many people around she might become
confused. Mrs. Smith was quite explicit in her introduc-
tions and in later contacts it was apparent that Annie had
remembered who belonged in her family.

When it appeared that Annie could get along alone
with the family, Mr. Roberts and I left telling her that we
would return in a couple of hours. We discussed the matter before returning and we determined that Annie should
stay in the hotel with me that first night. We felt this ad-
visable because of the confusion in the home. When we
returned to the home we found Annie getting along very
well. She was sitting with her shoes off, drinking root
beer and watching television. She was sitting very close
to Jane and whenever Jane moved, so did Annie. I felt
this a very good sign.

Mrs. Smith had a way of asking Annie questions
and giving her the answers at the same time. For example, "You don't want to go back to the hotel tonight,
do you?" In spite of Annie's answer to this question, we
took her back to the hotel. She went to bed early and
slept very well through the night. Just before she went
to sleep, after she had been reading to me, she stated
that she "really liked Jane." She was looking forward to
sleeping with her the following night.

The following morning I said nothing about going to
the new home. We had breakfast and I intended to walk
around the town with Annie before taking her to the
Smiths' home. This was intended to give her the opportunity to talk about the family and the home. Immediately after breakfast Annie asked, "When can I go back to
my family's?" I phoned Mrs. Smith and she came after
the child. (Mr. Roberts and I had arranged for this
earlier as Mr. Roberts was in _____ that morning.)

Later that evening Mr. Roberts and I went to the home
to see how things were going. Annie was playing with
Jane and some neighbor children and seemed to be enjoying herself. We had her suitcase with us and gave it to
her to unpack. We anticipated this would cause some
anxiety in the child, but there was none. She went up-
stairs with Jane and began unpacking the suitcase and putting her things in the drawer. I watched and listened
from a distance and Annie seemed to thoroughly enjoy
this operation. She was cheerful when she returned the
empty suitcase to me and apparently she was undisturbed
by this symbol of the fact that she was staying with her
"new family. "

On Friday morning, Mr. Roberts was working in
_____ so I went to the Smiths' alone to visit Annie and
her new family. When I arrived Annie was playing in the
barnyard and was enjoying herself immensely. I watched
her for a moment before she saw me. When she did see
me she came running up the hill to meet me. She ex-
citedly told me of all the things she had been doing, such
as riding the horse, driving the tractor, gathering eggs,
etc. I asked her to show me around her new home and
she did so. This gave us some time alone. As I would
probably be leaving the following morning, I asked her
if she was ready to stay with her new family. She said
she was. She was quick to leave the discussion and
point out things around the place. She showed me the
cows and told me not to be afraid as they wouldn't hurt
me. She even showed me where the milk came out. She
asked her brother to saddle the horse for her so she
could show me how she could ride. At this point she
seemed to be growing fond of her brother, Bill, the
fourteen year old. After the horse ride, she showed me
the rabbits, which were supposed to have babies any day
now, and the chickens. She took a stick and prodded the
chickens off their nests so she could show me how she
gathered the eggs. Again she told me not to be afraid
but to watch out for the rooster, "He was the mean
one. "

It seemed that the abundance of activity had helped
Annie to make a rapid adjustment to her new home. She
was becoming attached to other members of the family
now and she no longer seemed to fear Mrs. Smith or
Mr. Smith.

I had an opportunity to talk alone with Mrs. Smith before leaving that morning and things she told me indicated that Annie was adjusting well and that she had accepted this as her permanent family. Annie told Mrs. Smith that her "old family" had wanted to keep her but that Mr. Germain had told them he would bring them another little girl to take care of for a while. So then she had come to her "new family." Her reference to the foster parents as her "old family" and to the Smiths as her "new family" was viewed as a healthy sign. Mrs. Smith asked Annie if she would like Mr. Germain to come back next year with a baby brother for her to play with. Annie said no, she just wanted herself and Jane to be Mrs. Smith's children. After a little thought she added, "Maybe Stanley could come." This was the three year old boy in her foster home to whom she was very attached.

Annie had asked Mrs. Smith what they, being white people, would want with a "dark little Indian girl." Mrs. Smith gave a very good answer in explaining to Annie that they had asked for her especially and that it didn't matter what color her skin was, she wanted her for her very own. She told Annie that Indians were wonderful people and that Annie should be proud to have dark skin and Indian heritage. Mrs. Smith said her answer seemed to please Annie and she smiled and cuddled up to her a little.

Friday evening Mr. Roberts and I returned to the Smith home to tell Annie I was leaving. Annie was playing kick-ball with her brother and sister and some neighbor children. We had to go into the outfield to talk to Annie. She seemed unconcerned at my departing and we had to wait for her to chase a fly ball. We reminded her that Mr. Roberts was her new welfare man and he would be out to see her and help her get settled. Annie didn't leave the outfield when we drove away and she didn't miss a play.

From all indications Annie had made a good early adjustment to her new family and this placement would be very satisfactory. Although I had had some question about the family upon first meeting, before my departure I was quite convinced that this was a good adoptive home for Annie.

Mr. Roberts and his associates were most co-operative during the placement and it was a pleasure to work through this plan with them. It has been a genuine pleasure to work with you once again in this very worthy project for the placement of Indian children.

Sincerely,

Jack Germain
Child Welfare Worker

Background of the Research

This book is an account of the experiences of 97 American families living in 15 states who, like the Smith family, undertook to adopt children across racial lines. By adopting American Indian children, they embarked upon a relatively uncommon venture in American social life. They, in effect, became multi-racial families.

The children came from tribes located in 11 states. They reflected the broad range of physical types to be found among American Indians in the United States, showing great variation in coloring, physical features, and stature. They came from family situations where the oppression of poverty and the meanness of daily living--so familiar to American Indians--had exacted its toll. These were children identified by social workers on the reservations as being at great risk of growing up without any semblance of family life.

Arnold Lyslo provides background for the reader on the nature of the Indian Adoption Project which he directed. It served as the catalyst which brought together the American Indian children who are the concern of this study and their adoptive families. As he has indicated, a total of 395 American Indian children were placed for adoption in a nine-year period through this joint venture of the Bureau of Indian Affairs of the United States Department of Interior and the Child Welfare League of America. The children included in this study represent those placed in the earliest years of the cooperative effort.

The research described in this volume was undertaken for the purpose of portraying the nature of the experiences of the Indian children with their Caucasian

families over the five-year period following each child's
entrance into his adoptive home. In the course of a series
of annual interviews with the adoptive parents, I anticipated
that light would be shed upon their motives in departing from
the almost ubiquitous pattern of adoptive placement in the
United States whereby children are placed within families of
the same religious and racial backgrounds as their natural
parents. [1]

Since transracial adoption is still a relatively rare
phenomenon, it is important to become more knowledgeable
about the kinds of family backgrounds and social attitudes
that are characteristic of those who undertake such adoption. As I began to examine the phenomenon of transracial
adoptions, a number of questions began to get framed in my
mind: I began to wonder, for example, whether such adoptive parents tended to be politically more liberal than those
adopting within their own racial group. I hypothesized that
such parents would likely be more concerned than other
adoptive parents about the civil liberties of minority racial
groups. Given the individuality suggested by their choice
of ethnically different children, it seemed likely to me that
such parents would be relatively nonconformist in other
ways, e.g., in their orientation to religion, sex roles,
recreational interests and so forth. Thus, I was strongly
oriented in designing this research to get to know the
adoptive parents as people.

Another research objective in maintaining contact
with transracial adoptive parents was to learn as much as
possible about the nature of their living experience. I was
interested in learning all I could about the early "settling-
in" period experienced by the parents and the children.
I wanted to know how relatives and friends reacted to a
family's adoption of an American Indian child. I wanted
to ask the parents how the child was regarded by people
in the community and particularly by other children. Was
he treated in a fashion nondifferentiated from other children? Was he mistreated? I even wondered whether
parents might be worried that the child could perhaps be
regarded with excessive goodwill as some kind of pet.

I had a particularly strong interest in the matter of
the child's personal and social adjustment in the adoptive
home. I reasoned that the validity of each adoption agency's
decision joining together a Caucasian family and an Indian
child might be tested by the success of the parents in

helping the child to settle into the family and to develop a
sense of personal security and ease, and that this would be
reflected in the child's evolving personality and behavior.
Thus, a major emphasis of my research was upon various
aspects of the child's adjustment--his physical health, the
evolution of his personality, his mode of relating to other
children, the degree to which he was integrated within his
adoptive family, his social adjustment, his sociability, and
so forth.

Earlier Research in Adoption

This research did not suddenly emerge without ante-
cedents. My interest in adoption predated the project described here and my earlier experiences conditioned the way
I approached the study of Indian adoptions. My previous
work has included such research concerns as the experience
of Negro couples in seeking to adopt children, a comparative
analysis of emotional disturbance in adopted children as compared to other children known to out-patient psychiatric facilities, and a follow-up study of families who had adopted
children through four New York City adoption agencies 20 to
30 years before the study.[2] Some of the findings of my previous work, particularly the follow-up study, influenced the
kind of questions that I built into the interview schedules used
in the five annual visits to the adoptive homes. For example, Jaffee and I had found in our experience following up
adopted adults that the fact that a child was relatively older
at adoption and that he might have suffered several placement experiences was not, contrary to expectations, associated with a poor overall adjustment.[3] I was, therefore,
eager to assess adjustment in a variety of life-space areas
just as we had in the earlier study. The follow-up investigation had also failed to demonstrate any significant relationship between a variety of measures of the child-rearing tendencies of the adoptive parents and the kind of adjustments
shown by the children as they grew up. This surprising lack
of relationship seemed partly due to the weakness of the research design which required that child-rearing measures be
recorded, based upon the recall by parents of their modes of
caring for their children many years before. I expected that
some of the deficiencies of past research that I had been involved in would be corrected in the current study since it
was possible to interview the parents annually in relatively
early phases of their adoptive experience.

Time Perspective

        The research findings reported here should be seen
as only the beginning account of the experiences of our 96
families with transracial adoption. It has already been pointed
out that the research contacts with the families covered approximately a five-year period. The mean age of the adopted
children whose families were seen in the last series of interviews was six years and two months. Obviously I can only
describe how these adoptions are faring from the perspective
of early childhood. Yet, the use of the word "only" in connection with the research operations which took caseworker-
interviewers out into the field to widely scattered areas on
435 separate occasions is inappropriately modest. A block
of five years in the life of an adoptive family is, in fact, a
very substantial period of time, and since it represents the
crucial early experience, provides a significant preliminary
accounting of the adjustment of these families and their children.

        The research was built upon the model of the develop-
mental study which called for repeated data-gathering activity
over time. I saw several advantages of such a design over
a "one-shot" study in which the families would be seen on
only one occasion. A major positive feature was that repeated interviewing allowed for a picture to be developed of
the "settling-in" process--that is, the integration of the children into their adoptive families and the changes in their adjustment could be traced as they were displayed over a five-
year period. I felt that the reliability of parental reports
would also be more clearly established. Minimally, repeated
data gathering would make it possible to examine the stability
of child description measures as derived from parent interviews. It would not be surprising to have parents give rather
ecstatic reports of the course of the adoption in a single contact. Over five contacts, I would expect a "truer," less
emotionally colored account of the experience. I also expected that entry into the home on such a frequent basis
would increase the comfort of the adoptive families in cooperating with the research project, leading to greater rapport
and a more comfortable feeling about being the object of research scrutiny. From a long-range standpoint, it was my
hope that the willingness of the adoptive families to participate in the research would be sustained well into the adolescence and early adulthood of the adopted children when their
adjustment to work, courtship, and marriage could be surveyed.

American Indian Adoption as a
Particular Kind of Transracial Adoption

I should point out that this study does not pretend to
reflect upon the nature of the full range of transracial adoptions now being carried out in the United States, albeit on
modest levels. The reactions of the study families to questions about the kinds of minority group children they could
have considered for absorption into their homes makes clear
that the Indian child was not always viewed in the same manner as children of other minority groups. For example,
many adoptive parents indicated they could not have taken
Negro children. Thus, the present study sheds light on only
one form of transracial adoption. While what is learned
should have implications for agencies seeking to further transracial adoptions of a variety of kinds, the American Indian
child may have special sources of appeal to prospective adoptive parents not available to children of other racial minorities. For some people, the Indians are regarded with un-
abashed admiration as truly the "first Americans" or the
only "real" Americans. The Indian is the indigenous American rather than one who has his roots on foreign shores.
Not an insignificant number of Americans express pride in
having some Indian background in their family histories, however remote.

Even within the confines of an Indian adoption study,
some caveats about the "pureness" of transracial adopted
children ought be mentioned. Prior to the first research
interviews, it was anticipated that some of the parents would
raise questions as to whether their adoption was truly transracial. Some of the children placed were the offspring of
Indian mothers and white fathers and were not regarded by
their adoptive parents as being strikingly different in appearance. However, even where children were full-blooded and
obviously different looking, some parents might be inclined
to minimize the difference, perhaps on the grounds of their
being dark and swarthy themselves. Others might prefer
not to see the differences.

The Social Context of Adoption

Despite the affinity some Americans feel for the American Indian, this does not contradict the fact that prejudice
towards Indians, particularly in the southwestern section of
the United States, can be virulent. By taking the Indian child

great distances from the reservation on which he was born,
the Indian Adoption Project put him into a new social context.   More often than not, a child was placed in a community where he was something of an anomaly.   Most of the
children studied were the only, or one of a relatively few
Indian children in their respective localities.   In this investigation, I was interested in learning how the children were
received.   Were they well accepted by other children as
playmates?   Were they the object of staring in public places?
Did the adoptive parents anticipate that the children would
encounter problems in adolescence and later years when dating and courtship activities might put the matter of racial
difference into a new perspective?   I also had interest in
learning how the matter of their Indian background was handled with the children: would they be allowed to retain their
identity with their biological ancestors?   Would the fact of
the children's Indian background have a positive cathexis for
the parents and would this be transmitted to them?   Or,
would this feature of the children's past history be pushed
aside and handled perfunctorily or avoided entirely?

Why Adoption for Indian Children?

It is not my purpose in reporting upon this research
to demonstrate that transracial adoptions represent a solution for the problems of children living on Indian reservations.   Such an orientation would be absurd.   It is not difficult to establish, however, that some of the worst pockets
of poverty in the United States are those that afflict American Indians.   The following facts provide some perspectives
on this matter:

It was reported in 1962, when many of these adoptions
were being arranged, that the average reservation family had
an income of $1,500 and that unemployment on the reserva-
tions ran between 40 and 50 percent--seven or eight times
the national average.   Average schooling on the reservations
was only eight years--two-thirds of the national average.
Nine out of ten Indian families were reported to live in housing that was far below the minimum standard of comfort,
safety and decency.   More than half lived in one- or two-
room dwellings.   More than 80 percent of the Indians had
to haul or carry all the water for their household use.   Indian life expectancy was eight years below life expectancy
in the general population and the infant death rate was 70
percent higher than the rate for infants in the population as

a whole.   The tuberculosis death rate was almost six times higher than the rates of all the other races combined. [4]

In 1968, when the last of our interviews took place, the picture had not improved to any appreciable extent.   In his special message to the Congress on March 6, 1968, President Lyndon Johnson graphically portrayed the dismal condition of the "Forgotten American":

> There are about 600, 000 Indians in America today. Some 400, 000 live on or near reservations in 25 states.   The remaining 200, 000 have moved to our cities and towns.   The most striking fact about the American Indians today is their tragic plight:
>
> Fifty thousand Indian families live in unsanitary, dilapidated dwellings: many in huts, shanties, even abandoned automobiles.
>
> The unemployment rate among Indians is nearly 40 percent--more than ten times the national average.
>
> Fifty percent of Indian school children--double the national average--drop out before completing high school.
>
> Indian literacy rates are among the lowest in the nation; the rates of sickness and poverty are among the highest.
>
> Thousands of Indians who have migrated into the cities find themselves untrained for jobs and unprepared for urban life.
>
> The average age of death of an American Indian today is 44 years; for all other Americans, it is 65.

Among other grim facts revealed by this message are the following:

(With reference to education)--

> Ten percent of American Indians over age 14 have had no schooling at all; nearly 60 percent have less than an eighth grade education.

(With reference to health)--

The infant mortality rate among Indians is 34.5 per 1,000 births--12 points above the national average.

The incidence of tuberculosis among American Indians and Alaska natives is about five times the national average.

Viral infections, pneumonia, and malnutrition--all of which contribute to chronic ill health and mental retardation--are common among Indian children.

(With reference to economic conditions)--

Nearly 40 percent of the labor force on Indian lands is chronically unemployed, compared with a national unemployment rate of 3.5 percent.

Of the Indians who do work, a third are underemployed in temporary or seasonable jobs.

Fifty percent of Indian families have cash incomes below $2,000 a year; 75 percent have incomes below $3,000.

(With reference to housing and physical surroundings)--

Large areas inhabited by Indians are virtually inaccessible.

Most Indian housing is far worse than the housing in many slums of our large cities.[5]

The solution for the mass of Indian children suffering from long-standing national neglect and abuse certainly does not lie in being removed from their families. The children placed through the Indian Adoption Project were those who, from the perspective of the social workers who intimately knew their situations, were doomed to lives of stark deprivation. For most, it seemed destined that they would spend their childhood years in boarding schools or a series of foster homes. Some of the situations faced by the biological mothers of the children were horrendous, leaving them im-

paired not only in their maternal roles but also in their capacity to escape intense personal suffering in their everyday
existence.

While the representatives of the tribal organizations
gave their assent to the adoption of a limited number of children whose life circumstances seemed most dire, we must
bear in mind that this took place over a decade ago. They
may be less favorably disposed at the present time. As
Brieland[6] has observed, the increased self-pride and the
changing attitudes of minority ethnic groups may well lead to
increasingly vehement pressure against the release of their
children to white parents. The loss of a people's children
might well be seen as the ultimate indignity to endure.

It is difficult to predict what the future holds for
transracial adoptions in the United States. While minority
groups may be becoming less favorably disposed to the adoptive placement of their children across racial lines, there
are indications that more people are interested in undertaking
such adoptions. Thus, for example, there are signs of ex-
panding interest in the adoption of American Indian children
as a result of increased visibility of such adoptions.[7] We
know also that the adoption of Oriental children from abroad
has enjoyed considerable popularity since World War II. The
interest in transracial adoptions in the United States may be
further heightened if, as some professionals predict, the increased availability of legal abortions results in fewer white
children being born out-of-wedlock, thus diminishing the available pool of adoptable white babies.

Aside from the implications of the findings I report
here for adoption agencies, the research should have interest
from another perspective: it provides one barometer of where
we have moved as a nation in our attitudes about race. Are
we ready as a people to accept multi-racial families? We
know we can do this in Hawaii. But in New York? Vermont?
Iowa? By keeping in touch with these families we have an
opportunity to examine a phenomenon of perhaps more significance than the professional practice issues involved.

Research Orientations

In recent years, there has been a marked increase
in the publication of research reports dealing with adopted
children. The work of Witmer et al., Franklin, Lawder et

al., Kadushin, and Jaffee and Fanshel[8] all tend to have a
certain cast to them which would distinguish their approach
to description and assessment of adoptive families from those
one is apt to find in child development studies as typified by
the work of Kagan and Moss, Sears et al., Sarason and others.[9] Those who have contributed to the research literature
on adoption in recent years have tended to have a catholicity
of intellectual commitments, stemming from their base in the
social work profession and in child welfare as a field of practice. On the other hand, the child development investigators
have tended to reflect an orientation in their research stemming from their professional base in academic psychology.
In the work of the latter, there has been a relatively heavy
emphasis upon pursuing a central conception of child develop-
ment--as rigorously defined as possible--such as the assessment of specific personality characteristics of children as
they grow up. Thus, studies have focused upon such traits
as aggressiveness, anxiety, and motivation for achievement.
Child development investigators interested in these psychological domains have tended to invest considerable energy in
attempting to develop formal definitions of constructs and a
variety of test procedures which could measure them. The
main emphasis has been upon the development of psychometric methods for routine test procedures, the promulgation of
experimental tasks for children which would elicit behavior
of interest to the investigator, and the development of systematic observation of children in order to make more careful records.

In contrast to the research done by child development
psychologists, adoption studies have tended to be less focused
upon a specific domain of personality and more often than not,
the assessment procedures tend to place heavy reliance upon
parents as informants about their children's development.
Further, adoption studies tend to strive for multi-faceted
descriptive profiles of the adjustment of adopted children
based upon less rigorously defined developmental concepts.

The reader should not assume that because the two
orientations to investigative procedures appear to be so dis-
parate there are no areas of overlap of interest or that one
approach reflects rigorous science and the other rank empir-
icism. All investigators--child development and adoption re-
searchers--are faced with formidable, methodological difficulties. Bronfenbrenner and Ricciuti, in reviewing a number
of studies seeking to assess the personality characteristics
of children, point to major problems that plague child devel-

opment investigators.[10] Throughout their review, they refer
time and again to many blind alleys and sources of confusion
in measurement approaches. These include:

(1) Reliance on purely empirical approaches to the
construction and validation of measuring techniques without
prior and continuing conceptual clarification of the precise
variable or variables to be measured.

(2) Failure to consider and control the extraneous
variables that may in fact be measured by a particular tech-
nique. Common sources of such failure involve response
sets (such as acquiescence or social desirability), and factors associated with broader social influences (such as class
and culture). In particular, Bronfenbrenner and Ricciuti
note the tendency to interpret projective responses solely in
motivational terms; doing so may becloud the operation of
cognitive factors that account appreciably for individual differences in test performance.

(3) Reliance on measurements gained by a single tech-
nique applied in a single situation often far removed from
the context in which the variable appears in the day-to-day
life of the child. Given the fact that the behavior of children is even more likely to be affected by immediate environmental events than is the behavior of adults, they reason
that the practice of interpreting results of questionnaires and
projective techniques as reflecting enduring personality characteristics, without sufficient regard for the influence of mo-
mentary situational conditions or more stable social contexts,
has probably done much to retard the development of measuring techniques in which environmental variation could be
controlled or systematically varied through experimental ma-
nipulation. Bronfenbrenner and Ricciuti look to systematic
behavioral observation as one promising development in the
studies of children.

The study of the adoption of American Indian children
reported here falls within the tradition of adoption studies
previously cited. Explicitly, the series of interviews with
the adoptive parents was not undertaken with a single perspective regarding the development of child personality, such
as the emergence of aggressiveness, anxiety or, for example,
resolution of identity problems. Rather, the approach taken
here is a multi-dimensional one in which various facets of
the child's adjustment are covered in the research interviews
in order to create a composite set of measures dealing with

the overall adjustment of the adoptees.

A criticism which one might direct towards adoption studies such as this one is that they tend to be generated in a somewhat unsystematic, ad hoc fashion. However, such a criticism is valid only if one can accept the assumption that a single systematic theory exists whose use would prove more fruitful, based upon parents as the key informants about the adoptive experience. It was the judgment of this investigator that no single sociological or psychological theory would encompass all the factors relevant to adoption. As yet, the child development research literature has not generated such a powerful theoretical system and is not likely to in the immediate future.

The orientation here is one of interviewing parents about themes related to the experience of adoption--and to transracial adoption in particular--as a way of illuminating the experiences of these families and their children. Aside from the research of Yarrow and earlier research of Wittenborn, [11] the direct assessment of adopted children through psychometric procedures, has been a relatively untapped field in this recent period. In the main, most adoption agencies have been wary of intruding into the lives of adoptive families in such a significant way. Adoption studies which focus upon the reports of parents rather than the children themselves are more apt to be tolerated and accepted as less threatening to the families. In this study, involving the cooperation of agencies in 15 states, it seemed more reality-oriented to organize the research on the basis of parental perspectives. One should add, however, that by the time of the Fifth Series interviews with 60 of the families in this study, when inquiries were made about the future readiness of the families to permit the children to be seen directly, the response was guardedly positive.

Social Perspectives on Adoptive Parenthood

While the professional practice literature has focused upon the objective circumstances which made recourse to an adoption agency a necessary or desirable step for some couples--with infertility a paramount issue for investigation--the research literature shows little connection between the circumstances besetting couples at the time of application and the subsequent adjustment of their adopted children. [12] My own view is that the matter of assessing the way people experience the insult of infertility has been much too elusive a measurement task to encourage any appreciable investment in this direction. It would seem desirable to accept at face value the fact that application to an agency reflects a positive orientation to adding a child to the family and--except for a few instances of unusual circumstances--to assume that all applicants can be treated in relatively undifferentiated fashion in this regard. However, when one goes on to examine the phenomenon of transracial adoptions, one must deal with an added ingredient in the picture.

That an adoptive family goes beyond its own racial or ethnic boundaries in adding a child is a very significant social act. It is an affirmative statement which suggests that desire for a child is sufficiently strong to warrant the risk of being marked as a family different from its neighbors. It was my view at the inception of this study that one of the important sources of explanation of a couple's ability to be more venturesome in seeking of a child resides in their social perspective and life style. Minimally, I hazarded the assumption that an adoptive family is able to break the traditional boundaries imposed upon the adoption experience because of the social values it holds and because of its place in the social structure of the community. Within the perspective of viewing transracial adoption as an affirmative social act, there was no assumption that individuals who engage in transracial adoptions would necessarily reflect a homogeneous social orientation. Individuals might come to the experience from diverse social backgrounds and with different kinds of social supports. It was an important matter for investigation to secure their explanations of how they came to accept an Indian child for adoption.

From the above-stated perspective I undertook to include in the interviewing schedules items that could provide social profiles of the adoptive families, covering such domains as political orientations, life-style orientations, observance of traditional versus modern definitions of sex roles, and expression of religiosity, as well as demographic data which would help establish the social status of the families. The reader will note, as he goes along in this report, that the social profile data is linked analytically to matters that deal with the central task of the research, namely, assessing the experiences of the children with their adoptive families.

Perspectives on Parental Orientations and Behavior

There were several aspects of the orientations of the
adoptive parents which seemed relevant to this effort to chart
their experience over some five years with the children. One
of these related to specific aspects of adoptive parenthood:
the range of types of children the adoptive parents could have
considered at the time they first approached the adoption
agency. To better understand the decision to adopt an Indian
child, one needs to be able to view this within a larger perspective: the range of children of a wide variety of physical
and social types acceptable to the adoptive parents. Further,
it is important to have some perspective on the adoptive parents' specific orientation to the fact that the child is Indian,
and also to clarify whether an Indian child was particularly
sought out, whether his being Indian was valued or whether
this feature of his background was merely an unanticipated
development in their general search for a child. In addition,
it is important to scrutinize the kinds of supports and stresses
which adoptive parents involved in transracial placements experience from those close to them.

An additional perspective developed in this research
was related to the adoptive parents as parents. The work
of child development investigators such as Sears et al. provided some basis for the construction of interviewing schedules designed to examine the major child-rearing tendencies
of the parents, particularly with respect to the strictness-
permissiveness orientation identified in earlier research.

The parents in this study represent a very diversified
group with respect to education, life-styles and relative so-
phistication as interviewees in this kind of research. Therefore, interviews were created with an emphasis upon securing concrete descriptive information about their own orientations and their experiences, and questions were worded so
as to be suitable for such a diversified study population.

Having the opportunity to conduct a sequence of interviews
with the adoptive parents made it possible to develop several
approaches to the assessment of the condition of the children.
This will be fully developed as I proceed with the description
of each of the five series of interviews with the parents. Subsequent to this I assess the nature of the association between
the various kinds of information developed about the children
and their families in the early stages of the research and the
measures which reflect subsequent adjustment.

Notes

1. For exceptions to this pattern see bibliography on transracial adoptions at the end of this volume.

2. David Fanshel, A Study in Negro Adoption (Child Welfare League of America, 1957); Edgar F. Borgatta
   and David Fanshel, Behavioral Characteristics of
   Children Known to Psychiatric Outpatient Clinics
   (Child Welfare League of America, 1965).

3. Benson Jaffee and David Fanshel, How They Fared in
   Adoption: A Follow-Up Study (New York: Columbia
   University Press, 1970).

4. Carruth J. Wagner and Erwin S. Rabeau, "Indian Poverty and Indian Health," Health, Education and Welfare Indicators, March 1964.

5. Indian Record, Special Issue, March 1968, "President
   Johnson Presents Indian Message to Congress."

6. Donald Brieland, "Transracial Placements: Research
   Findings and Future Strategy," paper presented at
   the National Conference on Social Welfare, May 27,
   1969, in New York City.

7. The Adoption Resource Exchange of North America
   (ARENA) located at the Child Welfare League of
   America has reported a steady rise in the expres-
   sion of interest by potential adoptive applicants in
   American Indian children.

8. See: Helen Witmer, Elizabeth Herzog, Eugene Wein-
   stein, and Mary Sullivan, Independent Adoptions (New
   York: Russell Sage Foundation, 1963); David S.
   Franklin and Fred Massarik, "The Adoption of Chil-
   dren with Medical Conditions: Part I - Process and
   Outcome," Child Welfare, Vol. XLVII, No. 8 (October
   1969) pp. 459-467; "Part II - The Families Today,"
   Child Welfare, Vol. XLVIII, No. 9 (November 1969)
   pp. 533-539; Elizabeth Lawder, et al., A Follow-Up
   Study of Adoptions: Post-Placement Functioning of
   Adoption Families, (New York: Child Welfare League
   of America, 1969); Alfred Kadushin, Adopting Older
   Children (New York: Columbia University Press,
   1970); Benson Jaffee and David Fanshel, How They

Fared in Adoption (New York: Columbia University Press, 1970).

9. See: Jerome Kagan and Howard A. Moss, Birth to Maturity, A Study in Psychological Development (New York: John Wiley and Sons, 1962); Robert R. Sears, Eleanor E. Maccoby, and Harry Levin, Patterns of Child Rearing (Evanston, Ill.: Row, Peterson and Co., 1957); Seymour B. Sarason, et al., Anxiety in Elementary School Children (New York: John Wiley and Sons, 1960).

10. Urie Bronfenbrenner and Henry V. Ricciuti, "The Appraisal of Personality Characteristics in Children," in Paul H. Mussen, ed., Handbook of Research Methods in Child Development (New York: John Wiley and Sons, 1960).

11. Leon J. Yarrow, "Research in Dimensions of Early Maternal Care," Merrill-Palmer Quarterly of Behavior and Development, Vol. 9, No. 2, (April 1963) pp. 101-114; J. Richard Wittenborn, The Placement of Adoptive Children (Springfield, Ill.: Charles C. Thomas, 1957).

12. Benson Jaffee and David Fanshel, How They Fared in Adoption, op. cit.

Chapter II

BACKGROUND INFORMATION ON THE
INDIAN ADOPTION PROJECT:
1958 THROUGH 1967

Arnold L. Lyslo, Director[*]
Indian Adoption Project

The year 1967 marked the last full year in which the
Indian Adoption Project operated as a special project of the
Child Welfare League of America. With the beginning of
the Adoption Resource Exchange of North America (ARENA)
in early 1968, the Project became a part of this larger program for the adoption of all hard-to-place children in the
United States and Canada.

This report includes information about the Indian children placed for adoption through the Project from its inception in September 1958 through December 31, 1967. It also
highlights some of the major experiences of the Project, and
what we believe the Project accomplished for Indian children.
Problems encountered by the Project are cited as well as
recommendations for continued adoption services to Indian
children and their parents.

The Children Placed for Adoption

A total of 395 Indian children were placed for adoption through the Indian Adoption Project as of December 31,
1967. One hundred nineteen of the children were placed in
1967, compared with 67 in 1966 and 49 in 1965. Of all the
children placed, one child died prior to adoption, and two
children had to be returned to their home state because the

---

[*] Currently Executive Director, Talbot Perkins Adoption
Service in Brooklyn, New York.

33

placement failed.

The children ranged in age from birth to 11 years, with 37 of the children being five years and over at the time of placement. Approximately 50 percent of the children were under one year of age at the time of placement. Fifty of the children were sibling groups of two each, which included six sets of twins. Slightly over one-half of the children were full-blooded Indian. Fifty percent of all the children placed were the financial responsibility of the Bureau of Indian Affairs, meaning that the child's parent(s) had residence on an Indian reservation. The rest of the children were the responsibility of a state department of welfare, or in a very few cases, a voluntary agency.

The 395 children came from the following 16 states:

Alaska	2	New Mexico	8
Arizona	112	North Carolina	14
California	17	Oregon	1
Colorado	1	South Carolina	1
Minnesota	19	South Dakota	104
Mississippi	12	Washington	21
Montana	13	Wisconsin	48
Nevada	17	Wyoming	5
		Total	395

The Families Who Adopted

The 395 children placed for adoption through the Project were adopted by 341 families living in 26 states and one family living in Puerto Rico. Twenty-five families adopted sibling groups of two each, and multiple placements of non-related children included 34 families who adopted two unrelated children; three families who adopted three unrelated children; and one family adopted four children, two of whom were siblings.

The families who adopted the children lived in the following 26 states and one territory of the United States:

Eastern States		Midwest States	
Connecticut	6	Illinois	48
Delaware	13	Indiana	34
Washington, D.C.	2	Iowa	24

Maine	3	Michigan		1
Maryland	4	Minnesota		3
Massachusetts	31	Missouri		39
New Hampshire	3	Ohio		12
New Jersey	29		Total	161
New York	74			
Pennsylvania	33	Western States		
Rhode Island	1			
Vermont	15	California		1
Virginia	2			
West Virginia	2	Territory		
Total	218			
		Puerto Rico		1

Southern States

Arkansas	4	GRAND TOTAL	395
Florida	7		
Louisiana	2		
Tennessee	1		
Total	14		

The 395 Indian children placed for adoption were placed
by 50 agencies throughout the country.   Thirty-one were voluntary agencies and 19 were state departments of public welfare.   The agencies and the number of children placed by
them are set forth in Appendix A.

The Purpose, Background, Method
and Procedures of the Project

A.   Purpose.

The purpose of the Indian Adoption Project was to
stimulate the adoption of American Indian children on a nation-wide basis.   From 1940 to the early 1950's there had
been many programs designed to promote the adoption of all
children--the handicapped child, the child in the older age
group, and children of other racial groups both within the
United States and from foreign lands.   But the Indian child
requiring adoption services remained the "forgotten child,"
left inadequately cared for on the reservation, without a permanent home or parents he could call his own.   The results
of a 1957 nation-wide survey showed that there were approximately 1000 Indian children legally free for adoption who
were forced to live in foster homes and institutions because
adoptive resources had not been found for them.

The Indian Adoption Project originally proposed to select for purposes of adoption from 50 to 100 or more Indian
children deprived of families from all parts of the country,
to be placed through specialized adoption agencies primarily
with non-Indian families.   The adoptions of these children
were to be evaluated by qualified research personnel.   If successful, the over-all result would likely be a permanent interstate plan for the placement of Indian children requiring
adoption.   Equally important, however, would be the stimulation and encouragement afforded those social agencies then
responsible for the planning for Indian children, to develop
new and intensive programs for their adoption within their
own states.

B.   Background.

It had been apparent for some time, from the reports
of the Area and Agency Welfare Staff of the Bureau of Indian
Affairs, that many children who might have been firmly established in secure homes at an early age through adoption
had been passed from family to family on a reservation or
that they had spent years at public expense in federal boarding schools or in foster care.   They had never had the security of family life to promote their development and assure
their future.   Bureau of Indian Affairs social workers had
reported that planning for the adoption of Indian children had
been difficult, largely due to a lack of facilities for finding
families who were interested in adopting these children, and
therefore the adoption of homeless Indian children had not
been widespread.

American Indians living on reservations number approximately 380, 000.   More than half, however, are minors.
Most of these Indians live in some 154 identifiable tribal ju-
risdictions which come within the responsibility of the 51
agency offices of the Bureau of Indian Affairs.

We learned that the number of out-of-wedlock births
to Indian unmarried mothers had never been accurately determined, but reports by health, education, and social work personnel on the reservations indicated that the figure was high.
For a small percentage of these children, a plan was developed on the reservation for their care; but for the majority,
resources outside the reservation had to be found.

Illegitimacy among Indian peoples is frequently accepted without punitiveness, and the extended family is by no

means extinct. The unwed mother may bring her child home
to be cared for by herself, her family, or some relative, and
he (she) may be successfully absorbed by the tribe. However,
there are situations where this is not the case and children
are left uncared for. The Indian unwed mother seldom re-
ceives the assistance from social agencies usually available
to the non-Indian. Isolation and a general attitude that her
situation is "natural" have precluded the counseling indicated
to give her any choice in planning for herself and her child.
From the experience of the Bureau of Indian Affairs, many
of these children were left unsupervised on the reservation
without proper care, and no permanent plan was made for
them. If the mother chose to keep her child or place him
with relatives, she accepted the only resource available to
her--Aid to Dependent Children.

In consultation with social agencies, we learned that
services to Indian unmarried mothers had been extremely
limited. Because the Bureau of Indian Affairs itself was not
authorized to engage directly in the field of adoption, and because adoptive applicants had been so limited in number, very
few unmarried mothers were ever given any choice but to
keep their children.

There had also been an increasing interest shown on
the part of the American public in the adoption of Indian children. Letters of inquiry to both the Central and Area offices
of the Bureau of Indian Affairs had increased through the
years. Many came from people in non-Indian states. Therefore, it was evident that non-Indian families were interested
in the adoption of Indian children. Part of this increased interest in adopting an Indian child may have been attributed
to the previous experience of adoption of European and Oriental children by families in the United States; and also to
the year-long, nation-wide study of the American Indian, conducted by the National Council of Protestant Churches, which
was completed in 1957. As a result of this study, many inquiries were made concerning the general welfare of the Indian child, including his availability for adoption.

Because of the joint concern of the Bureau of Indian
Affairs and the Child Welfare League of America, the Bureau, in 1957, sent inquiries to all of its reservation social
workers, asking the approximate number of children then in
care who might be available for adoption. They also interviewed state departments of public welfare in the states containing Indian reservations. The reports received from these

workers presented conclusive evidence that there were many
children badly needing adoptive placement who were then free
or who could be made free for adoption if adoptive resources
were available.

With the employment of an experienced social worker
as Project Director, one who had worked for several years
with Indians on reservations, a thorough study of tribal laws
and appropriate state laws was made; other background data
were incorporated. Indian leaders on reservations were interviewed concerning the problem of children needing adoption. On the basis of these studies, the Child Welfare League
and the Bureau of Indian Affairs were convinced that this pi-
lot project could be successfully carried out.

It was realized that a program of this type dealt only
with the end result of complex social problems. However,
no community is fully exempt from problems of neglect and
illegitimacy, nor from the need for an adoption program.
Therefore, it was felt that this project to help a small segment of children was justified. As the League engaged in
the project, its intent was to become more deeply involved
in basic problems in the care of Indian children and to help
improve the general conditions among Indians.

C.   Other Objectives of the
     Adoption Project Included:

1.   A demonstration that adoptive homes could be se-
     cured for homeless or rejected Indian children as
     an alternative to foster care.

2.   The Bureau of Indian Affairs would immediately im-
     prove and stress services to unmarried mothers,
     and through this experience would generally improve
     its social work practice in relation to planning for
     children.

3.   The project was to establish regular procedures for
     the future adoption, by non-reservation families, of
     Indian children in need of such planning. This would
     include older children.

4.   The existence of an available resource would stim-
     ulate earlier court action in the case of grossly neg-
     lected babies.

5. The interest of public and private agencies would be stimulated to give better service to the Indian unmarried mother and her child.

6. Helpful information would be provided to the public and to child welfare agencies concerning the experiences of these adoption agencies in planning for the adoption of Indian children.

7. The project could be used as a possible basis for comparing the adoption of Indian children, its problems and successes, with the adoption of children of other races.

D. Method.

1. As funds were available, reservations were selected where the project was to operate. Criteria used for selection of Indian reservations to be included in the project included:

   a. A qualified social worker on the staff.
   b. A permissive attitude on the part of the tribe.
   c. An interested administrative personnel.
   d. Evidence that a number of children on that reservation would benefit by adoption and that they could be made legally free for adoption.
   e. A public health facility and a cooperative attitude on the part of its staff.
   f. Interest and cooperation of state and county welfare agencies and private agencies wherever possible.

2. In the areas in which the project was to operate, the laws were studied, and the legal framework in which the adoption process was to take place was established.

3. Initially, two high-standard private adoption agencies in the east were selected to participate in the project. However, with minimum publicity about the project, families from other areas expressed interest in adopting an Indian child which necessitated recruiting other adoption agencies to participate.

4. The criteria for selection of an Indian child for purposes of adoption were as follows:

a. The child be one-fourth or more degree Indian blood.
b. The child be considered adoptable both physically and emotionally.
c. The parent or parents, after careful casework counseling, released the child for adoption because it was the best plan for the child.
d. In those situations of abandonment or neglect where the child needed permanent removal from his parents, adequate court protection be provided through state courts to assure the child's adoptability.

E. Procedure.

1. Referral of Indian Children Needing Adoption. Any Indian child in need of adoption who met the criteria was referred to the project director, who in turn referred the child to an adoption agency willing to assume the responsibility for adoption of the child. The project director acted as liaison between the agency having responsibility for the child and the adoption agency planning for him, assisting in whatever manner necessary until consummation of the adoption. Duplicate case records were kept by the Child Welfare League of America for research purposes. Referrals of Indian children to the project were made in the following ways:

a. Direct Relinquishment. The adoption agencies under special contract with the Child Welfare League of America to participate in this project agreed that certain Bureau of Indian Affairs social workers on Indian reservations could act on their behalf in obtaining a voluntary relinquishment of a child from his parent(s) to the adoption agency, when it was felt that adoption was the best plan and when the agency agreed to assume responsibility for his adoption.

The child may have had a short period of foster family care at League expense prior to adoptive placement.

Contract agencies participated fully in the research aspect of the project. Their records were available to the League, and families who

adopted Indian children through their agency, if
they consented, were included in the research
sample.

b. Inter-Agency Agreement. A child already removed from his parent(s) either by voluntary
relinquishment or termination of parental rights
was referred to the Indian Adoption Project by
the agency having custody of the child (usually
the state public welfare department or some private agency in the state). The adoption agency
willing to plan for the child acted as agent for
the referral agency, and an agreement was entered into for the adoption of the child. The
referral agency usually held legal custody of the
child until consummation of the adoption, unless
otherwise agreed upon.

2. The Responsibility of the Referral Agency. It was
the responsibility of the referral agency to provide
adequate social information about the child and his
family to enable the adoption agency to plan for him.
This summary of the record included services provided, and a compilation of the pertinent facts with
the necessary documentation. Special emphasis was
given as to how, through casework service, it was
determined that adoption was the best plan for the
child and his parent(s).

It was presumed that the child who was relinquished
for adoption would be placed in a home where the
religion of the adoptive parents was the same as
that of his own parent(s) unless the parent(s), or
the mother, if she was not married to the child's
father, specified that the child should or might be
placed with a family of another religion. A statement as to the parent's preference or non-preference
for the religion of the child was included in the referral.

Consideration of tribal enrollment was of paramount
importance and protection of the child's rights in
this area was part of the casework planning with the
parent(s). Aside from the financial implications for
the child, the retention of his tribal rights was seen
as having potential importance in helping him to retain a positive identification with his Indian back-

ground. If the child was enrolled in a tribe, the
superintendent of the Indian agency provided a statement concerning any tribal monies that might be
coming to the child either then or in the future. A
statement of real and personal property which might
come to the child through inheritance or tribal rights
was also included. If the child was eligible for any
tribal benefits, it was the responsibility of the adoption agency to establish a guardianship or trust arrangement to protect the funds until the child reached
majority. Procedures were worked out with the Bureau of Indian Affairs which protected the confiden-
tiality of the adoptive parents in these matters.

It was the responsibility of the referral agency to
assume the responsibility for travel and any incidental expenses of the child and escort from the
state of the child's residence to the adoption agency,
unless this cost was borne by the adoptive parents.
Arrangements for medical and foster family care of
the child, if they were needed, were agreed upon
prior to transporting the child.

Written agreement was secured from the referral
agency that should any child prove unadoptable for
health reasons, the referral agency agreed to plan
for the return of the child to his home state at
their expense, thereby relieving the adoption agency
of any further responsibility for the child.

The referral agency also had the responsibility to
provide: (1) two or three color pictures of the child
which could be shown to adoptive applicants; (2) adequate clothing for the trip, including diapers, blan-
kets, formula and other essentials as required; (3)
medical examination of the child 24 to 48 hours
prior to departure; and (4) an evaluation of the current situation of the child--his whereabouts, daily
routine, general characteristics, and so forth. If
the child was in foster home care, impressions
about the boarding parents and their handling of the
child was included.

3.   Referral of Approved Adoptive
      Families for Indian Children:

Any licensed adoption agency had the opportunity to

refer an approved family for an Indian child to the
Project Director. A résumé of the adoption study
was sent, pointing out those factors which led the
agency to believe the family had the capacity to adopt
an Indian child. The age, sex and color tolerance
of the child the family would accept were expressed,
and pictures of the family, their home, etc., were
furnished.

The Project Director referred the approved families
to agencies having Indian children in need of adoption
and decision of the suitability of the family for a
particular child was the responsibility of the agency
having custody of the child. Prior to placement of
the child, matters of inter-agency, interstate agreements had to be worked out between the two agencies.
Other considerations included: (1) preparation of the
child and family for placement, (2) exchange of all
legal documents necessary in the adoption, (3) consideration of travel for child to the adoption agency,
and (4) agreements concerning supervision of the
child in the adoptive home, with periodic progress
reports.

It was expected that each agency would inform its
own State Department of Welfare of the planning for
the adoption of an Indian child. In those states having regulations governing the interstate placements
of children, it was the responsibility of the placement agency to see that all appropriate policies and
laws were compiled with.

Perceived Consequences of the Project

One can no longer say that the Indian child is the
"forgotten child," as was indicated when the Project began in
1958. As already reported, resources for the adoption of
Indian children were developed in 26 states and one territory
of the United States. The adoption needs of Indian children
have been well publicized through a variety of national media,
and over the years the League has referred well over 5,000
prospective adoptive families for Indian children to agencies
in every state in the Union. The Indian child's reception in
the East was primarily one of "sentiment for our first Americans." The prejudice which prevented his adoption in his
own state greatly decreased, due mainly to the receptivity of

families in other states to adopt him.   This reaction caused
social agencies in the child's home state to take a "new
look" at the Indian child's adoptability with the result that
many more Indian children were placed for adoption in their
own state.   The effects of the Project in South Dakota were
expressed in a letter from the Area Social Worker, Mr. Edgar Lautzenheiser, from the Bureau of Indian Affairs in
Aberdeen:

> Before the advent of the Indian Adoption Project
> adoption opportunities for the Indian children were
> practically nonexistent.   So much so that our so-
> ial workers felt inhibited in talking with Indian
> mothers about the future of their infants because
> the worker knew that all that could be offered was
> a succession of foster homes.   All this has been
> changed in the few short years that you have been
> working with the problem.
>
> An area in which I think you and the Project have
> been given insufficient credit is the stimulation
> that has been given the local, state and private
> agencies in Indian Country to expand and develop
> their own adoption activities for Indian children.
> Here in South Dakota these activities have expanded
> to such an extent that we really no longer consider
> the Indian infant a hard-to-place child.

Increased social services were made available to Indian unmarried mothers to enable them to make a satisfactory plan for themselves and their children.   Many unmarried mothers preferred to live in maternity homes awaiting
the birth of their children, rather than stay with their own
families or relatives on a reservation.   As adoption opportunities became increasingly available, unmarried mothers
were more willing to release their children for adoption,
knowing that adoption could afford the child greater opportunity for a better life.

Many Indian tribes, through their experiences in working with the Indian Adoption Project, learned the advantages
of agency adoptions for their children.   The use of state
courts rather than tribal courts, whose jurisdiction off the
reservation may be questioned, was reinforced as a more
desirable procedure.   In a few states, such as Montana,
Arizona and New Mexico, the fact that an adoptive family
was available for a particular child enabled the tribal court

to secure the cooperation of the state court to make the child legally free for adoption. These cooperative procedures worked out well in those states where, traditionally, the jurisdiction of the state court over Indian children whose parents resided on an Indian reservation had been questioned.

It would appear that more and better adoption services were developed for Indian children in their own states. These services included the voluntary as well as the public agencies. Lutheran Social Services of South Dakota, as an example, placed 77 Indian children for adoption through their special Indian adoption program during an 18-month period. The majority of these children were placed in South Dakota, but through the help of other Lutheran agencies placements were made in 19 states.

In Los Angeles, California, the Los Angeles County Department of Adoptions placed 12 Indian children through the Indian Adoption Project in 1967 and four in 1966. The increasing number of Indians moving into the area for employment reasons increased the need for a network of social services for them. Indian unmarried mothers were referred to social agencies by the workers of the Bureau of Indian Affairs and Indian organizations. The Los Angeles County Department of Adoptions served 48 unmarried mothers in 1967. The Indian Adoption Project encouraged the development of these services and if adoptive families were not readily available for Indian children in California, assistance was given in finding homes for them in other sections of the country.

The League, through the Indian Adoption Project, was instrumental in helping some states change their adoption laws. Wyoming was one such state. Through participation in the Project, agencies in several states discovered that their adoption law was obsolete and not conducive to the interstate placement of children. Ways were found in most states to place these children, however, mainly by special interagency agreements.

Participation in the Indian Adoption Project contributed to greater understanding by agencies of the differences in practice among adoption agencies. They learned that there may be many extenuating circumstances involved in the placement of a child and that there need not be only one way a child may be placed. While every precaution was taken to protect the child and adoptive family, the flexibility of agencies in effecting these placements as the Project progressed was noteworthy.

The steady expansion of the Indian Adoption Project
was the most obvious measure of its success. In 1967, sev-
en additional states and one territory and 21 more agencies
participated than in 1966. Five of the 21 agencies had never
before worked with the Indian Adoption Project. Four of
these were public agencies and one was voluntary.

It was common for an agency to increase its participation once it had the satisfaction of providing a home for
an Indian child. The New England Home for Little Wander-
ers in Boston furnished homes for two children in 1966. The
following year this increased to 14 homes for children and a
representative of the agency stated that the agency had become very enthusiastic about such adoptions. Another example was the Indiana Department of Welfare which furnished
homes for three children in 1966 and 11 in 1967.

Major Problems of the Project

Adoption services for families wanting to adopt Indian
children were not available in all states. This lack of service usually extended to families wishing to adopt any out-
of-state child, including the foreign child. The rationale, as
stated by social agencies, was that their first obligation was
to serve children who were residents of the state. Some
agencies objected to the "red tape" involved, and a lack of
trust between agencies was also evident. As a direct result
of agencies refusing service, in one area some families or-
ganized themselves into an adoptive parent group for minority
children. Through their efforts, services became available
for Indian and children of other racial minorities.

Many more Indian children could have been placed for
adoption in 1967 had they been on referral to our Project.
All that year the Project had from 50 to 65 approved adoptive families on referral, with far fewer children referred.
There were still many Indian children needing adoption who
had not been referred to our Project. The Bureau of Indian
Affairs and state departments of welfare need to have frequent periodic reviews of Indian children in foster care to
make sure that those children who, in essence, are without
parents receive services to make them eligible for adoption.

One of the problems in referring Indian children to

our Project for adoption purposes was that the majority of
state departments of welfare did not have sufficient personnel to keep up with the increased caseload of Indian children
needing adoption.   For states like Arizona, which placed 41
Indian children through our Project in 1966, the workload to
get these children placed on an interstate basis was great.
The Bureau of Indian Affairs commendably worked out a plan
with the Arizona Department of Public Welfare at that time
to subsidize the employment of one adoption worker to assist
the Department of Welfare in processing the Indian adoptions.
An added responsibility of this worker was to review all children living in foster family care to see whether adoption was
a suitable plan for any child.   This plan to assist state departments of welfare could well have been used in other
states having a large number of Indian children for adoption.

Health services in some areas were difficult to secure, primarily because some families lived so far away
from the Division of Indian Health facilities.   Specialized
services such as pediatric, psychological and other special-
ties were available in some areas only in the larger public
health facilities.   This meant that a child might have had to
spend one or more nights away from home in order to receive these services.   Adoption had to be delayed for some
children referred to our Project because adequate diagnostic
and medical services were not readily available to them.

Agencies involved in the placement of Indian children
should have been in closer communication with each other
about all aspects of a case.   Telephone conferences would
have speeded up many placements and would have established
a one-to-one relationship which is so meaningful in the development of trust between agencies.   Placement agencies
frequently asked for additional material and/or legal documents.   The need for this was not always obvious to the
agency responsible for the child.   A telephone conversation
explaining why the material was needed would have solved
the matter.

Religious matching was a requirement in many states.
The policies and regulations of some agencies were frequently more restricting than the laws.

General Recommendations for Continued Services
for Indian Children and Their Parents

Improved counseling services to Indian families are

needed to better enable parents to provide a wholesome environment for their children, giving them the opportunity to
grow and develop within their own family. Several children
who were placed for adoption through the Project had suffered
extreme physical and emotional neglect, which required their
removal from their natural families. Had adequate counseling services been provided these families, perhaps the children could have grown up in their own homes. In addition,
the Indian community needs to be educated to accept responsibility for the protection of their children.

Tribal courts should be encouraged to request civil
courts to handle all civil matters relating to the Indian child.
When a state court does not have jurisdiction of Indian children residing on a reservation, these children frequently are
not relinquished for adoption.

Much more work needs to be done educationally with
the Indian unmarried mother to encourage her to use both
prenatal and postnatal health services. She should be encouraged to use available counseling services to enable her
to make a satisfactory plan for herself and her child and, if
she decides to keep her child, she should receive continuing
services which would include education in good standards of
child care. An interesting research project could be developed with Indian unmarried mothers who keep their children,
to see what happens to the child in later years.

The quality of foster family care for Indian children
should be improved. Occasionally agencies apologized for
the poor quality of foster family care provided for children
referred to the Indian Adoption Project. The foster parent
may have been an aged grandmother, or the foster family
may have lived in near poverty, so that the substitute care
offered was marginal at best. Reflecting the unhappy condition of foster care for Indian children were referrals we received of older children when agencies suddenly realized that
the foster families had not provided adequate stimulation for
the children to enable them to develop commensurate with
their capabilities. We are aware of instances, also, where
agencies replaced children in more adequate foster homes in
order to evaluate a child's true potential, or to prepare him
for adoptive placement.

The Indian Adoption Project encouraged agencies to
develop specialized foster homes for children to help prepare them for adoption. Periodically, foster families should

be revaluated to determine whether they are still able to help prepare a child for adoption. If not, the home should be closed.

We are aware that, on occasion, infants and young children are still placed in child-caring institutions which operate under conditions which are damaging to them. Three Indian children placed for adoption through the Indian Adoption Project spent considerable time in their early infancy in an institution. The placement agencies reported that these children had considerable difficulty in establishing relationships with their adoptive families, apparently because of the early emotional deprivation they experienced in the institution.

Child Welfare League of America Standards state that institutional care is not appropriate for preschool children. From this perspective, an infant or a child under the age of six is not ready to profit from group living, and needs the warm, continuous physical care from the same person which cannot be provided in a group setting.

Uniform adoption laws among the states would greatly facilitate the adoptive placement of children.

At the time of this writing, almost two years after the closing of the Indian Adoption Project, there are still many families waiting to adopt an Indian child. No Indian child who can benefit from adoption should be deprived of this opportunity. Our objective for all Indian children remains the same as when this Project began in 1958: that all Indian children have the opportunity for a good life within their own family, or at least with a family of their own tribal heritage. This is by far the most preferred plan for caring for deprived Indian children. But if this is impossible, then on the basis of the good adjustment made by most Indian children placed with non-Indian families, as reported in this research study, we should continue these transracial adoptive placements of Indian children.

Chapter III

STUDY DESIGN, PROCEDURES AND SUBJECTS

The research subjects of this study were the adoptive parents and their adopted children. While the children were not themselves subjected to research interviewing or direct examination, interviews with the parents were designed to chart their progress from a variety of perspectives. The physical health of the children, their developmental progress, the status of their emotional health, their behavioral dispositions, and their social and family relationships were assayed in considerable detail. At the same time, the parents were of interest in their own right. I wanted them to tell us the motives that had led them to adopt an Indian child. I also wanted to learn from them about social attitudes and life-styles that might influence how they functioned as adoptive parents of Indian children.

The research was designed to trace the experiences of the children and their families until the latter had been in the adoptive homes for approximately five years. Five annual interviews were scheduled with the adoptive families with the following general perspectives about their content:

Series One: The interview was conducted jointly with the adoptive father and the adoptive mother. I encouraged the interviewers to be flexible in the conduct of the interview and to concentrate upon establishing rapport with the adoptive parents. I wanted to insure the latter's cooperation with the plan for repeated annual contacts. The interview was not designed to garner specific data but was instead seen as having a "getting acquainted" function. The interviewers produced a rather lengthy prose summary at the end of this interview and this became part of the corpus of information available for rating tasks at a later stage.

The topical outline developed for the interview covered such topics as:

1. The circumstances leading to the decision of the couple to apply to the agency for the adoption of a child.
2. The couple's experience with the agency study process.
3. How the couple came to adopt the child presented to them.
4. The couple's reaction to the child's Indian background.
5. The life style(s) of the couple including cultural and extra-curricular interests, religious activity, employment or other income-producing activities, friendships, and so forth.
6. The quality of the child's adjustment in the home since first placed.
7. The reaction of the couple to participating in the research.

Series Two: The second interview was designed to be carried out with the adoptive mothers exclusively. The interview took about two hours to complete. It was a more structured interviewing situation involving the use of a schedule in which questions were presented in exactly the same wording and in the same order to all respondents. Many of the questions were of the "fixed-alternative" kind in which the responses of the mothers were limited to stated alternatives. Open-ended questions were also included. The interviewers were trained to stay within the confines of the formal questions while at the same time attempting to put the mothers at ease to reduce defensiveness. The interviewers were asked to write a summary of their impressions subsequent to the interview, a practice maintained for the entire series of five interviews. Among the many areas touched upon were:

1. The progress of the adoptee to date (e.g., problems shown, degree of security demonstrated, etc.).
2. Behavioral traits of the child.
3. The child-rearing dispositions of the mother (building upon the work of Sears, Maccoby and Levin[1]).
4. The nature of the child's manner of relating to his / her parents, siblings, and other children.
5. The quality of the father's relationship with the adoptee.
6. The mother's feelings and perspectives about the child's Indian background.
7. The community's reaction to the child.
8. The mother's attitudes about the types of children she could have considered at the time the couple approached the agency.
9. The family's life-style, e.g., use of leisure time ac-

tivity, the degree of sharing of chores between husband and wife, etc.
10.   The political and social views of the adoptive mother.
11.   The personal biography of the mother including the
      degree of deprivation she experienced as she grew up.

Series Three: The third interview, of about two hours' duration, was conducted exclusively with the adoptive fathers.
It closely resembled in form and content the interviews with
the adoptive mothers.   The interview was designed to give
the adoptive fathers an opportunity to tell how the family had
come to the decision to adopt an Indian child and what the
nature of their living experience with the child had been up
to the time of the interview.

Series Four: The fourth interview was designed as a return
to the joint husband-wife interviewing format used in Series
One.   An interviewing guide served as a basic frame of reference for the interviewers.   There was ample latitude allowed for the interviewer in the way inquiries were made, to
offset the more formal approach in the prior two series.
However, unlike Series One, which was not created to provide categorical data which could be utilized in some form
of quantitative analysis, Series Four information was recorded by the interviewers in a codebook prepared for this
purpose.

      The content of the Series Four interview was almost
exclusively devoted to the task of developing a multifaceted
portrait of the child's adjustment and the way in which the
parents performed their child-rearing tasks.   The topics included in the interview were:

1.   Developmental progress of the child.
2.   Health status of the child.
3.   Physical appearance of the child.
4.   Child's personality and general disposition.
5.   Child's social relationships.
6.   Problems of child attributable to his Indian or adop-
     tive status.
7.   School adjustment.
8.   Child rearing patterns.
9.   Family climate.

Series Five: The fifth interview was the last in the series and was held exclusively with the adoptive mothers. It was, like the second and third in the series, a structured interviewing situation involving the use of an interviewing schedule with "fixed alternative" responses. The major emphasis was upon the adjustment of the child and the performance of parental roles. Areas covered by the interviewers included:

1. Major events in the life of the family during the preceding year.
2. The child's developmental progress.
3. The child's pre-school experience.
4. The child's school adjustment.
5. Behavioral description of the child.
6. The child's health status.
7. Social relationships of the child.
8. The adoptive mother's child-rearing behavior.
9. The role of the child's Indian background in his/her adjustment.
10. The family's life-style.
11. The attitude of the family to the research and attitudes toward future direct involvement of the child in the research.

It should be noted that while a number of families adopted more than one Indian child, the design of the research called for the study of the first child placed. While some information was collected about the other adoptees, it was not feasible to treat them as research subjects in as complete a manner as with their older siblings. Therefore, this report does not deal with the adjustment of Indian children who entered the adoptive homes after the primary subjects were placed.

Selection of the Subjects

The families participating in the study constitute only 29 percent of the 341 families who adopted children from the Indian Adoption Project during the decade 1958-1967. The promotional effort started at a modest pace and built up momentum over time so that 119 children were placed in the last year of the project. The research effort coincided with the early phase of the project when the number of placements were limited. The build-up of the study population proceeded slowly. As Table III-1 shows, it took about 5 1/2 years to complete the full round of Series One interviewing. Some families were having Series Five interviews at the same time that others were experiencing Series One.

Table III-1

DATES OF FIRST AND LAST INTERVIEWS
COMPLETED IN EACH SERIES

Dates	First Family Interview	Last Family Interview
Series One	11/7/60	5/22/66
Series Two	11/9/61	10/28/66
Series Three	12/3/62	12/29/66
Series Four	3/16/64	6/27/67
Series Five	2/17/65	3/8/68

Aside from the matter of the timing of the placements, the study population was also restricted by the need to arrange the travel schedules of interviewers within reasonable geographic bounds. The cooperation of the study families was only solicited if they lived sufficiently close to a population center to permit a cluster of families to be interviewed on a single field trip of about one week's duration. Thus, clusters of families for interviewing were created around such cities as St. Louis, Chicago, Indianapolis, Des Moines, Wilmington, Del., and New York. Families who lived in isolated areas, distant from population centers were not included in the study.

The enlistment of families in the research was arranged through the cooperation of the adoption agencies. Participation was voluntary and not a precondition for the placement of the children in their adoptive homes. As far as is known from the reports of the agencies, only two families refused to participate in the study when invited. One hundred families were recruited for the study. One family was eliminated when an anticipated placement did not take place. One additional family refused further participation after their Series One interview and a second family withdrew after their Series Two interview. Thus 97 families constitute the basic study population about which this report is focused.

Table III-2 provides the reader with an overview of the interviewing experience of the 97 families. One mother was not interviewed during Series Two because of serious

Table III-2

INTERVIEWS COMPLETED WITH ADOPTIVE PARENTS OVER FIVE SERIES; MEAN AGE OF CHILDREN, EACH SERIES

Series	No. Families Interviewed	Mean Age (in Months) of Children		Time Interval (in Months) Between Interview and Date of Placement		Interval Since Prior Interview	
		$\overline{X}$	S.D.	$\overline{X}$	S.D.	$\overline{X}$	S.D.
One (both parents)	97	31.4	27.2	10.3	8.7	--	--
Two (mother)	96	40.4	28.1	19.1	11.2	8.9	6.8
Three (father)	94	52.4	29.9	30.9	13.6	11.8	7.1
Four (both parents)	88	61.9	27.0	42.5	13.5	12.2	3.1
Five (mother)	60	73.5	29.8	52.9	14.1	12.4	6.8
(Tot.)	435						

illness and three fathers missed their Series Three interviews because they were temporarily out of range for interviewing; two were abroad on sabbatical leave and one was on a work assignment in California. The Fourth Series interview was completed with 88 families; four were unavailable and four had adopted relatively late so that the time that had elapsed since the Series Three interview was too short to warrant the next series. The Series Five interview was completed with only sixty adoptive mothers. One mother was too ill to be seen for the last interview and 25 were not seen because their adoptions had been arranged later than the other families and their scheduled Fifth Series interviews came after the date when field data-gathering activities had to be brought to a close.

Table III-2 shows that the mean age of the adoptees

when the parents were first seen was 31.4 months, and that
this was some 10.3 months after the adoptive placement.
Subsequent interviews were arranged at approximately twelve-
month intervals between each interview.

The Interviewers

The interviewing was carried out by three caseworkers
with graduate social work training who had substantial experience in child welfare.   One interviewer, Mrs. Rhoda Fishleder, was assigned to the New York metropolitan area and
had annual interviews with about 20 families.   A second interviewer, Miss Mary Davis, did much of the interviewing in
states other than New York and New Jersey.   Mrs. Trude
Bettelheim relieved Miss Davis of some of the arduous travel
involved in field trips by undertaking interviews in the mid-
West for Series Three to Five.   The interviewers were in-
structed on the procedures to be utilized in each of the five
series of interviews.   As they completed interviews, their
return schedules were monitored to insure that uniform procedures were being employed at each phase of the study.

Coding Operations and Statistical Analysis of Data

All of the interviews except the First Series required
the development of codebooks and coding procedures.   The
Second, Third and Fifth Series interviews involved major coding operations by coders, whereas the Fourth Series called
for the filling out of a codebook by the interviewers themselves.   All interviews were coded twice to insure reliability.
Where discrepancies in coding were revealed, the differences
were resolved by the author making the final decision.   Except for a few ambiguous items which were dropped, the reliability of the coding appeared to be of a high order.   While
no coefficient of reliability was computed, the number of disagreements in coding which required a third judgment were
under 5 percent of the items.   Most disagreements in coding
were located in the areas of schedules which involved open-
ended questions.

All codesheets were punched on IBM cards and the
punching verified.   The cards were subjected to "out-of-
range" scrutiny to remove errors in coding or punching.   The
cards were sequenced for each case under a computer program designed to permit statistical analysis even where there

was missing data on a case, i.e., where one of the five series of interviews was missing. The specific statistical routines employed in the analysis of the data will be discussed in the context of later chapters in which findings are presented.

Other Sources of Data

The background characteristics of the adopted children and their parents were secured from a research form filled in by the agency. In addition, the referral summaries prepared for the Indian Adoption Project by agencies with respect to the children and the adoptive families were systematically reviewed and selected areas of information were coded. In addition, as will be discussed in Chapter IX, professional rating procedures were developed for characterizing the adjustment of the adoptees on the basis of a review of all of the available research protocols.

DESCRIPTION OF THE SUBJECTS

The remainder of this chapter is devoted to a portrayal of the adoptees and their natural families. I will describe for the reader the deprived conditions from which the children came and the kinds of homes in which they were placed. While the data is essentially demographic, anecdotal references will be used to create some of the flavor of the stark circumstances endured by the children before adoption. I will also present demographic data concerning the adoptive parents.

The Adoptees and Their Backgrounds

In Table III-3, there is presented the tribal origins of the adoptees. Children from the Sioux and Apache tribe constitute the largest sub-groups within the study population but other tribes are also represented. These tribes reflect all of the diversity and broad range of physical types which is characteristic of the American Indian. The reservations from which the children came were located in 11 widely scattered states.

Table III-4 contains information of a demographic nature about the background characteristics of the adoptees.

Table III-3

TRIBAL ORIGINS OF THE ADOPTEES
(N= 98)

State	Tribe	Reservation	Number of Children in Study
Alaska	Tsimshian	Annette Islands	1
Arizona	Apache	Fort Apache	12
	Apache	San Carlos	6
	Pima	Gila River	4
	Papago	Papago	1
Minnesota	Chippewa	*	1
Missouri	Apache		1
Mississippi	Choctaw	Choctaw	3
Montana	Assiniboine	Fort Peck	1
	Blackfoot	Blackfoot	1
	Northern Cheyenne	Northern Cheyenne	2
	Flathead	Flathead	1
	Chippewa-Cree	Rocky-Boy's	2
Nevada	Shoshone	Pyramid Lake	1
	Paiute	Pyramid Lake	2
North Carolina	Cherokee	Cherokee	7
South Dakota	Oglala Sioux	Pine Ridge	7
	Sioux	Sisseton	15
	Sioux	Rosebud	3
	Sioux	Crow Creek	1
	Sioux	Yankton	1
	Sioux	Flandreau	2
	Sioux	Cheyenne River	1
	Sioux	(Other)	5
Wisconsin	Oneida	Oneida	2
	Menominee	Menominee	7
	Winnebago	Winnebago	3
	Chippewa	*	
Wyoming	Arapahoe	Wind River	1
	Shoshone	Wind River	2

*There are several reservations in Minnesota and in Wisconsin occupied by Chippewa Indians. The specific reservations from which the children came are not identified.

Nine out of ten biological mothers[2] were full-blooded Indian women; eight were part Indian and two were Caucasian (the fathers of the children being Indian). Two-thirds of the mothers were Protestant and about one-third were Catholic. By and large, they were a relatively young group of women at the time of their children's placement in adoptive homes, their mean age being close to 25 years. Only 10 percent were 35 years or older while 28 percent were 19 years or under. Their educational levels were low; 9.0 was the mean number of years of schooling.

The marital histories of the biological mothers are also set forth in Table III-4. Almost half had never been married while 37 percent had contracted one marriage in their lives. Ten women had been married at least twice. Two-thirds of the adoptees were born to parents who were not married; 19 percent were born to married parents living together and 6 percent had parents who were divorced or separated. Coding and tabulation of the information obtained from the agency referral letters to the Indian Adoption Project revealed that 36 percent of the relationships between the biological parents were apparently long-term ones and 22 percent were somewhat sustained. About two out of five situations involved fleeting, casual relationships between the biological parents.

Forty-two percent of the biological mothers had given birth to only one child, the adoptee, whereas 27 percent had had four or more children. About two out of five of the mothers had experienced two or more out-of-wedlock births.

Table III-5 presents a count of the disabling conditions which afflicted the biological mothers. The frequency count must be seen as a conservative estimate of the disabilities suffered by these women since they were identified in referral summaries which were not written with a research purpose in mind. Nevertheless, the table suggests that many of the biological mothers were highly troubled, unhappy women overwhelmed by a variety of demoralizing experiences. The summaries indicated that many had obviously suffered stark deprivation all of their lives. Forty-two percent of the mothers had serious drinking problems; 17 percent had been in prison, usually on minor charges associated with their drinking. Almost 45 percent were described in terms which indicated that they suffered from quite severe personality disorders. One in every five of the mothers was strikingly neglectful of the children.

Table III-4

BACKGROUND CHARACTERISTICS
OF THE ADOPTED CHILDREN
(N= 98)
[where information is missing in a category
it is given as a "blank"]

A. BIOLOGICAL MOTHERS

Race

	%
Indian	89.8
Part-Indian	8.2
Caucasian	2.0
	100.0

Religion

Catholic	30.2
Protestant	67.4
Jewish	1.2
Other	1.2
(blanks = 12)	100.0

Age

15 to 19 years	28.1
20 to 24 years	25.0
25 to 29 years	20.9
30 to 34 years	15.6
35 to 39 years	7.3
40 to 45 years	3.1
	100.0

Mean   = 24.9 years
Median = 24.0 years
S.D.   = 6.6

Education

Grade school, graduate or less	46.2
Some high school	38.5
High school graduate	15.4
	100.0

(blanks = 7)

Mean   = 9.0 years
Median = 9.0 years
S.D.   = 2.1

<u>Marital History</u>   %

Marital History	%
Single, never married	46.8
Common-law marriage	5.3
Single marriage	37.3
Two marriages	8.5
Three marriages	2.1
	100.0

(blanks = 4)

B.   PARENTS' RELATIONSHIP

<u>Relationship Between</u>
<u>Biological Parents</u>

Paternity not established	1.0
Married, living together	18.6
Married, separated	3.1
Married, divorced	3.1
Married, common-law	3.1
Not married, some considerations of marriage, but dubious	3.1
Not married, marriage unlikely	68.0
	100.0

(blanks = 1)

<u>Nature of Relationship</u>
<u>Between Biological Parents</u>

Paternity not established	1.0
Fleeting, casual	41.2
Somewhat sustained	21.7
Long-term	36.1
	100.0

(blanks = 1)

C.   CHILD

<u>Number Children Born</u>
<u>to Biological Mothers</u>

One	41.7
Two	15.6
Three	15.6
Four	10.4
Five	3.1
Six	2.1
Seven	5.2

Eight	2.1
Nine	4.2
	100.0

Mean   = 2.8
Median = 2.0
S.D.   = 2.3

Number of Children Born
Out-of-Wedlock
to Biological Mothers

None	10.4
One	49.0
Two	16.7
Three	9.4
Four	9.4
Five	3.1
Six	1.0
Nine	1.0
	100.0

Mean   = 1.8
Median = 1.0
S.D.   = 1.5

An index of the biological mother's disability was created by summating the conditions reported in the referral summaries. The index scores proved to be normally distributed. The reader is alerted to the fact that this index will be shown in Chapter X to be linked to a major measure of the overall adjustment of the adoptees.

The nature of some of the circumstances surrounding the biological mothers' surrenders of their children will perhaps be made more graphic for the reader by summary abstracts prepared from the referral letters sent to the Indian Adoption Project. The following are illustrations of conditions where the mothers appeared least impaired.

> The mother has never married. She is the mother of three children. She is regarded as intelligent. She works as a waitress.

>   *   *   *

> A quiet, intelligent young woman. Better than average student in high school. She has had three children out-of-wedlock--all placed through the pro-

Table III-5

FREQUENCY OF SELECTED DISABLING CONDITIONS
OF BIOLOGICAL MOTHERS OF ADOPTEES
(IDENTIFIED IN CASE HISTORIES)
AND SUMMATED PROBLEM SCORES[1]
(N= 98)

Condition	Reported	Not Reported
Drinking problem or alcoholism	39	59
Mental illness (diagnosed)	3	95
History of jail incarcerations	16	82
Physical health problem	18	80
Personality disorder	41	57
Neglect of children	18	80
Abandonment of children	5	93
Abuse of children	1	97
Severe neglect or mistreatment by own family	11	87
Other problem	43	55

Summated Scores:[2]

Value	0	1	2	3	4	5
Freq.	10	25	33	19	8	3
Percent	10.20	25.51	33.67	19.39	8.16	3.06
Cum. %	10.20	35.71	69.39	88.78	96.94	100.00

Mean = 1.99   Median = 2.00   S.D. = 1.214
Skewness = 0.367
Kurtosis = 0.232

[1]Conditions were coded from referral summaries sent by agencies serving the mothers to the Indian Adoption Project at the Child Welfare League of America.

[2]Conditions coded as being identified in the summaries were assigned values of one point. Where no condition was reported a value of zero was assigned. The values for the ten conditions identified in the table were added to secure a Summated Problem Score for each case.

ject.   The father is described as friendly and ca-
pable but the mother has no intention of marrying
him.

*   *   *

The mother has an IQ of 100 and has had fairly de-
cent grades in high school.   She graduated from
high school and then worked as a waitress.   She
is a moody person--gay one moment, depressed
the next.   She has much guilt about this illegitimate child even though it is not uncommon among
the families that she knows.   She would not describe the father of the child.

*   *   *

This mother appears intelligent.   She is married
to the child's father.   She works at housekeeping,
scrubbing, and dishwashing in cafes.   She has been
treated for TB.   She has had nine other children.
The child was put into a foster home because of
the mother's illness.   The parents showed little
interest in getting the child back.   The mother is
meek and timid.   There are strong family ties
despite the difficulties.   The father is described
as a disturbed personality who does a lot of drinking.   He has been treated for TB.   He is under
emotional stress and is conflicted.   He is able to
see his problems and reason them through but can't
do anything about them.   He presents himself as a
defeated personality.   He has very close ties to
his wife, children and family.

*   *   *

This mother has a ninth-grade education.   She is
legally married to the child's father.   He has five
children by a previous marriage and two by this one.
He was employed at a fish hook factory.   Before the
birth of the child the couple came to the agency to
ask to have it placed for adoption.   The mother
said she was unable to care for an infant due to
the presence in her home of an older child who
was sick and required constant care.   They love
their children and have given this step a good deal
of thought.   They feel adoption would give their

child the best home possible.   The father is unemployed.   He lacks finger dexterity for the fish
hook factory and no other permanent job is available to him.

*   *   *

This mother is alert and observant and is unusually
thorough and reliable.   She is a conscientious student.   She completed nine years of education and
plans to enter nursing school.   She never married
and this is her first pregnancy.   She was forced
to quit school because she was pregnant at 16. The
father shows an outgoing personality and is able to
express his feelings easily and intelligently.   He
has an eighth-grade education.   He is married and
separated and has three children from this marriage.   The pregnancy occurred within the context
of a brief affair.

Mothers showing problems somewhat more serious in
nature are typified by the following vignettes:

This mother was cooperative at school and achieved
a tenth grade education.   She never married and
has not been employed.   She appears very immature
for her age.   She has a nice personality but lacks
judgment.   When she was not at boarding school,
she was frequently in jail for drinking.   The child
was born as the result of a very brief affair.

*   *   *

This mother has never married.   Her work in
school was above average; she was considered
"exceptional."   Her adjustment in boarding school
was excellent.   She was considered tense and self-
conscious.   She had an unsettled life due to the
separation of her parents.   She was shunted between both parents' homes.   There was considerable drinking in the home of each parent.   She herself was brought to court for drinking and being
out at night.   She appears moody and unhappy.

*   *   *

This mother is above average in intelligence--she

was an exceptional child in school achieving straight
A's.   She was in a non-Indian boarding school.
She was born out-of-wedlock and raised by a grandmother who died when she was nine.   She felt lone-
some and unwanted in her adolescence.   She never
had emotional security.   She feels guilty about the
pregnancy.

*   *   *

This mother is of average intelligence.   She wanted
to study nursing.   This is her second illegitimate
child.   She is a quiet, retiring girl.   She has evidenced problems of lying and stealing.   She man-
ifests apparent feelings of insecurity.   She was
raped by a relative who had been drinking.

*   *   *

The mother had lived in a two room shack housing 12
people.   She had no financial income in order to
provide for the child.   She had received very little
attention in growing up.   The children in her family were frequently separated and sent to boarding
school.   Mother had a previous child out-of-wedlock.
She was a poor student and this was the result of
a lack of attendance rather than intelligence.

Very severe cases of personal disorganization are
typified by the following illustrative narratives:

The mother does not seem dull but has rather childlike attitudes and ways of reasoning.   Completed
seventh grade.   She had previously married and is
now separated.   She has six other children; three
were born out-of-wedlock.   She roams around a
great deal.   Her own mother died when she was
nine.   Her home life was unhappy and insecure.
She is very quiet and withdrawn.   She appears to
have considerable guilt about her conduct and her
neglect of the children.   She drinks and this has
been especially heavy since she separated from her
husband.   She is often in jail.   She is able to be a
good housekeeper and, when she is in good condition, appears to have a good deal of pride and is
able to carry through a plan.   She has tried to
stop drinking but is unable to do so.

*   *   *

This mother appears to be emotionally and intellectually retarded. She is married to the child's father. She had two earlier children born out-of-
wedlock. She has experienced a great deal of social and familial disorganization. She is very shy
and dependent. Her immaturity and lack of judgment cause her to function at a childlike level and
she had been characterized clinically as a simple
schizophrenic. Her children were taken into court
custody due to neglect. She is utterly incapable of
handling family and child-rearing responsibilities.
The father is dull normal with a quite low verbal
ability and average performance ability. He is er-
ratic and unstable. He works sporadically at physical labor. His mother died when he was eleven.
He lived with his grandmother under limited supervision. He drinks excessively, has frequently been
in jail and is regarded as irresponsible.

*   *   *

The mother has been married but is now divorced.
She had three other children. She has never held
a job. She has had frequent jail sentences and is
known as a heavy drinker. She was unfaithful to
her first and only husband. She appears to be unconcerned about her problems and her children.
The father divorced the mother and remarried. He
has a mixed work history. He has often been
jailed for beating his wife on her complaint. He
was given a year's prison term for stabbing another
man in a quarrel over his wife. After second
child, wife began to be unfaithful. Husband tried
to solve the problem with the traditional method of
wife-beating.

*   *   *

This mother has been married and divorced. She
remarried her husband and separated again. She
has a serious drinking problem and has a prior
background history of delinquency as a child. There
has been a steady pattern of deterioration. The
father is described as being very dependent on his
mother. He had a drinking problem but seems to

have overcome it. He is described as being stoi-
cal with a rather passive personality and lacking
depth.

*   *   *

This mother had a seventh-grade education. She
was married to the child's father. Both mother
and father were unable to focus on the needs of
the child and were anxious to be rid of the responsibility for him. At age 14, this mother had set
her clothes on fire because her grandmother was
drunk and angry at her. She required hospitaliza-
tion for several months. She drinks too much as
do her husband and father. She and her husband
were jailed twice; they fight often and he beats her
severely. The parents appear fond of the older
children but reject this one. The father appears
average in intelligence. He had two marriages
previous to the present one to the mother of the
child. He usually works as a cowboy for cattle
associations and is a fairly reliable worker. He
does all right when he is at home in the country
but drinks too much when he comes to town for
supplies. When he is in town he is frequently in
jail.

For the 90 biological fathers where the information
was known, it was determined that 63 percent were identified
as Indian and a few as part-Indian. Almost 25 percent of
the fathers of the children were Caucasian and another 7 percent were of other racial identifications. The mean age of
the fathers was 28.4 years.

Because the information about the biological fathers
was not consistently available in the summaries, no effort
was made to tabulate the presence of disabling conditions.
The summaries prepared by social workers referring the
children for adoptive placement give the distinct impression,
however, that the fathers of the children were as beset with
personal and social difficulties as were the biological mothers. There was frequent mention of problems of alcoholism,
imprisonment, and lack of stability in personal living arrangements.

The Adoptive Parents and Their Backgrounds

The adoptive parents were widely scattered geographically in 15 states located primarily in the East and Midwest.
As indicated earlier, the families were selected for inclusion
in the study on the basis of their proximity to population centers which could serve as the hub of interviewing field trips
made by the research interviewers. Some lived within cities
and others in medium-sized towns. A not insignificant group
of families--about 20 percent--were located in small towns
or rural areas.

Table III-6

STATE OF RESIDENCE OF ADOPTIVE FAMILIES
AT TIME OF ADOPTIVE PLACEMENT

State	No. of Families
Connecticut	1
Delaware	3
Illinois	6
Indiana	11
Iowa	6
Maryland	2
Massachusetts	8
Missouri	14
New Jersey	8
New York	20
Ohio	1
Pennsylvania	12
Tennessee	1*
Vermont	3
Virginia	2
TOTAL	98

*Moved soon after placement.

In Table III-7, selective demographic information about
the adoptive parents is set forth. It seems clear that there is a
broad range of social class representation in the study population. Twenty-three percent of the fathers were professional
men (e.g., professors, scientists, ministers) and 16 percent
were secondary professionals (e.g., teachers, accountants,
journalists). These two groups, totalling 39 (cont. on p. 72)

Table III-7

DEMOGRAPHIC CHARACTERISTICS
OF THE ADOPTIVE FAMILIES*

A. Occupation of Father

	No.	%
Professional	22	23
Manager, broker, etc.	13	13
Secondary professional	15	16
Small businessman, salesman	8	8
Skilled labor, clerical	27	28
Semi-skilled labor	12	12
	97	100

B. Education

	Father	Mother
5-8 years grammar school	5	4
Some high school	12	15
Finished high school	24	29
Some college	12	18
Finished college	10	21
Some graduate training (M.A)	15	8
Ph.D. or equivalent	18	--
Other	1	2
	97	97

C. Father's Yearly Income

Under $5,000	3
$5,000 - $7,499	30
$7,500 - $9,999	24
$10,000 - $14,999	23
$15,000 or over	11
Unknown or unemployed	6
	97

*where N of 97 is given instead of the 98 originally enlisted
in the study, the missing case is of an adoptive family that
withdrew from the study after the First Series interview.

Table III-7 (cont.)

D. Religion

	Father	Mother
Protestant	69	72
Catholic	10	10
Jewish	13	11
Other	4	3
No religion	1	1
	97	97

E. Number of Children in Family and Ordinal Position of Primary Research Subject

Ordinal Position — No. of Children

	1	2	3	4	5	6	7	8	Total
First	6	23	9	1	-	-	-	-	39
Second		14	5	-	-	-	-	-	19
Third			11	5	-	-	-	-	16
Fourth				7	9	-	-	-	16
Fifth					4	1	-	-	5
Sixth						1	1	-	2
Seventh							-	1	1
TOTAL	6	37	25	13	13	2	1	1	98

F. Identification of Primary Research Subject

Only IARP child placed	60
Oldest of two IARP children placed	31
Oldest of three IARP children placed	5
Oldest of four IARP children placed	1
	97

percent, included six college professors (one of whom was
a college president), five grade or high school teachers, six
ministers, a writer-playwright, a sculptor, four scientists,
an attorney, two social workers, and several in other professional categories. Thirteen percent of the fathers were
managerial employees including a newspaper supervisory administrator, an assistant plant manager, a training director,
an administrator of a manufacturing firm and the executive
of a social agency. Eight percent of the fathers were small
businessmen or salesmen. Skilled laborers or foremen
were well represented among the fathers, accounting for 28
percent of the study group. They included machinists, elec-
tronic technicians, printers, factory foremen, and so forth.
Twelve percent of the fathers were unskilled blue collar workers employed as mill workers, truck drivers, and as small
farm workers and operators. While the occupations of the
mothers are not displayed in the table--many having been
homemakers for some years--their occupational backgrounds
tended to be as varied as those of the fathers, albeit on a
lower level of occupational achievement. The diversity of
the group suggests that the adoption of Indian children has
attracted Americans from many walks of life.

The educational levels achieved by the adoptive fathers and mothers was quite high. Forty-four percent of
the fathers had graduated from college and 18 percent had
been awarded the Ph.D. or its equivalent. Twenty-nine percent of the mothers had graduated from college. Only 17
percent of the fathers and 19 percent of the mothers had
achieved less than a high school education.

The adoptive families were a relatively comfortable
group financially with a third of the fathers reporting earnings over ten thousand dollars a year during 1966 or 1967.
It should be noted, however, that a sizable group of fathers
had quite modest earnings; a third of the group had salaries
under $7,500 a year.

The religious composition of the group was heavily
weighted toward Protestant with 69 percent of the fathers and
72 percent of the mothers reporting such identification or affiliation. Ten percent of the adoptive fathers and mothers
were Catholic while 13 percent of the fathers and 11 percent
of the mothers were Jewish.

In Table III-7, there is displayed a sub-table indicating the number of children in the adoptive families, in-

cluding the adoptee and his ordinal position. The reader will observe that as of the end of field interviewing in 1968, in only 6 percent of the families was the adoptee an only child. Thirty-eight percent of the families had two children and 26 percent had three. Twenty-nine percent of the families had four or more children. The adoptee who was the focus of research interest was either the only child or the oldest of siblings in 39 of the cases. He was the second oldest child in 19 of the cases. In the remaining 40 cases, the adoptee was third or lower down in his ordinal position. I shall subsequently have occasion to look at the relationship between various outcome measures and the ordinal position of the adoptee.

Sixty of the adoptive families had adopted only one child through the Indian Adoption Project. In most cases, the adoptee helped complete the size of the family desired by the parents. In 31 cases, the adoptee was the oldest of two Indian children placed and in five cases, he was the oldest of three Indian children placed. One family adopted four Indian children.

An Index of Socioeconomic Status (SES) was developed based upon three items of information about the adoptive father: his occupation, education and income. In Table III-8, there is displayed the intercorrelations among items. Occupation and education are highly correlated (r=.70), occupation and income more modestly but significantly correlated (r=.48) as is the case between education and income (r=.39). Cronbach's Alpha was utilized to assess the reliability of the scale and it proved to be fairly substantial (Alpha=.76).[3]

When I compared Protestant, Catholic and Jewish families with respect to a number of demographic characteristics [see Table III-9], using the one-way analysis of variance as the statistical test, only the Index of Socioeconomic Status showed significant differentiation among the three groups. The Jewish families were significantly higher in status than both the Protestant and the Catholic families. With respect to the ages of parents, most of the fathers were in their mid- to late-thirties while their wives averaged a few years younger. Jews, Protestants and Catholics were not significantly different with respect to age. Jewish parents, however, tended to enter the adoption experience three to five years earlier in their marriages than their Protestant and Catholic counterparts.

Table III-8

INDEX OF SOCIOECONOMIC STATUS
OF FATHERS OF ADOPTIVE FAMILIES
(N= 98)

Item	Response Categories (with examples)	%
1. Occupation	Unskilled or semi-skilled worker (factory worker, truck driver)	12.2
	Skilled worker (foreman, book-keeper)	27.6
	Small businessman, salesman	8.2
	Secondary professional (teacher, social worker, optometrist)	15.3
	Large proprietary manager (bond salesman)	13.3
	Primary professional, top managerial	23.4
		100.0
2. Education	Grammar school or less	5.2
	Some high school	12.4
	High school graduate	24.6
	Some college	12.4
	College graduate	10.3
	Some graduate work	15.5
	Ph.D. or equivalent	19.6
		100.0
3. Yearly income	Under $4,999	3.3
	$ 5,000 - $ 7,499	32.5
	7,500 - 9,999	27.2
	10,000 - 14,999	25.0
	15,000 or over	12.0
		100.0

Intercorrelation Among Items				Cronbach Alpha= .76
1	2	3	Total Score	
1.00	.70	.48	.92	
	1.00	.39	.86	
		1.00	.69	

Low Score   High Score
LOW SES   ⟵——————————⟶   HIGH SES

Table III-9

DEMOGRAPHIC DATA ABOUT ADOPTIVE FAMILIES
ACCORDING TO RELIGIOUS BACKGROUNDS*

Variable		Jewish (13)	Catholic (10)	Protestant (67)	F-test for significant differences in group means
Father's age at placement	$\overline{X}$	35.69	38.60	35.74	0.918 N.S.
	S.D.	5.68	4.62	6.61	
Mother's age at placement	$\overline{X}$	33.23	35.00	33.19	0.395 N.S.
	S.D.	6.69	4.19	6.18	
Years parents married at placement	$\overline{X}$	7.70	13.10	11.90	2.218 N.S.
	S.D.	4.60	3.04	7.69	
Socioeconomic status index	$\overline{X}$	14.77	11.20	10.87	7.327***
	S.D.	1.83	3.08	3.62	
Age of child at adoptive placement (in months)	$\overline{X}$	14.23	17.50	20.07	0.494 N.S.
	S.D.	12.99	15.39	21.51	

*Two families listed under Jewish involved a Jewish adoptive father and a Protestant mother. Six families not included in the analysis included a couple affiliated with the Ethical Culture Society, another with Bahai, and four couples who had other affiliations or none at all.

Notes

1. Robert R. Sears, Eleanor E. Maccoby, and Harry Levin,
    Patterns of Child Rearing (Evanston, Illinois: Row,
    Peterson and Co., 1957).

2. Reference to "biological mothers" might strike the reader
    as an odd or offensive way to describe the women
    who gave birth to the adoptees. I use the term for
    lack of a better one. Some authors refer to "natural
    mothers."

3. The Cronbach Alpha Coefficient was used to assess the
    reliability of the index. The formula for this is:

$$\left(\frac{k}{k-1}\right)\left(1 - \frac{\sum\limits_{i}^{k} S_i^2}{S_x^2}\right)$$

    where k stands for the number of items in the index,
    $\sum\limits_{i}^{k} S_i^2$ for the sum of the item variances and S_x^2 for

    the variance of the total score. See: Lee J. Cron-
    bach, "Coefficient Alpha and the Internal Structure of
    Tests," Psychometrika, Vol. XVI (1951), pp. 297-
    334.

Chapter IV

SERIES ONE INTERVIEWS WITH ADOPTIVE PARENTS:
BACKGROUND TO ADOPTION AND THE EARLY EXPERIENCE

Number of couples interviewed: 98
Date of first interview in series: 11 /7 /60
Date of last interview in series: 12 /28 /66
Mean age of children: 31. 4 mos.
Mean time interval between
     interview and date of placement: 10. 3 mos.

This chapter reviews the impressions gained from the initial interviews with the adoptive parents. Since the first interview was designed to be a kind of warm-up procedure giving the adoptive parents an opportunity to become related to the research enterprise, considerable latitude was given the interviewers regarding the order and manner in which questions were to be framed. An interview outline provided a guide to the interviewer about the content areas to be covered.

Because of the nature of the interview, I made no effort to quantify the material. Rather I decided to treat the interviews as qualitative data that would offer insight into the nature of the beginning experience of these families with the adoption of an American Indian child. Thus in this chapter, I permit the reader to read what the parents actually told us about several key questions by quoting them extensively.

-- What motivated the adoptive parents to undertake the adoption of an American Indian child?

-- What was the nature of their experience with the adoption agency in working through the arrangements to adopt?

-- What was the nature of the early experience with the child?

77

Background for Adoption

Before I present the adoptive parents' explanations of
what motivated them to adopt American Indian children, I
will examine one domain of background information which is
a major source of differentiation among the families, namely,
the prevailing patterns of family building. Some of the families came to the adoptive experience after having had a number of children born to them. Others had experience with
adoption through having adopted a Caucasian child; yet a smaller
number had previously adopted other types of minority group
children (i.e., Oriental, Puerto Rican, and Mexican). Another
group of parents had adopted an American Indian as the first
child to enter their families. Thus there is considerable
variability in the kinds of experience the respondents had in
a parent role prior to the adoption. Some were venturing
into parenthood for the first time; others were "old timers"
with five or six children already in their homes. Some were
new to adoption while others had already worked successfully
with agencies.

In Table IV-1, I have symbolized the family composition of the 98 families with whom Series One interviews were
completed. At first sight, the manner of symbolizing the
patterns among families might seem strange, but it is easily
made comprehensible. Take a family with the following pattern, for example:

$$AI_1 \rightarrow AO_2 \rightarrow AC_3 \ .$$

This family's first child is an adopted Indian child, the second an adopted Oriental child and the third an adopted Caucasian child. Or take the following example:

$$N_1 \rightarrow N_2 \rightarrow N_3 \rightarrow N_4 \rightarrow AC_5 \rightarrow AI_6 \ .$$

This family had four children born to them. They adopted
a Caucasian as the fifth child and then adopted an American
Indian as the sixth child in the family.

Analysis of Table IV-1 reveals the following features
of the 98 families:

1. Twenty-nine families were "pure types" in that the only children in their families were adopted American Indian children.

2. Eleven additional families had adopted American Indian children as their first children. Thus 40 of the families had commenced their careers as parents with American Indian children as their first children.

3. Only six families were one-child (American Indian) families.

4. Forty-seven families had their own natural children born to them; seven of these involved births after the Indian child was placed as the first child in the family and three had additional births after the placement of American Indian children who were not first.

5. Thirteen families had adopted American Indian children after first having adopted a Caucasian child; four after adopting Oriental children, and one after adopting a Puerto Rican child.

6. Six families represented mixtures of natural, adopted American Indian and adopted Caucasian and/or Oriental children. One family had adopted a Negro child as their eighth child in a family which had the following pattern:

$$N_1 \rightarrow N_2 \rightarrow AO_3 \rightarrow N_4 \rightarrow AO_5 \rightarrow AO_6 \rightarrow AI_7 \rightarrow AN_8 .$$

The table should make amply clear that the demographic features of families involved in the transracial adoption of American Indian children is extraordinarily complex. For many families, the adoption of an Indian child was not the first venture into parenthood; for others, it was not the first venture into adoptive parenthood; and for yet others, it was not the first venture into transracial adoption. The ways in which combinatorial patterns can be arranged to reflect the various kinds of parenting roles is obviously enormously large. It would be even more complex if one added the sex of children as an additional variable. As far as I am aware, researchers in this field have not yet begun to show interest in family patterns as an important perspective about the adoption experience.

Table IV-1

PATTERNS OF FAMILY COMPOSITION
IN ADOPTIVE FAMILIES
(N= 98)

Symbols:

N = natural child
AI = adopted American Indian child
AC = adopted Caucasian child
AO = adopted Oriental child
AP = adopted Puerto Rican child
AM = adopted Mexican child
AN = adopted Negro child

The subscript after the symbols designates the
ordinal position of the child in the family.

Exclusively Adopted American Indian Children

Pattern	No. of Families in Pattern
AI_1	6
$AI_1 \rightarrow AI_2$	18
$AI_1 \rightarrow AI_2 \rightarrow AI_3$	5
$AI_1 \rightarrow AI_2 \rightarrow AI_3 \rightarrow AI_4$	1
TOTAL	30

Exclusively Adopted: American Indian, Caucasian, Oriental, Puerto Rican, and Mexican Children

Pattern	No. of Families in Pattern
$AC_1 \rightarrow AI_2$	7
$AC_1 \rightarrow AC_2 \rightarrow AI_3$	2
$AC_1 \rightarrow AC_2 \rightarrow AI_3 \rightarrow AI_4$	1
$AC_1 \rightarrow AI_2 \rightarrow AC_3$	1
$AI_1 \rightarrow AM_2$	1
$AO_1 \rightarrow AI_2$	2
$AO_1 \rightarrow AO_2 \rightarrow AI_3$	3
$AI_1 \rightarrow AC_2$	1
$AI_1 \rightarrow AO_2 \rightarrow AC_3$	1
$AC_1 \rightarrow AM_2 \rightarrow AI_3$	1
$AC_1 \rightarrow AC_2 \rightarrow AC_3 \rightarrow AI_4 \rightarrow AO_5$	1
$AP_1 \rightarrow AP_2 \rightarrow AI_3$	1
TOTAL	22

Table IV-1 (cont.)

Exclusively Natural Children and Adopted American Indian Children

Pattern	No. of Families in Pattern
$N_1 \to AI_2$	5
$N_1 \to N_2 \to AI_3$	3
$N_1 \to N_2 \to N_3 \to AI_4$	7
$N_1 \to N_2 \to N_3 \to N_4 \to AI_5$	4
$N_1 \to AI_2 \to AI_3$	1
$N_1 \to N_2 \to AI_3 \to AI_4$	3
$N_1 \to N_2 \to N_3 \to AI_4 \to AI_5$	5
$N_1 \to N_2 \to N_3 \to N_4 \to AI_5 \to AI_6$	1
$N_1 \to N_2 \to N_3 \to N_4 \to N_5 \to AI_6 \to AI_7$	1
$N_1 \to AI_2 \to N_3$	3
$N_1 \to N_2 \to N_3 \to AI_4 \to N_5$	1
$AI_1 \to N_2$	2
$AI_1 \to AI_2 \to N_3$	1
$AI_1 \to N_2 \to N_3$	2
$N_1 \to N_2 \to AI_3 \to N_4$	1
TOTAL	40

Mixture of Natural Children, Adopted American Indian Children and Other Adopted Children

Pattern	No. of Families in Pattern
$N_1 \to AI_2 \to AI_3 \to AO_4$	1
$N_1 \to AC_2 \to AC_3 \to AI_4 \to AP_5$	1
$N_1 \to N_2 \to AO_3 \to N_4 \to AO_5 \to AO_6 \to AI_7 \to AN_8$	1
$N_1 \to N_2 \to AC_3 \to AI_4 \to AI_5$	1
$N_1 \to AC_2 \to AI_3$	1
$N_1 \to N_2 \to N_3 \to N_4 \to AC_5 \to AI_6$	1
TOTAL	6

Motivation for Adoption

In reporting upon the motivations articulated by the parents for adopting an American Indian child, I shall organize the narratives provided by the parents according to some of the patterns displayed in Table IV-1. Within this context, the variability of motives will be displayed. It is

my view that family patterns taken alone do not explain the
motivation for transracial adoptions. Obviously the patterns
are interactive with value systems regarding children, race,
the American Indian, and so forth. (Names used in the following remarks from parents are disguised.)

Father ($AI_1 \rightarrow AI_2$): We had come to adopt a child
and when Nora was discussed with us, there was
no hesitation at all, as we were ready to take any
kind of child. You can't contemplate your navel
too much in this kind of thing.

*   *   *

Mother ($AI_1 \rightarrow AI_2$): We could have accepted any
child. We had seen pictures of other Indian children and when we saw Timmy we fell in love with
him immediately. We had no reservations at all.
We were interested in Indians. My husband has
worked with a full-blooded Indian and we are friends
with him still. I also have a sister-in-law who is
one-third Indian. If our economic circumstances
made it possible, we could have taken half a dozen
American Indians and we can never repay Timmy
for all he has done for us.

*   *   *

Mother ($AI_1 \rightarrow AI_2$): During the process of adoption,
the worker called us telling us that an Indian baby was
available. We were ready to accept the child immediately. I had no feelings about an Indian child
being a problem and I have always thought of the
American Indians in the same way I think of anybody else. You know, my husband's ancestry goes
back to the founding pilgrims and we have heard
over and over again about the mixed-breeding that
took place way back with the Indians.

Father: I really did not feel that I was pressured
into taking Seth. I thought we had a good chance
of getting another child if we did not want him.

*   *   *

Mother (AI_1): When the social worker at the adop-

tion agency asked us about taking an American Indian child, I felt it would be all right although I
knew nothing about such children. My husband had
met Indian boys in the service. When I saw a few
snapshots of Harry, I had made up my mind to
take him even before seeing him. When my husband and I saw him through a one-way screen, I
wanted to go in then and there and take him into
my arms. I looked at him and I knew he was for
me. My husband and I did very little talking about
adopting an Indian child and I never thought of him
as being different until my neighbors began to mention this to me.

[Interviewer: There is an openness of manner
about her which made me feel that she really feels
no emotional reaction to the difference, although
she may see it visually. When I asked her whether
she felt that she had done anything unusual, she
said she knew it was unusual, but not unusual for
them.]

*   *   *

Mother (AI_1): We became interested in adopting an
American Indian child when I heard a TV appeal for
adoptive homes for the hard-to-place child. We
had no reservations whatsoever and needed no time
to discuss the pros and cons because when we saw
our daughter's picture, we both just knew that she
would be great for us. Her background has nothing to do with the satisfaction we get from caring
for her. Other people think that we have done
something unusual in adopting an Indian child, but
for us this is an insignificant aspect.

*   *   *

Father ($AI_1 \rightarrow AI_2 \rightarrow AI_3$): Andy was the first
child discussed with us by the agency. We could
have adopted any child offered us. We were just
thrilled and we were not going to be choosy--if we
had our own child, we could not be choosy. I was
particularly impressed with the information they
gave us about Andy's background. His tribe sounded
very interesting. I have always felt that the Indians in this country had a tough break and even

as a boy I would root for the Indians rather than
the cowboys.

*   *   *

Father (AI$_1$ → AI$_2$): I do not regard our adopting
an Indian child as a heroic act.   I got involved in
this strictly through my own self-interest.   I don't
feel like some other people that I have a particular
moral obligation to make amends for the wrongs
done to the Indians in the past and I certainly did
not get involved in adoption on this basis.

Some families were quite firm in the view that their
motives for adopting an Indian child stemmed from the positive appeal of the child's deprived situation.   It was not
just any child that appealed to them--they wanted the youngster for whom the odds against achieving a normal, healthy
life were overwhelming.

Mother (AI$_1$ → AI$_2$): When the agency worker told
us about Indian children, we became interested and
pursued it.   One of the biggest appeals to us was
the fact that these were children who other people
did not want as easily, whereas, we never really
cared what children looked like because we just
wanted children.

Not all of the families claimed that it was easy to overlook
skin color as a factor in adoption.   Some parents were also
inconsistent with each other.

Father (AI$_1$): The agency had asked us if we would
consider an Indian child and we thought about it and
decided that it would be okay as long as the child
would be light-skinned.   Since I come from the
South, I would have hesitated to consider a dark-
skinned child because people might jump to the
wrong conclusions.   We did not want the child to
be taken for part-Negro.   The agency had said we
would have a better chance of being accepted if we
took an Indian child.

*   *   *

Father ($AI_1 \rightarrow AI_2$): We had not applied for an Indian child but when they asked us, we readily indicated our willingness. I suddenly got very taken with the notion of adopting a full-blooded American Indian--there was something that moved me about the idea. I couldn't care less about the color of a child's skin.

Mother: My only concern was the darkness of skin coloring. I knew I could love such a child but would always wonder about the attitudes of the other children.

*   *   *

Mother ($AI_1 \rightarrow AI_2$): When they first showed me a picture of Billy, I was quite upset. During the first visit with him, I guess I was quite subdued and I had a hard time reaching out to him. However, I thought long and hard about my feelings and I resolved them. I think I was more caught up with the fact that I needed to adopt rather than the fact that Billy was an Indian child. We had waited a long time to have a child. As time went on, Billy's being Indian became very exciting to me. It opened up new areas of interest for us even though we had not gone out looking for this aspect of adoption. I guess I was ready to accept the difference intellectually, but when they showed me the picture of Billy, I realized there was a difference between emotional acceptance and the intellectual acceptance I already had. However, once I made the decision, there was no problem.

A small number of families articulated motives in which the racial difference of the child was said to be unimportant whereas the interviewer sensed that the underlying feelings were actually conflicting.

Mother ($AI_1 \rightarrow AI_2$): I had not cared about the background information which the social worker gave us and which I considered irrelevant. But when I saw the pictures of the child, I was thrilled. I do not think we have done anything unusual in adopting Indian children.

Father: I guess what we have done is different,
though, in our circle, if people are going to adopt,
they usually adopt blond, blue-eyed children.

[Interviewer: The adoption of these two children is
more a gratification of a seemingly emotionally immature woman in order to compensate for her in-
ability to have her own child than a conviction about
adoption and concern for well-being of children.
There is evidence that this mother sees placement
of American Indian children as placing them in a
kind of second rate category and she does evidence
a need to deny the children's Indian identity.]

An occasional parent observed that the problem of the
child's color was more evidenced by the caseworker at the
adoption agency than they themselves showed.

Mother ($AI_1 \rightarrow AI_2 \rightarrow AI_3$): My husband and I immediately consented to an Indian child without any
need to discuss this or to see pictures of the child.
We just love children and therefore we were able
to love the child even before we saw him. I am
the kind of person who is not frightened by anything
new and, on the contrary, I find new things chal-
lenging and exciting. It really annoyed me to see
how gingerly the agency social worker handled the
question of our adopting an Indian child. They
present the children as if they are unadoptable.
Why do they talk so much about the darkness of
the children? Even if they are dark, what difference does it make? If I had the slightest reservation about taking a child because of his skin color,
I would never think of adopting him!

Exclusively Adopted Children:
Caucasian Child Adopted First

The families who had adopted Caucasian children first
were in a similar position to natural parents who had not
yet adopted transracially. They were at a juncture in their
lives where they had to decide whether to become a multi-
racial family or to remain homogeneous. The affirmative
decision to adopt an American Indian child was related to a

variety of considerations: religious values, fear of not being
considered for a Caucasian child, a desire to "save" deprived
children, and so forth.

Father $(AC_1 \rightarrow AI_2)$: When the worker asked us
about it, we were able to give an affirmative reply.
We just had no problem in accepting the idea.   We
knew that a child would have difficulties and that he
would be faced with prejudice but felt that he would
have less of a problem facing the world if he were
reared in a good home.   I also felt that it was a
very definite challenge and that, if anything, he
needed us more than we needed him.   I wasn't
particularly struck with the idea that it was an unusual thing to do.

[Interviewer: I had a feeling that the whole question of doing something worthwhile in his life was
a strong factor in his adoption of Zeke.   His deep
sense of religiosity seems to have affected his decision to adopt a different child.   He went along
with his wife who felt so sure and unquestioning re-
lying upon his religious faith to confirm for himself that they were doing something which they felt
is objectively worthwhile and charitable.   I think this
gives them a great deal of satisfaction over and
above the real satisfaction that they are getting
from him just as a child.]

*   *   *

Father $(AC_1 \rightarrow AI_2)$: We like all children.   We
made up our minds long ago on adoption and we
didn't particularly care much about what kind of a
child we adopted.   When a couple wants the child
to resemble them it's because they want to confuse
the world into thinking that these children are their
own by natural birth.   We were firm from the beginning that we did not have to engage in such a
pretense.   We just accept the fact that our child is
Indian and we take no more satisfaction in adopting
her because she is Indian than if she were any other nationality.   We like everything about her as a
person.

Mother: We could have taken any child.   However,

I was aware that we were doing more for a child
when we were adopting an Indian child. Little has
been done for the American Indian and it's about
time something more was done. I feel Kathy has
more of a "glow" inside her than she would if she
were a white child. The big hurdle in the decision
is the initial decision to adopt--not what kind of
child to adopt.

*   *   *

Mother ($AC_1 \rightarrow AC_2 \rightarrow AI_3$): We wanted to have a
third child. The agency worker asked if we could
consider an Indian child; we had already applied
for a handicapped child. I saw no particular advantage or disadvantage in the fact that Mary was
Indian, but felt that taking her was a chance to increase our family and bring happiness to another
child. I don't feel that we have done anything unusual in taking an Indian child. I think prejudice
is fastly disappearing. As a religious person, I
could not have prejudice.

Father: I think we were able to take Mary because,
first of all, such a child would be more readily
available to us and also I think we enjoyed our
first two children so much that we wanted to give
something to a child who might not have such an
easy time being placed. The social worker's sug-
gestion that we might be interested in taking an Indian child was a jolt at first and I was taken aback.
I knew nothing about American Indians and wanted
to find out just how different such a child would be.
The fact that an Indian child is an American, had
a lot to do with my positive resolution of this question. I felt an American Indian child would encounter less prejudice than other kinds of children. Of
course, ideally, a baby is a baby and once you have
brought a child up, they are your own regardless
of color or background.

A number of families were keenly conscious about the
fact that according to objective criteria such as their older
age or the fact that they already had children of their own
that they were unlikely to be considered for a Caucasian infant. They are the people who, in Kadushin's terms, have

"marginal eligibility" for adoption.[1]

> Mother (AC$_1$ → AI$_2$): The question of an Indian
> child arose when we were informed that the agency
> that had placed our first child with us, only placed
> second children who were special kinds of children.
> We pursued the possibility of adopting an Oriental
> child and eventually contacted the worker at the
> agency who told us they had an Indian baby at that
> time. I was immediately thrown into tremendous
> conflict. I did not know anything at all about In-
> dian children. I could not refuse the child since I
> felt this meant we would not be given another chance
> for any other kind of child. On an intellectual
> level, I guess, I had fully approved and felt this
> was very exciting and a good thing to do. At the
> same time, as I look back upon it, I was pulled
> by another side of myself which could not disre-
> gard what other people think. I think the worker
> made a mistake in promoting an Indian adoption
> with us because she did not see that there was a
> frightened side of my personality, although I no
> longer have these fears.

> Father: When they asked us if we would accept an
> Indian child, we were ready to discuss the possi-
> bility although we had never seen an Indian child.
> As I look back upon it, we did not really think
> through the situation sufficiently. When I saw
> Tina, I felt troubled and continued to feel troubled
> even after taking her. When I am really being
> honest with myself, I have to recognize that I am
> essentially a prejudiced person.

*   *   *

> Father (AC$_1$ → AC$_2$ → AI$_3$ → AI$_4$): We had not ap-
> plied specifically for an Indian child but had the
> understanding that it would be easier to adopt if
> we did so. On the basis of the information we
> got and the pictures they showed us, we did not
> have any questions about the two boys. The only
> thing that gave us pause was my concern about the
> darkness of their skin. I was afraid they might be
> thought of as "colored" and abused for this. I was
> concerned that my wife not be hurt in the process

because it would be very painful for her to see the
children treated this way.

Mother: What appealed to me most about the boys
was that they were in a very unhappy situation and
there was indication that they had been mistreated.
I don't think we have done anything unique in adopting our boys but I am aware that it is different
from the usual adoption.

Families with Natural Children of Their Own

Forty-one families adopted an American Indian child
after having had one or more natural children of their own.
All but six had at least two natural children making it unlikely that they would be considered by an adoption agency
for a Caucasian infant. Their motives in adopting an American Indian child were varied: concern for deprived children,
the desire for larger families with race being unimportant,
the realization of their marginal eligibility, and so forth.

Father ($N_1 \rightarrow N_2 \rightarrow AI_3 \rightarrow AI_4$): Above all, we
wanted a child who might not have as wide a chance
for adoption as the traditional blond, blue-eyed baby. We wanted a child who needed a home. We
felt our chances for getting a hard-to-place baby
would be better. We asked for an older child of
mixed race, or one with a slight handicap. When
we were told about American Indian children, we
realized that we had never had a particular interest in the American Indian, but we felt people are
people. We have a special sense of satisfaction in
this adoption, but not because of the ethnic difference. Rather, we feel good because we have been
able to provide a home for a child who needed one.
We have enlarged our family and made ourselves
happy in the process.

[Interviewer: Michael is not by far, second-best
for this family. He seems to be, as far as their
feelings are concerned, just what they would hope
for in adoption and over and beyond what they expected. The principal reason lies in their deep
feelings for children as well as philosophical ones;
they are sensitive to the needs and to the sorrows

of children.   They wanted equally to open their home
to a child who needed parents and they wanted more
children in their own family.]

*   *   *

Mother ($N_1 \rightarrow N_2 \rightarrow N_3 \rightarrow AI_4 \rightarrow AI_5$):   We had
adopted an Indian child quite accidentally.   The
fact that Lisa was Indian was as much a surprise
to me as to anyone else because frankly I never
had given much thought to Indians.   My basic motivation was that I wanted to adopt a child--almost
any child.   I had such a strong drive to be a mother.   I had seen reports about a speech given by a
person about Indian children being available for
adoption in the newspaper.   My drives for being a
mother were so strong I probably could have adopted
any kind of child.   As a matter of fact, I am glad
that Lisa was selected for me rather than having
to go through the original procedure that was suggested in which I would go to an Indian reservation.
I would have been likely to take the most woebe-
gone, disabled child on the reservation.   I'm glad
someone else selected the child for me.   I have a
very strong identification with children and I feel
their suffering intensely.

*   *   *

[Interviewer ($N_1 \rightarrow AC_2 \rightarrow AC_3 \rightarrow AI_4 \rightarrow AO_5$):   This
couple did not apply specifically for an Indian child
but were most interested and delighted when they
learned there might be a possibility.   They have a
sense of social justice and feel that the Indians
have been much mistreated.   The father spoke of
the lack of understanding on the part of white persons in regard to ethnic minorities.   They do not
think they have done anything unusual.   They don't
feel as if they are "crusading" or that they have
made a "sacrifice."   Mr. B. quoted the scripture:
"To us a son is given," and they feel that Paul is
their own son.   Neither do they feel they are aton-
ing for what was done to the American Indian.
However, their heavy investment in church activity
and their long involvement in missionary work gives
them a special compassion about minority children.]

*   *   *

Father $(N_1 \rightarrow N_2 \rightarrow N_3 \rightarrow AI_4 \rightarrow N_5)$: At the time
we applied to the Department of Public Welfare, we
wanted to adopt a Caucasian child, but because of
our ages, it did not look as though one would be
forthcoming. We considered the possibility of
adopting an Indian child and were somewhat worried
about what our neighbors would think and what some
members of our families would say. However,
they were very understanding and the agency was
able to assure us that the child would not be too
dark or have any Negroid features. It is not that
we have prejudices about dark children but in this
community it would be difficult to get such a child
accepted.

*   *   *

Mother $(N_1 \rightarrow N_2 \rightarrow N_3 \rightarrow AI_4 \rightarrow AI_5)$: When the
plight of the American Indian child available for
adoption was called to our attention by the agency
social worker, we decided that if these children
needed homes, we would wish to make our home
available.

Father: We had applied for an Oriental child.
After the caseworker talked with us about the Indian Adoption Project, we promptly decided to apply for an American Indian child. We have always
been very moved by the story of the plight of the
Indian and we gave up the idea of adopting a child
from abroad on the basis of "Let's solve our own
problem first." We feel that the American Indian
owns the country by right and he has been pushed
around and never given a break. In accepting the
child, we feel we have done a little bit for the
American Indian.

*   *   *

Mother $(N_1 \rightarrow N_2 \rightarrow N_3 \rightarrow AI_4)$: We learned that
there was an enormous waiting list for the Protes-
tant, Caucasian children who were available for
adoption. It was at this point that we became
aware of the fact that our best possibility would be
to consider a child of mixed racial background or
a Caucasian child who was physically handicapped.
We both eliminated the possibility of the physically

or emotionally handicapped child from the beginning because we had to consider what this would mean to our own children who are very normal and alert. When the caseworker suggested the possibility of an American Indian child, we were both immediately enthusiastic. We had previously lived in Montana where we had developed strong affection for the American Indian who we feel was here first. We then discussed the possibility with our own children and they thought it was a marvelous idea. However, we were careful to stress with them the possible difficulties we might encounter with a child who was not Caucasian. They were nevertheless enthusiastic and we all went into this together. I do not think that we were prompted in this adoption through religious considerations, but more out of our love for children.

Not all of the parents of natural children entered the adoption experience without ambivalence:

Father ($N_1 \rightarrow AI_2$): Frankly I was hesitant when they raised the question of placing an Indian child with us. I wondered if he would be full-blooded and if his skin coloring would be dark or light. I asked my wife if she could love an Indian baby as much as a white one to which she had replied, "Why not?" I concluded that if she could do so, I could also. My case is a little unusual in that I was born on an Indian reservation where my father ran a general store. I had played with Indian children as much as with other children and learned to speak some words of Indian dialect from my father who spoke twelve Indian dialects. Although my wife had had no contact with Indians, she felt assured that she would feel no resentment towards them. I do believe that we have done something unusual in adopting an Indian child to the extent that I do not think that many other people would have done so, given a choice between an Indian child and a white child. It may be that I was motivated to some extent by my religious and social beliefs. I do belong to a church that preaches love for all regardless of race. Further, my mother was a kind of missionary among Indians and maybe some of this rubbed off on me.

*   *   *

Mother ($N_1 \rightarrow AI_2 \rightarrow N_3$): I had read publicity from
the local agency which had indicated that the re-
strictions were not as great for adoptive families
for American Indian children as I understood they
were otherwise. My first preference had been for
a little girl but then I changed my mind because I
was afraid of taking an Indian girl as a first child
to be adopted. I thought that it matters more to a
girl than to a boy where one comes from and since
this would be my first experience in adopting a
child of a different ethnic background, I felt that I
was not altogether certain if I would be able to handle the problems which might be involved in having
a child whose skin color was darker than my own
and that of my own child. We therefore decided
that the adoption of an Indian boy instead of an Indian girl would present less social problems to be
dealt with. I certainly felt unusual in wanting to
adopt such a child. It may be that I was influenced
to some extent in this adoption by religious considerations.

[Interviewer: Although couple seems to have thought
through carefully their decision to adopt an Indian
child, one wonders if they would not have adopted
a child more like themselves if they had been given
a choice.]

The Experience with the Agencies

During the Series One interviews, the adoptive parents' perspectives were obtained on their experience with the
adoption agencies. It has been clear for some time now that
the agencies are viewed with mixed feelings in the community
at large. There are those who view adoption agencies with
considerable misgiving, feeling that they are arbitrary in
their standards, bureaucratic in their manner of dealing with
applicants, and too prone to probe into sensitive and private
domains of individuals.[2] The adoptive parents were encouraged to report on what they liked about their encounters with
the agency caseworkers as well as what may have irritated
them. In the main, what came across most strongly was

that they had anticipated some difficulty and discomfort in dealing with agencies and had been pleasantly surprised to find the caseworkers to be friendly, warm, and accepting. While features of the experience irritated some parents, only a few--less than 10 percent--were left with a basically negative view of the agencies. By and large, there was an enthusiastic response on the part of parents reflecting, no doubt, the fact that they had been successful in securing children who pleased them.

> Mother (AC$_1$ → AI$_2$): We had been advised by friends when we lived in California not to get involved with agencies in that state because they were offensive. We had also heard of troubles couples had because they were artists and agencies were not sympathetic to artists. However, as I look back upon it, the experiences of these couples were probably influenced by their own attitudes. When we had gone to the agency, we had expected it would take ages and ages to adopt a child and I guess I approached the social worker expecting institutional rules and red tape. We were a little apprehensive because we had the impression that the people who made the decisions were hardly sensitive and were playing God. Much to our pleasant surprise, we were not treated in this way by the agency. Throughout the experience, we developed a relationship of mutual understanding and friendship with the social worker and everything went smoothly in relationship to our application. The caseworker was a woman with exceptionally mature judgment and concern who was very friendly and we all got to like each other. We were always honest with her and as a result, she got to know us as we really were. We were fully aware of what was involved in the agency's attempt to relate the child's background, both physically as well as emotionally, to that of our family. In the beginning, I felt this was a lot of hocus pocus, but having lived through it, I now see the basis for the agency's concern.

> *　　　*　　　*

[Interviewer (AC$_1$ → AI$_2$): The adoptive mother's reaction to the adoption experience insofar as the

agency is concerned seemed to be a positive one.
She said it had taken about six months to get Carole
and a little over a year to get John. She did not
feel that there was much psychological probing and
nothing in the interview situation had been disturbing to her. She thought that the caseworkers were
gracious and did get to know her. She felt that
they were dealing with professional people who knew
what they were about. The hardest thing had been
deciding that they wanted to adopt. In going to the
agency there had been a good deal of anxiety about
whether they would get a child or not and at times
she had felt that they would be turned down. There
was a sense of hopelessness inherent in the situation and she spoke about mortals playing God with
the implication that this is not a role they can easily take. She knew that someone had to do the job
and yet it did leave you at the mercy of someone
who, after all, was just a person.]

*   *   *

Mother ($AI_1 \rightarrow AI_2$): On the basis of the experience of
a friend of mine had who had adopted, I realized
that the agency was going to look at our personal
lives in a way I wasn't used to. I also knew that
we would have to pay a fee. The experience at
the agency was just the way my friend prepared
me. However, I found that it didn't really bother
me. The social worker who dealt with us was a
real nice young person who seemed to have a genuine interest in helping us. She sorta fit in with
us. The purpose of the interviews was to find out
if a couple like us really liked children. They just
weren't going to give children to anyone who came
along asking for a baby. I expected that they
would want to make sure that a child would fit in
with us, be loved, and that they would want proof
that we really couldn't have a baby of our own.

Father: I expected a lot of red tape; someone told
me that a representative of the agency would visit
every day. I was pleasantly surprised when all
that red tape didn't materialize. I consider the
caseworker who was assigned to us one of the
nicest and most understanding persons I have ever
met. She got to know us as individuals. In the

beginning, we were both so anxious that we'd not
get a child that we'd call her a lot; she always
assured us that things were moving along and that
she was hopeful we would get a baby. I think she
was as happy as we were the day Laura was placed
in our home.

The following comment was made by a professional
man who was close to the behavioral and social sciences in
his interests:

> Father ($AC_1 \rightarrow AI_2$): We were both favorably im-
> pressed with the way our application was handled
> by our local agency from the beginning. I would
> describe the caseworker as thorough and someone
> who knew of the availability of Indian and foreign
> children. She was an enthusiastic woman and we
> both felt she conveyed an overall philosophy of con-
> cern and warmth for the children. We respected
> the priority she placed upon the welfare of the
> children rather than upon our needs. She made a
> genuine effort to get to know us as people and I
> think she succeeded fairly well. There were times
> when she was obviously probing us for soft spots
> to see if we could withstand the social pressures
> that people sometimes experience when they adopt
> across ethnic lines. My overall reaction was that
> I was impressed with the quality of the experience
> we had with the agency.

A similar comment was made by the following parent:

> Mother ($N_1 \rightarrow N_2 \rightarrow AC_3 \rightarrow AI_4 \rightarrow AI_5$): Our ex-
> perience with the agency was a happy one. Our
> social worker was a very warm kind of person.
> She was tactful and seemed to be able to find out
> what she needed to know by just coming and getting
> to know us and talking to us rather than asking a
> number of personal questions.

A small group of parents--between five and ten per-
cent--were more critical of agency practices. They found

the inquiry into their personal lives and the whole style of
discourse in their dealings with the caseworker a source of
ambivalence or outright anger.

> Mother ($AO_1 \rightarrow AI_2$): Since we had adopted a Ko-
> rean child through another organization, we ex-
> pected that we would have to be looked at carefully
> before a child would be placed with us. I must ad-
> mit that I thought there were times when the ques-
> tions were too personal and irrelevant. For exam-
> ple, I was asked if our sex life was satisfactory,
> but my husband wasn't. I was also asked questions
> about my childhood which I thought had nothing to
> do with my being a good parent. Also, how I would
> react to an Indian child--when I already had a Ko-
> rean child! Aside from this, I must say that the
> worker was basically a decent sort of person who
> obviously wanted to be helpful. I just wish she
> hadn't been so anxious to know personal things.

> Father: The experience with the agency was as I
> had expected although we had more interviews than
> when we had adopted our first child. I had the
> impression that the agency was much less rigid
> than I thought it would be. I didn't think there was
> as much emphasis on everything being just so in
> our home as I was prepared for. They obviously
> were more concerned with who we are as people--
> which is correct from my standpoint. I must say
> that I developed more respect for their way of
> working after the experience.

> *   *   *

> Mother ($AI_1 \rightarrow AI_2 \rightarrow AI_3$): I do have some feeling
> about the psychological probing that took place in
> our interviews at the agency. Maybe it wasn't the
> question of probing so much as the parrying that
> they did. Why don't they just come out and say
> what they want? I am a mature woman. I had
> the feeling that I was being handled and manipulated
> and I resented it. The first time we met Billy I
> was a little reserved and had not gotten right down
> on the floor the way my husband did and I was
> called into the agency to discuss this the next day.
> I sensed that the worker wanted me to demonstrate

that I could be actively responsive to the child and
I fitted in as well as I could with what I thought
she wanted. I found myself in the peculiar position
of trying to figure out what the worker wanted and
acted accordingly and I have a feeling that all people do this. In a sense, we kind of had to cope
with the agency so that we could get a baby. We
had applied and when nothing seemed to be happen-
ing, we decided to look into foster home placement.
I did not want to do anything behind the agency's
back and so I called the worker to tell her what we
were doing. The next day she called and told us
that Billy was available for adoption. I really feel
that our putting pressure on them in this way had
made the difference. If I had not done this, we
might have had to wait endlessly. The thing that
bugs me the most about the way social workers
deal with people like us is that they tend to judge
too quickly from little things. This can become a
very serious problem since they have the power to
give or withhold a child from a couple.

Despite this strong criticism, this adoptive mother
went on to comment favorably about the caseworker:

Mother: Even though I feel quite critical about the
agency's practices, I must say that I did feel very
warmly towards the social worker who was the kind
of person I would like to be friendly with socially.

The following mother was even more severe in her criticism:

Mother ($N_1 \rightarrow N_2 \rightarrow AI_3$): I do not feel that the
interviews we had with the agency impressed me
favorably because the caseworker kept stressing
the fact that Peggy was Indian. I recognize that
she was forcing me to look at all the facts, feeling
that if I did not face them, I would withdraw my
application. However, I can't see the validity of
this; I would not have agreed to take an Indian child
if I really was afraid of the idea. I don't see why
they insist that people ponder about the matter.
Either you do it spontaneously or you don't. I have

a great many friends or acquaintances who have
adopted and I must say that their experience fits in
with mine in very definitely leaving a negative impression about social work.

Child's Entry into the Home
and the Beginning Experience

        Most of the parents were pleasantly surprised at how
well the children made the transfer from their foster homes
to their adoptive homes. Considering that the mean age of
the children was about 21 months--and some were adopted
at three and four years of age--one might have anticipated
that the children would be more disoriented and traumatized
than most of the parents reported. Yarrow, for example,
has shown that the older a child is at the time of being trans-
ferred from a foster home to an adoptive home, the more
apt he is to display symptoms which reflect disturbance in
personality and behavior.[3]   That the children described here
showed, in the main, a relatively easy transfer to their
adoptive homes does not of course preclude the possibility
that they were paying a price whose evidence was deeply
submerged and not really visible to the parents.

        The relatively sanguine reports about the transfer
process is all the more remarkable considering the nature
of the arrangements required to bring children and families
together. The distance between the child's foster home and
the home of the adoptive parents was always considerable.
The children were often transported thousands of miles with
a social worker from the foster care agency, or one they
had never met before from the adoption agency, to meet their
adoptive parents at an airport. Other children met their
adoptive parents in their foster homes and flew back with
them in several days after only a beginning relationship had
developed. The experience was full of high drama for all
concerned and the adoptive parents obviously were still caught
up at the time of the Series One interviews with the remarkable emotionality and dream-like quality of it.

        The following is the interviewer's account of one
adoptive family's report in the Series One interview that typified the many that went rather smoothly from the start.
This one involved an infant child:

[Interviewer (AI$_1$ → AI$_2$): The child adopted was
the first one discussed with them. They were told
she was part Apache and probably part Spanish due
to the curling of her hair. However, it was later
established by papers which came with her that she
was full-blooded Apache. They both said that from
the beginning, even before they saw the child's pictures, they had made up their minds that they
wanted to adopt this child. When they saw pictures
of her, they were most enthusiastic about her and
felt they could love her. The father referred especially to her long black hair and dark eyes and
olive complexion, which had impressed him in the
picture. The mother later said that they had been
most impressed by the fact that she was a baby
girl and an Indian. At no time did they have any
reservation about proceeding to adopt this child
from the time they heard about her.]

[The adoptive mother said that she had always
heard that it was a mother's wonderful feeling when
she first had her baby placed in her arms, and she
would certainly say this was her experience when
she first saw the child at the airport. When she
saw the caseworkers who had brought the child to
them come off the plane, she went to them and
asked to take the child. She said she just cried
with delight. The father found it hard to describe
his initial reaction when he first laid eyes on her
but said that he was too 'choked up' and was
'standing on his head with delight.']

[The adoptive mother spoke of the ease with which
the child adjusted to their home. She said that
from the time the child was brought into the house
for the first night, she settled in as though she had
always been their child. There had been no feeding
or sleeping problems from the very beginning. They
had expected her to react to the strangeness of
coming into a new place and being with new people.
However, they both commented on the fact that from
the time the mother took the child into her arms
at the airport, she responded to her as if she knew
she belonged to the couple.]

[Both parents described the pleasure they received
in doing things for the child, even the smallest

chore. The adoptive father commented that it
seems they are happier and more settled than before the child came into the home. It is just a
pleasure for him to work and save for her. The
adoptive mother added that the child is now their
'whole life.']

   Other placements that went well almost from the start
had the following flavor:

Mother ($N_1 \rightarrow AI_2$): Terry was the first child the
caseworker talked to us about and he could not have
been more well-chosen for us. We had been told
that his own mother had loved him but because of
being unable to care for him she had put him up
for adoption. We had no hesitation in making our
decision to proceed with our application to adopt
Terry after we heard of him and saw his picture.
We very much appreciated, at the beginning, the
care and concern of the caseworker who brought
him from Montana. Someday I would like to take
him back to the reservation to show her how well
he is doing.... From the beginning, he adjusted
very easily in our home and my husband and I had
no difficulty in getting used to him. As a matter
of fact, he adapted so easily that it is hard to realize that he has not always been with us.... When
we first saw Terry it was late at night--he looked
just as we had expected. I had anticipated that
separating from his foster mother would be hard
for him. However, because of his easy adjustment, I realize my fears were groundless.

                    *   *   *

Mother ($AC_1 \rightarrow AC_2 \rightarrow AI_3$): We feel we owe a great
deal to the foster home in South Dakota; those peo-
ple got our child off to a good start.

                    *   *   *

Mother ($AI_1 \rightarrow AI_2 \rightarrow AI_3$): Even though he had
been so very young when he came to us, he had
reacted to being handled over to us by the foster
mother with hysterical screaming which went on

for hours. However, he quickly adjusted to our
home and after a few weeks of catering to his every
whim, we realized he was well on his way to getting spoiled, and we began to clamp down a bit so
that now things are going very smoothly.

    Not all of the initial experiences went so smoothly.
About one in five couples reported moderate to severe tur-
bulence in the early settling-in phase. The following reflect
situations in which the beginning of the adoptive experience
was hardly auspicious:

> <u>Mother</u> ($AC_1 \rightarrow AI_2$): The agency from which we
> had adopted our first child could not offer us an-
> other baby other than a handicapped child or a
> child from a racial minority. We mulled it over
> and, with reservations, approached the agency and
> were told about an Indian baby we could take right
> away. The caseworker obviously wasn't in tune
> with our uncertainty and rushed us along at a pace
> that was bad. We were afraid that we would not
> be considered for another child if we turned her
> down.... The baby was particularly cute but she
> was tiny and it wasn't long before we got concerned
> because she was born prematurely and might be
> retarded. Also, I knew nothing about Indian chil-
> dren and later realized that it was one thing to
> have intellectual acceptance about racial difference
> but it was another to have it right in your own
> family. I realized that I found it very painful to
> have people stare at me when I went out with the
> baby. I couldn't disregard other people's attitudes
> as well as I expected I would. The caseworker
> had never appreciated the other side of me that
> was so frightened of difference.... For a time
> the agency wanted to take the child back but my
> husband and I found that there was something pull-
> ing us to her even though we were upset about peo-
> ple staring. I finally decided to get psychiatric
> help so that I could resolve what was going on for
> me in this adoption. I went weekly for about nine
> months and finally got to the bottom of my difficul-
> ties. I think I have worked out my problems about
> Sally looking different. I have come to realize that
> I had other kinds of problems that were getting in

the way of my being a loving mother to her. We
got off on a bad start but I now feel that everything
is going to work out well. I now find so many
things I can enjoy in Sally.

*   *   *

Mother ($AC_1 \rightarrow AI_2$): We went through a long period of adjustment with Fran and my orientation to
parenthood with her was different from my experience we had with our first adopted child. I just
was not prepared for what would be involved in
taking an older child into our home and having two
children to care for simultaneously. I had tended
to minimize the time that would be involved before
Fran could settle down. In the beginning, she did
not respond to me very well and was much more
responsive to my husband and to men in general.
However, there suddenly came a time, after six
months, when I became aware of a great change in
Fran's responsiveness to me. I attributed the difficulty she had initially partially to the fact that
she is very sensitive and was reacting to some extent to being removed from a foster home in which
there were only two women and in which she had
felt the need of a father person.

*   *   *

Mother ($AC_1 \rightarrow AI_2$): The child has been defiant
from the beginning. She would have temper tantrums and pass out completely. She continued to
have bowel movements in her pants and would remove the feces and put them under her brother's
bed.

*   *   *

Mother ($N_1 \rightarrow N_2 \rightarrow AI_3$): The social worker had
wanted us to go down South where April was in a
foster home and I fought against this because I
abhored the South, didn't want my own children
exposed to the bigotry there and because I felt that
it was better for the worker to handle the child's
separation from the foster parents. We finally
consented to go to North Carolina where we all had
an absolutely ghastly experience. We realized

quickly that April thought of her foster parents as
her own parents. She was two years old at the
time and had been in the foster home for most of
her life. She was a very happy child and very attached to her foster parents and I realized it would
be very difficult to remove her. The caseworker
was completely unprepared for April's hysteria and
panic about moving out of the foster home. I was
ready to give up the idea since I felt like a kid-
napper until the caseworker convinced me that in
the long run the adoption was a better plan for the
child.... It still is hard for me to talk about what
happened. April was terrified and was hitting,
screaming and kicking all the way back to our home.
That night we found she had 102 degree temperature
and was covered with sores. She needed penicillin
immediately and we discovered that she had severe
hives, which she had been scratching constantly....
The child was bewildered by our home--she had
never been in a tub bath and had never seen a toilet before.... After this, we felt pretty abandoned
by the caseworker. For two weeks, April remained
in my lap and hit out at anyone who came near her.
She would not let my husband put her to bed and
seemed to distrust men. For the first two nights,
April slept with me, then I put her in the same
room with my oldest child as she was accustomed
to being in a room with other children. For three
days we could not take her clothing off.... It took
a very long time before April developed any security with us and it was hell for all of us.

Notes

1. Alfred Kadushin, "A Study of Adoptive Parents of Hard-
    to-Place Children," Social Casework, Vol. 43 (May
    1962).

2. Rael Jean Isaac, Adopting a Child Today (New York:
    Harper and Row, 1965).

3. Leon J. Yarrow, "Research in Dimensions of Early Ma-
    ternal Care," Merrill-Palmer Quarterly of Behavior
    and Development, Vol. IX, No. 2 (1963) pp. 101-14.

Chapter V

SERIES TWO INTERVIEWS WITH ADOPTIVE MOTHERS: SOCIAL PERSPECTIVES ON TRANSRACIAL PARENTHOOD

Number of mothers interviewed:	97
Date of first interview in series:	11/9/61
Date of last interview in series:	10/28/66
Mean age of children:	40.4 mos.
Mean time interval between interview and date of placement:	19.1 mos.
Mean time interval since prior interview:	8.9 mos.

In this and the following three chapters, the findings from the Series Two through Series Five interviews with the adoptive parents are presented. As previously indicated, these interviews were more structured than those in Series One and hence could be treated in quantitative fashion. A variety of indexes relevant to the purposes of the study are discussed in the chapters.

First, however, I have created small vignettes based upon reports of three of the adoptees whose progress I would like to present over the series of four interviews. The cases were chosen to reflect a case of a "well-adjusted," "average adjusted," and a child whose adjustment was viewed as "guarded" seen from the perspective of the final interviews. In this way, it is hoped the reader can capture some of the flavor of a developmental study in which a child's progress can be charted over the course of repeated annual interviews.

Progress of Child Rated as "Well-Adjusted" at the End of the Five Series

[Is there anything you want to tell me about your overall experience with Cal?] Everything has been

just great and we love him so much. He is such
a loving child. It has just been a terrific experience. Everything has gone as if we had brought
him home from the hospital and everything has been
A-OK. [Since I saw you last, what progress would
you say Cal has shown?] He is growing in every
way. His physical progress is apparent and his
mind absorbs so much. His talking is not just a
matter of mimicry. One can just see what an
amazing little fellow he is. He adjusts well to people. He is so very secure. [To what do you at-
tribute this?] The fact that we have given love to
him so freely. He is just Number 5 in the family.
He has a terrific personality. [Have you had any
problems about Cal eating enough or eating the kind
of foods he needs?] No, he has a wonderful ap-
petite. [What do you expect from him in the way
of table manners?] I do not consider table manners for the child too important now. I am more
interested in having him enjoy his food. [What
sort of things do you enjoy in Cal?] We get along
just beautifully. I get a real thrill out of his beau-
tiful, happy disposition and his love of life. I cannot think of any way in which he becomes a problem. We enjoy playing together. When I clean
the living room, he follows me around with his own
dusting mop. We take time out when I am clean-
ing or baking to listen to one of his sister's music
boxes. We also enjoy caring for the animals--
dogs, cats and other creatures together. He also
enjoys the birds outside with me. [Would you tell
me something about how Cal gets along with his
brother and sisters?] He is real affectionate with
them and they are with him. There is give and
take among them. When they get into a squabble,
it usually irons itself out without my getting in the
middle. [Will you tell me something about the way
Cal and his father act towards each other?] Cal
is real happy when he sees his father's car turn
into the road. He just runs up and greets him.
He likes to go right along with his daddy. If his
father is working on the tractor, he likes to ride
on it with him. They wrestle and they play ball.
He likes to go to the bathroom with his father together and he is beginning to be proud of standing
up to urinate like a man.

(Cal was two years old at the time of this interview.)

Child Rated as "Average Adjustment"
at the End of the Five Series

[Since I last saw you, what progress would you say
Danny has shown?] He has grown tremendously.
He has become more socialized since playing with
the same children in the summer play group and
nursery school has helped tremendously. He went
through a bad hitting stage. He has always been
boisterous and aggressive. He has always found it
difficult to play with children because he blows up
quickly. [What problems does Danny show?] He
attempts to dominate children. He is aggressive
in that he is rough and he tends to push children
and is hyperactive. [What is your reaction to this?]
I am somewhat concerned but I think with the help
of the school, he should make progress. He is a
very secure boy. We are with him constantly and
we love him so dearly that I am sure he is going
to grow up to be a substantial young man. The
fact that he is mischievous and stubborn and sometimes destructive doesn't particularly disturb me.
I associate that with being a boy. He is somewhat
tense at times and about a year ago, we discovered
that he is very fearful of physical punishment. He
cringed and started to cry when he saw my husband changing a belt on his pants. It may be that
he was beaten in the past but he doesn't seem to
remember this. [Could you tell me more about
how you and Danny get along together? What sort
of things do you enjoy in him?] We get along very
well when we are alone together. He is a suave,
polished conversationalist. He is very good with
one adult. Life is never dull with him. He is
good company. He plays lustily--is interested in
things. I very much like his general vivacity.
[In what way do you get on each other's nerves?]
The excessive noise and the dawdling and the drift-
ing away during meals sometimes provokes me.
His roughness with his baby brother can also get
my dander up. [In general, how does Danny get
along with the neighbor children?] His boisterous-
ness frightens them a bit. Generally, he is okay
though. He has gone through a fighting stage periodically and I would say that he gets along less
well than the average child because he is so rough.
I think this will even itself out in time. [How of-

ten do you spank Danny?] He gets a real spanking
about once a month. He gets a slap on the hand
fairly frequently. However, we have stopped most
of this since the belt incident. My husband particularly is concerned that Danny not be frightened
of him and he merely uses verbal reprimand when
it is necessary. [Can you tell me something about
Danny and his father and how they act toward each
other?] His father is very strongly attached to
Danny and very proud of him. They are very happy doing things together. My husband expects more
of Danny in terms of good behavior and he often
gets it.

(Danny was four years old at the time of this interview.)

Child Whose Adjustment was Rated as "Guarded"
at the End of Series Five Interview:

[First of all, is there anything you want to tell me
about your overall experience with Gary?] He has
been fun and we have all enjoyed him most of the
time. His improvement has been satisfying. [Since
I saw you last, what progress would you say he
has shown?] Physically he is in better shape; he
used to have colds a lot. He has become more
grown-up and is beginning to be kind of independent. His kindergarten teacher has felt that his
behavior has improved a great deal. [What problems does he show?] He cannot remember the
only two rules about playing out of doors. He
seems unable to resist the temptation to play out
of bounds and he does not seem sorry except when
he is caught. He has a little trouble telling the
truth. I am inclined to feel that his being disobe-
dient must be connected with his seeming lack of
emotional attachment to our family. I have the
feeling that he does not feel identified emotionally
with us and he could just as easily live with another family on the block. I am somewhat concerned about whether he will ever be able to have
a meaningful relationship with us. [Is there anything else you want to tell me about his personality?] He is restless and has many needs. He
wants things very much--like toys--then in a short
time he is not interested or does not care about

them. [How much attention does he seem to want
from you?] He demands an awful lot of attention,
talking rather than asking to be helped to do something.

(Gary was six years old at the time of this interview.)

The Series Two Interview

The Series Two interview was designed to survey the
adoptive mothers in several important areas: the progress
of the child's integration within the family and his adjustment, the nature of the family's deliberations about adopting
an Indian child, and the child-rearing orientations of the
adoptive mother. In addition, since the adoption of a child
across racial lines was viewed to be as much a social act
as a personal venture, emphasis was placed upon illuminating the social attitudes and life-styles of the mother. This,
together with attitudinal data secured from the adoptive fathers, would form a social portrait of the families.

The interview called for a prescribed sequence of
questions standardized with respect to wording, and required
approximately two hours to administer. Appointments were
scheduled with the adoptive mothers after first notifying the
agencies that had placed the children in the home of the pend-
ing research visit. If active work was going on with the
families, the agency would thus be able to forestall the appointment until another time. The contact also made it possible for the agency to inform the research staff about any
recent developments in the lives of the adoptive families that
might make an interview difficult. In only three cases was
it necessary to delay scheduling an appointment. Once clear-
ance was received from the agency, a letter was sent to the
adoptive mothers to arrange for the interviewer to visit at a
mutually convenient time.

Since the interviewing involved use of a standardized
instrument, it was possible to develop a codebook to treat
all responses in either categorical form or as continuous
variables. An extensive statistical analysis of the mothers'
responses was undertaken with a computer.

The analytic procedure I used was the division of the
Series Two interview into three domains: (a) child description, (b) parent behavior and parent attitudes relative to

adoption, and (c) social psychological attitudes of the parents. A factor analysis was completed for each of the three domains and the results were used in an empirical manner as a guide for the construction of indexes.[1] The intent was to create indexes which were consistent with the factorial structure of the phenomena studied. There was no attempt to create more rigorous measures in which, for example, items would be weighted in the indexes according to their factor loadings. Such a refinement seemed pretentious in view of the small size of the sample and the nature of the data.

Using the factorial structure as a guide, indexes were constructed as follows: the items to be included in the index were identified; since items varied in the number of categories and would be disproportionately weighted if they were simply summated, each item was subjected to the procedure of "reciprocal sigma weighting" whereby each item was divided by its standard deviation. Where items were negatively loaded in the factorial display after rotation, they were reflected in the creation of the index so that the high point became the low point.

The responses of the adoptive mothers are displayed here in a somewhat unusual fashion in the interest of brevity and to spare those readers who are not particularly concerned with the refinements of attitude analysis or elaborate discourse about the nature of the statistical properties of these attitudes. The responses of the mothers are set forth within the context of the indexes constructed from their interview material, and the reader can therefore quickly scan the way these responses have been distributed. I have also taken the step of displaying the intercorrelation matrix for each index as well as the correlation of each item with the summary score for the index. To test the reliability of the index, I have calculated Cronbach's Alpha Coefficient cited in the previous chapter. The experience of developing indexes displayed in this chapter reveals that many of the summary measures were of a high order of reliability. This was particularly true of indexes created on the basis of quite strong and unambiguous factorial structures. Some indexes were retained even though their factorial structures were ambiguous (and their reliabilities accordingly low), because there was theoretical interest in the domain and, within the context of an essentially exploratory investigation, it appeared valid to test whether any kind of illumination came from these less adequate measures.

The Characteristics of the Adoptees
and Their Progress to Date

In the main, the adoptive parents were quite glowing
about the nature of their experience. When asked about the
progress shown by the adoptees thus far in their living together, only two our of 97 adoptive mothers said that things
had worked out somewhat worse than they had expected.
About a quarter of the mothers reported their experience to
be just as they had anticipated it. Almost three-fourths of
the adoptive parents reported with pleasure that the experience
was somewhat or much better than they had anticipated. The
overall flavor of their responses was almost euphoric. There
were frequent expressions of extreme delight with the adoptees and, some nineteen months after the adoptive placement,
the children seemed well imbedded within their families. Fully
85 percent of the children were described as showing themselves to be very secure with their parents and only three
youngsters were described as being either somewhat insecure
or quite insecure. This is not to say that the children were
problem-free or that the developmental problems one would
expect in any sample of children taken from the population
at large were missing. They simply didn't seem to take on
great importance. When the parents were asked about the
problems the child had shown since the last interview, almost one in four children was described as having some personality or developmental problems and 38 percent spoke of
situations in which a character trait of the child was mentioned as problematic. However, in only 29 percent of the
cases were the parents very or somewhat concerned about
this.

Index of Child Adjustment

Table V-1 displays an index of child adjustment which
is based upon only two items. The index provides a crude
measure of how the mothers perceived the progress of the
child, as indicated by their reports of the child's problems
and the mother's degree of concern about these problems.
One might well wonder whether the portrayal of the children's
adjustment on this limited basis relatively early in the placement would have any predictive value. It can be reported
that there are significant correlations between this obviously
modest Series Two Index and summary measures developed
for Series Four information some two years later $(r=.39)$
and for Series Five interview material $(r=.37)$. Further,

the correlation between the Index of Child Adjustment from
Series Two and an Overall Adjustment Rating summarizing
all of the information known about the children for all of the

---

Table V-1

INDEX OF CHILD ADJUSTMENT
(N= 97)

Question	Response Categories	Percent Response
1. Since I saw you last, what problems has your child shown?	Personality or developmental problems mentioned	25.8
	Character trait mentioned	38.2
	Child has shown no problems	36.0
		100.0
2. What is your reaction to child's problems?	Very concerned or somewhat concerned	28.9
	Slightly or not at all concerned	38.9
	No problem whatever to be concerned about	32.2
		100.0

Product-moment correlation
between items = .70

---

interviews conducted with the families was fairly impressive
(r= .40). The overall impression is that, even within the
second year, one begins to get information which portends
the later adjustment measures and there is indication of some
stability in the way in which the children are perceived over
time.

Child Behavior Characteristics

Table V-2 provides the frequency distributions of the
mothers' responses when presented with an adjective checklist containing various behavioral characteristics of the children. Some of the items proved, not unexpectedly, to be

Table V-2

MOTHERS' DESCRIPTIONS OF BEHAVIORAL DISPOSITIONS
OF ADOPTEES DURING SERIES TWO INTERVIEWS

(N= 97)

Characteristic	Very Much	Somewhat	Hardly or Not at All	No Response
		(Percentaged Across)		
Happy	96.9	3.1	—	
Active	91.7	7.3	1.0	
Mischievous	25.0	52.1	22.9	
Stubborn	21.9	37.5	40.6	
Quiet	14.6	30.2	52.1	3.1
Explosive Temper	8.3	32.3	59.4	
Shy	4.2	32.3	63.5	
Agile	66.7	18.8	13.5	1.0
Bright	82.3	15.7	1.0	1.0
Graceful	41.7	32.3	25.0	1.0
Trusting	74.0	19.8	3.1	3.1
Destructive	7.3	16.7	76.0	
Friendly	83.3	15.7	1.0	
Talkative	62.5	24.0	11.5	2.0
Tense	1.0	14.6	83.4	1.0

very skewed in the direction of highly positive reports. Thus,
almost all of the children were described as being happy
youngsters who were very active. On other items, there
was more of a spread in the distributions of responses and
these were useful for developing specialized indexes for behavioral descriptions of the children.   Thus, a fourth of the
children were seen as mischievous and at least two out of
five were described as having somewhat explosive tempers.
Two out of five children were portrayed as somewhat shy and
almost a fourth were said by the adoptive mothers to be
somewhat destructive or worse. Very few children were
described as being tense or not trusting.

Child Activity Level

Based upon the factor analysis of the child description
material, a four item index was created, the Index of Child
Activity Level. The Alpha Coefficient was calculated as .62.
A high score on this index would describe a child who tends
to be stubborn, explosive in his temper and mischievous. He
is apt to be spanked more than other children.   While there
is not necessarily a connotation of pathological behavior involved here, the association with the previously discussed
Index of Child Adjustment is significant ($r= -.39$), suggesting
that the more aggressive children were regarded by the adoptive mothers as being more problematic in their behavior.
The association between this measure and the subsequently
developed Series Four and Series Five summated symptom
scores and the Overall Adjustment Rating developed on the
basis of all interview material was modest (for all three
summary adjustment measures the correlations were about
.20).   Surprisingly, there was not a significant difference
between the boys and the girls in the sample on this measure.   However, age appeared to be a related factor in that
the older children tended to be described as more aggressive
and the association with the age of the children at the time
of the adoptive placement was significant ($r= .21$).

Index of Child's Friendliness and Outgoingness

Four items were clearly linked in the factor analysis
and these were merged into an Index of Child's Friendliness and
Outgoingness displayed in Table V-4. This measure seemed
relatively stable, having an Alpha Coefficient of .95. There was
a modest association between this index and the (cont. pg. 118)

Table V-3

INDEX OF CHILD ACTIVITY LEVEL
(N= 97)

Question	Response Categories	Percent Response
1. Stubborn*	Not at all or hardly	40.6
	Somewhat	37.5
	Very much	21.9
		100.0
2. Explosive*	Not at all or hardly	59.4
	Somewhat	32.3
	Very much	8.3
		100.0
3. Mischievous*	Not at all or hardly	22.9
	Somewhat	52.1
	Very much	25.0
		100.0
4. How often does mother spank her child?	Rarely or not at all	35.5
	Occasionally	44.1
	Fairly often	11.8
	Frequently	8.6
		100.0

Intercorrelation Among Items					
	1	2	3	4	Total Score
1	1.00	.46	.42	.25	.79
2		1.00	.15	.26	.69
3			1.00	.13	.63
4				1.00	.61

Cronbach
Alpha= .62

Low Score $\longleftarrow$ $\longrightarrow$ High Score

PASSIVE   AGGRESSIVE

*Respondents were told: "I am going to show you a card which lists characteristics of children. For each characteristic, please tell me whether your child is very much, somewhat, hardly, or not at all like this."

Table V-4

INDEX OF CHILD'S FRIENDLINESS AND OUTGOINGNESS
(N= 97)

Question	Response Categories	Percent Response
1. Friendly*	Not at all	--
	Hardly	1.1
	Somewhat	15.6
	Very much	83.3
		100.0
2. Quiet*#	Not at all	3.1
	Hardly	52.1
	Somewhat	30.2
	Very much	14.6
		100.0
3. Shy*#	Not at all	--
	Hardly	63.5
	Somewhat	32.3
	Very much	4.2
		100.0
4. Talkative*	Not at all	2.1
	Hardly	11.5
	Somewhat	23.9
	Very much	62.5
		100.0

Intercorrelation Among Items					
	1	2	3	4	Total Score
1	1.00	.34	.47	.20	.85
2		1.00	.35	.47	.66
3			1.00	.19	.69
4				1.00	.58

Cronbach Alpha= .95

Low Score ⟵⟶ High Score

RETIRING OR WITHDRAWN   OUTGOING

* Respondents were told: "I am going to show you a card
which lists characteristics of children. For each characteristic, tell me whether your child is like this."

When included in index, item has been "flipped" so that 4
becomes 1, 3 becomes 2, etc.

overall Adjustment Rating (r= -.22) developed at the end of
the study, and similar associations with Series Four and Series Five summated scores.   In the main, what is of interest
is that the child's activity level as described by the previous
index and the child's friendliness and outgoingness are essentially orthogonal, with the correlation between the two measures being close to zero.   This would of course be predicted
from the knowledge that the two indexes were derived from
factor analytic treatment of the mothers' responses.

I am well aware of the fact that the relatively young
age of the children would make it unlikely that many of them
would be in any serious difficulty so early in their adoptive
experience, despite their having experienced maternal deprivation and a separation from their original biological mothers
and their foster mothers.   The three indexes we have displayed here represent relatively modest efforts to portray
the children along dimensions that make sense for such a
relatively young group.

Orientations to the Adoptive Parent Role

Although the adoptive mothers and fathers had been
interviewed in the Series One sessions about the manner in
which they had approached adoptive parenthood in general and
the adoption of an Indian child in particular, some aspects of
this required refinement and were included as part of the
Series Two interview.   For example, since these adoptive
parents had availed themselves of the opportunity to adopt a
child across racial lines, did this signify that there was a
broad range of types of children that they might have adopted?   Or had they specifically desired an Indian child in approaching the adoption agencies?   Only one adoptive mother
in five reported that she had approached the agency specifically desiring an Indian child, whereas an additional 24 percent indicated that they were open to a child of mixed or
minority group parentage.   A substantial number of the parents had not originally considered a child with a mixed background but had no reservations, or only minor ones, about
the idea when it was presented by the agency.   For many
adoptive mothers, the desire for a child was so strong that
ethnic background was an insignificant matter.

Attributes of Acceptable Children

In Table V-5, are presented the percentage distribu-

tions of the mothers' responses regarding their willingness
to adopt certain kinds of children as presented on a hypothetical list of children they might have considered. The
list includes children with physical handicaps, those with
problems in their background, as well as youngsters who are
of minority racial groups. Of the 13 characteristics posed
to the adoptive mothers, the child who was regarded by most
parents as the one they could have adopted easily was the
Oriental child (e.g., a Chinese child). About 71 percent of
the adoptive mothers said they could have easily adopted such
a child and about one in five said they would have had minor reservations about such an adoption. Only six percent
of the mothers said they could not consider such a child. It
was obvious that the racial characteristics of the Indian child
were not considered too different from the Oriental child and
a large number of the adoptive mothers reported that they,
in fact, were often stopped on the street by people who in-
quired as to whether the Indian child was Korean. Similarly,
a child whose appearance was somewhat marred by injury
due to forceps delivery was, by and large, regarded as easily adoptable. Only three percent of the mothers indicated
they could not consider such a child.

Children with physical handicaps were also relatively
acceptable, although with increased reservation if the handicap was more serious and not correctable. The child who
was regarded as most difficult to adopt was one of mixed
Negro-white parentage. This was true whether or not the
child was specified as being obviously Negro in features and
skin color. Only about 15 percent of the adoptive mothers
indicated they could have easily adopted a child who was obviously Negro, and 22 percent expressed similar views about
a child not obviously Negro in appearance. Fifty-eight percent of the mothers said they could not consider a child of
mixed Negro-white parentage who was obviously Negro in appearance and 48 percent made the same response to a child
who was not Negro in appearance. More often than not, this
posture on the part of the adoptive mother was accompanied
by the explanation that while she did not have any emotional
aversion to adopting a black child, she felt that community
pressures and hostility would be so stressful for the adoptive
family that the child's welfare would be interfered with. This
view was typically expressed in the words of one adoptive
mother:

> Mother: I would have had no misgivings about
> accepting a child of mixed Negro background, but
> (cont. pg. 122)

Table V-5

MOTHERS' RESPONSES TO TYPES OF CHILDREN
COUPLE MIGHT HAVE BEEN ASKED TO CONSIDER
WHEN APPROACHING AGENCY*

	Adopted Easily	Minor Reservations	Major Reservations	Could Not Consider
		(Percentaged Across)		
1. Slightly retarded child	9.4	30.2	18.8	41.6
2. Normal older child (e.g., eight years old)	39.6	20.8	14.6	25.0
3. Child with mild handicap, not correctable (e.g., deaf in one ear)	61.5	26.0	4.2	8.3
4. Child with fairly serious handicap, correctable (e.g., cleft palate)	43.2	23.2	12.5	21.1
5. Child with serious handicap, correctable (e.g., club foot)	44.8	18.8	15.6	20.8
6. Child with serious handicap, not correctable	12.5	13.5	32.3	41.7

7.	Child of mixed Negro–white parentage (obviously Negro in features and skin color)	15.6	6.3	19.8	58.3
8.	Child of mixed Negro–white parentage, but not obviously Negro in appearance	21.9	14.6	15.6	47.9
9.	An Oriental child (e.g., Chinese)	70.8	17.7	5.2	6.3
10.	A child with mental illness in his immediate background	37.5	28.1	16.7	17.7
11.	A child whose looks are somewhat marred by injury due to forceps delivery	67.7	24.0	5.2	3.1
12.	A withdrawn, shy child (four years old)	64.6	20.8	6.3	8.3
13.	An aggressive, hyperactive child (four years old)	58.3	20.8	10.4	10.4

*The number of subjects responding to the items varies from 97 to 92.

I felt my husband would have had difficulty because
of his "Upstate New York background." Also, the
attitudes of the community that we live in would
have worked against the interests of the child.

The minority that indicated they could have adopted a
black child generally took the position that they could cope
with such problems, and several evidently had left it up to
the agency as to what kind of child to place in their home.
One such mother commented:

Mother: It seems to me we would have taken any
child presented to us, even if we had some reservations. We had some question even before approaching the agency about whether we could take
a Negro child, because of the attitude of society.
But here, too, if we had been presented with a
Negro child, I am sure we would have taken him.
In a sense, I guess having an Indian child will be
much easier, because the prejudices against the
American Indian are not as intense as against Negro people.

Adopting Handicapped Children

In the factor analytic treatment of the parental responses, it was discerned that there were three major clusters of foster mother responses to types of children they
could adopt.[2] One factor revealed responses related to the
adoption of handicapped children; another defined children
with psychological problems; and finally, there was a separate factor relating to the ability to adopt Negro children.

Table V-6 shows the Index of Adoptive Mothers' Orientations to the Adoption of Handicapped Children. Five of
the seven items deal with physical handicapped, one deals
with the adoption of a mentally retarded child, and one with
the adoption of an Oriental child. While one does not con-
ceive of an Oriental child available for adoption as being
handicapped, the factorial structure of the items tended to
implicate Oriental children with the handicapped children in
the responses of the adoptive mothers. The table shows that
a child with a mild handicap which is not correctable would
apparently still have a very easy time of being adopted:

Table V-6

INDEX OF ADOPTIVE MOTHERS' ORIENTATIONS
TO THE ADOPTION OF HANDICAPPED CHILDREN*

Question	Response Categories	Percent Response
1. A child with mild handicap, not correctable (e.g., deaf in one ear)	Could not consider	8.3
	Major reservations	4.2
	Minor reservations	26.0
	Adopted easily	61.5
		100.0
2. A slightly mentally retarded child	Could not consider	41.6
	Major reservations	18.8
	Minor reservations	30.2
	Adopted easily	9.4
		100.0
3. A child with correctable, fairly serious handicap (e.g., cleft palate)	Could not consider	21.1
	Major reservations	12.6
	Minor reservations	23.2
	Adopted easily	43.1
		100.0
4. A child with a serious handicap (e.g., club foot)	Could not consider	20.8
	Major reservations	15.6
	Minor reservations	18.8
	Adopted easily	44.8
		100.0
5. A child with a serious handicap, noncorrectable	Could not consider	41.7
	Major reservations	32.3
	Minor reservations	13.5
	Adopted easily	12.5
		100.0
6. An Oriental child (e.g., Chinese)	Could not consider	6.3
	Major reservations	5.2
	Minor reservations	17.7
	Adopted easily	70.8
		100.0

INDEX OF ADOPTIVE MOTHERS' ORIENTATIONS
TO THE ADOPTION OF HANDICAPPED CHILDREN*

Question	Response Categories	Percent Response
7. A child whose appearance is somewhat marred by injury due to forceps delivery	Could not consider	3.1
	Major reservations	5.2
	Minor reservations	24.0
	Adopted easily	67.7
		100.0

Intercorrelation Among Items								
	1	2	3	4	5	6	7	Total Score
1	1.00	.27	.44	.46	.41	.15	.20	.67
2		1.00	.28	.27	.36	.11	.19	.55
3			1.00	.86	.46	.13	.32	.77
4				1.00	.47	.16	.27	.78
5					1.00	.15	.33	.72
6						1.00	.14	.42
7							1.00	.55

Cronbach Alpha= .74

Low Score ←——————————→ High Score

MAJOR RESERVATIONS   EASILY ADOPTED

*The subjects were told the following: "As you may know,
the agency has many kinds of children to place for adoption.
Now, I would like you to think back to the time when
you first came to the agency to apply for adoption. Suppose children of the following types had been offered to
you for consideration. I would like you to tell me whether
you might easily have adopted such a child, would have had
some reservations about adopting, had major reservations,
or would not have been able to take such a child under any
circumstances."

three-fifths of the mothers said that he was adopted easily and 26 percent would have only minor reservations. A child with a correctable handicap which is either serious or fairly serious would have somewhat more difficulty; only about two-fifths would have easily adopted such a child and about a fifth would not consider such a child at all. A child with a noncorrectable serious handicap would have a much more difficult time of it: almost 42 percent of the adoptive mothers indicated they could not consider such a child and almost a third would have had major reservations. Only about 12 percent indicated they easily could have adopted such a child. Cronbach's Alpha Coefficient for this index is fairly high (Alpha = .74) and one has the impression of a quite stable index. That the verbal responses of the mothers had some validity is indicated by the significant correlation between the index scores and the age of their adopted children at the time they entered the home (r = .21).[3] That is, mothers who indicated that they could adopt handicapped children of various degrees of disability were also those who had been able to adopt the somewhat older children in the sample.

Table V-7 is the five-item index comprising the Index of Adoptive Mothers' Orientation to Adopting a Child with Psychological Problems. It included such items as adopting a slightly retarded child (an item which was included in the previous index), a normal older child, a child with mental illness in his immediate background, a withdrawn child, and an aggressive, hyperactive child. Of these cited characteristics, the withdrawn child and the aggressive child apparently were seen as easiest to adopt, almost two-thirds of the mothers responding positively. Only one mother in ten indicated she could not consider such types of children. A child with mental illness in his background was seen as somewhat more difficult to adopt, although 37 percent indicated they could have adopted him easily and 28 percent had only minor reservations. Somewhat similar findings were reported for the normal older child. The largest proportion of mothers indicated they could not have considered a slightly retarded child. The reliability of the index again seems fairly strong, with the Alpha Coefficient being .75. By and large, parents indicating that they could adopt such children tended to adopt older children and the correlation between the index and the age of the adoptee at placement is significant (r = .35). There was also a significant correlation between this index and the index relating to handicapped children, even when the item related to adopting a mentally retarded child was dropped out (r = .47).

Table V-7

INDEX OF ADOPTIVE MOTHERS' ORIENTATIONS
TO ADOPTING A CHILD WITH PSYCHOLOGICAL PROBLEMS*

Question	Response Categories	Percent Response
1. A slightly retarded child	Could not consider	41.6
	Major reservations	18.8
	Minor reservations	30.2
	Adopted easily	9.4
		100.0
2. A normal older child (e.g., eight years old)	Could not consider	25.0
	Major reservations	14.6
	Minor reservations	20.8
	Adopted easily	39.6
		100.0
3. A child with mental illness in his immediate background	Could not consider	17.7
	Major reservations	16.7
	Minor reservations	28.1
	Adopted easily	37.5
		100.0
4. A withdrawn, shy child (four years old)	Could not consider	8.3
	Major reservations	6.3
	Minor reservations	20.8
	Adopted easily	64.6
		100.0
5. An aggressive, hyperactive child (four years old)	Could not consider	10.4
	Major reservations	10.4
	Minor reservations	20.8
	Adopted easily	58.4
		100.0

| Intercorrelation Among Items | | | | | |
1	2	3	4	5	Total Score
1 1.00	.34	.29	.30	.21	.61
2	1.00	.30	.45	.45	.72
3		1.00	.33	.32	.64
4			1.00	.74	.80
5				1.00	.77

Cronbach
Alpha=.75

Low   High
Score ←——————————→ Score

MAJOR RESERVATIONS   EASILY ADOPTED

*The subjects were told the following: "As you may know,
the agency has many kinds of children to place for adoption.
Now, I would like you to think back to the time you first
came to the agency to apply for adoption. Suppose children
of the following types had been offered to you for consideration. I would like you to tell me whether you might easily
have adopted such a child, would have had some reservations about adopting, had major reservations, or would not
have been able to take such a child under any circumstances.

Table V-8 provides information on the Index of Adoptive Mothers' Orientations to the Adoption of Negro Children.
This is a two-item index in which the items were correlated
strongly (r = .85). In the main, the adoptive mothers indicated they could not have adopted such a child. Only 22
percent said that they could have easily adopted a child who
was obviously Negro or had minor reservations about this,
and about 37 percent where the child was not obviously Negro in appearance. People who were more favorably disposed to adopting Negro children tended to have higher socioeconomic status; the correlation between the two measures
was .32 (significant at .01 level). They tended to be middle-
class professionals living in large urban areas. It is of
further interest to note that the ability to adopt Negro chil-

dren was significantly correlated with the Overall Adjustment
Scores developed for the children at the end of all of the
field interviewing. The correlation was modest but significant (r = -.21). Also, the correlation between the ability
to adopt Negro children and the index measuring the ability

Table V-8

INDEX OF ADOPTIVE MOTHERS' ORIENTATIONS
TO THE ADOPTION OF NEGRO CHILDREN*

Question	Response Categories	Percent Response
1. A child of mixed Negro-white parentage (obviously Negro in features and skin color)	Could not consider Major reservations Minor reservations Adopted easily	57.9 20.0 6.3 15.8 100.0
2. A child of mixed Negro-white parentage but not obviously Negro in appearance.	Could not consider Major reservations Minor reservations Adopted easily	47.4 15.8 14.7 22.1 100.0

Correlation Between Items = .85

*The subjects were told the following: "As you may know,
the agency has many kinds of children to place for adoption. Now, I would like you to think back to the time you
first came to the agency to apply for adoption. Suppose
children of the following types had been offered to you for
consideration. I would like you to tell me whether you
might easily have adopted such a child, would have had
minor reservations, major reservations, or would not have
been able to take such a child under any circumstances."

---

to adopt handicapped children was significant (r = .21) but
there was no such significant association with the index of
the ability to adopt children with psychological problems
(r = .05).

Child's Indian Background

The adoptive mothers were queried about how the adoptive family viewed the adopted child's Indian background. For
example, they were asked whether there were any sources of
hesitation about adopting an Indian child.   Twenty-two percent expressed some concern and hesitation over whether the
child would be accepted in their community.   Another ten
percent expressed other sources of concern about an Indian
child.   Two-thirds of the study population said they had no
hesitation about moving forward in adopting an Indian child
even though many of them had not come to the agency specifically wanting an Indian child.   However, for many of the
adoptive mothers, the child's being Indian was not something
that they would regard as making him "something special."
About half of the sample said that their love for the child
was unrelated to his ethnic background and their affection for
him was not particularly enhanced because he was American
Indian.   Another group, almost equally as large, did respond
very positively to the Indian aspect of the adoption, once they
had embarked upon this course.   A number of the adoptive
mothers spoke of the great sense of pride they felt in the
child's heritage, while others particularly admired the child's
Indian appearance and personality factors that they associated
with Indian people.

When questioned about whether there was any aspect
of the child's Indian background which caused them concern
at the present or for the future, one in five adoptive mothers
expressed fears, usually of a mild order.   One in ten anticipated prejudice against the child, while a similar size
group expressed some concern about what the deprivation the
child had experienced before coming to them might have done
in the way of affecting his growth as a healthy personality.

Table V-9 is an index that relates to the mother's
description of the child's Indian appearance and the degree
to which she was aware of people staring at him and of the
family's being an object of particular curiosity.

Based upon the factor analysis of the child description
items, the four items included in the index appeared to be
interrelated as part of a central construct.   The first question dealt with the matter of whether neighbor children tended
to make comments about the Indian child's background or
appearance.   Only in about ten percent of the cases were
unpleasant incidents cited.   For about two children out of

Table V-9

INDEX OF CHILD'S INDIAN APPEARANCE
(N= 97)

		Percent Response
1. Have neighbor children made comments about your child's background or appearance?	Unpleasant incidents cited	10.6
	Good-natured teasing	3.2
	Friendly curiosity	38.3
	No comments of this nature	47.9
		100.0
2. Do people in general ever comment about your child's appearance or his looking different from you?	Frequent comments received	28.2
	Comments made fairly often, perhaps 2-3 times a month	21.8
	Such comments rarely received	50.0
		100.0
3. In general, would you say that your child's Indian characteristics make him strikingly different from you in appearance?	Feels child looks strikingly different	39.8
	Feels child looks somewhat different	26.9
	Feels child does not look different	33.3
		100.0
4. Do you ever get the feeling that when you are in public places people tend to stare at you and your child?	Yes	48.9
	Yes, but less so now	9.8
	No	41.3
		100.0

Intercorrelation Among Items				
	1	2	3	4	Total Score
1	1.00	.65	.17	.21	.73
2		1.00	.19	.24	.74
3			1.00	.46	.65
4				1.00	.68

Cronbach Alpha= .69

Low Score ⟵————⟶ High Score
DIFFERENT   DOES NOT LOOK DIFFERENT

five, there was evidence of friendly curiosity; that is, the interest in the child's Indian background was purely benign. For 48 percent of the sample, there were apparently no comments reported about the child's Indian background at all. With respect to adults, it was reported that almost 50 percent of the families received comments from strangers about the child's Indian appearance either frequently or fairly often. For 50 percent of the sample, such comments were rarely received. About half of the adoptive mothers reported that when they were in public places, people tended to stare at them and the child; two out of five mothers reported that this did not take place. It is interesting to observe that this index correlated significantly with a similar index created from the Series Three interviews with the fathers ($r = .51$), indicating that there was quite good agreement between parents about the child's appearance.

Twelve adoptive mothers reported that when they encountered people staring at them or being intrusive, they would get annoyed about it.

> Mother: Every so often we did get hostile reactions from people while riding in public transportation, or even walking along the street. I would notice people looking from one to the other and the expression on their faces would sometimes be extremely hostile and bitter. However, I did not feel particularly threatened by all of this.

Most mothers indicated that they either did not mind the questions of strangers or that they enjoyed them. The overall impression is that, in the early phase of the adoptive experience at least, the fact of the child's ethnic difference did not loom particularly large in the adjustment of the adoptive families. Further, almost all of the mothers reported that the child seemed oblivious to the fact that they were being stared at; there were only three cases where mothers reported that the child might be uncomfortable about this. In the main, the children were just too young to be particularly cognizant of this.

Occasionally, the interviewers would note what they considered a tendency on the part of a parent to deny that her child looked Indian:

[Interviewer: I had the feeling, as she discussed
it, that she didn't think of the child as Indian although he is full-blooded and clearly so.   When,
for example, we were talking about the question of
their religious participation, she mentioned that
they had taken Billy to a synagogue during the hol-
idays and Billy looked more Jewish than many children.   I found after awhile that every time I mentioned the child as being different or spoke about
Indian children, there was a reaction on her part,
as though saying in effect, 'What again?']

When the adoptive mothers were asked whether they
expected their children to experience discomfort because of
their Indian background, 27 percent said that they did indeed
anticipate this.   Another 18 percent of the mothers saw this
as a distinct possibility but did not see it as of major importance.   One out of five adoptive mothers responded that
they knew that when the children reached the dating and
courtship period, there might be an issue of acceptance of
the child by others.   They also seemed to be aware that the
child might encounter racial prejudice when he was older.
A few respondents felt they already saw signs of this.

Mother: I feel that my child is not as accepted
as a white child would be in certain circles. Some
of my old childhood friends have expressed the
view that what we have done in adopting an Indian
child is terrible.   Some people have mentioned
what they regard as a fact: that Indians have bad
tempers.

The overall perspective of the parents seemed to be
optimistic and hopeful that attitudes towards persons of different races would have improved in the United States by the
time the child was older and more conscious of the way people were treating him.

Mother: We feel that as the child grows up and
makes wider contacts, she may be aware of the
rejection of others.   Therefore we must prepare
her for the fact that there may be problems.

An important line of inquiry in the interview was the matter of the way in which the adoptive family planned to treat the child's Indian heritage. For example, they were asked whether they planned to tell the child about his Indian background. About half of the adoptive mothers spoke of their plan to make a special effort to acquaint the child with his heritage so that he would be proud of it. They indicated that they were learning all they could about the child's tribal background and planned to give him every opportunity to get connected with the history of his own people.

> Mother: We want to give him as complete know-
> ledge of his heritage as we can. We don't want
> him to have nationalistic pride but we don't want
> him to be ashamed either.

*   *   *

> Mother: I suppose he will experience some dis-
> comfort when he is older. He may want to date
> a certain girl whose mother may object because
> of his background. We have tried to prepare him
> by trying to make him proud of his Indian back-
> ground which is his only defense. We have several
> books about Indians in the house and last summer,
> we took a trip to the West visiting several Indian
> reservations but not the one from which he came.
> We talk about his Indian heritage as it comes up.

*   *   *

> Mother: Our child may have to seek out an iden-
> tity for himself besides being a member of our
> family. He is different from us in two ways: He
> has experienced being adopted and he is an Indian.
> In a sense, that makes him a different person and
> he and we have to be comfortable with that differ-
> ence.

One in five mothers reported that they would tell the child but did not plan to make any special effort. Rather, they thought they would follow his lead and give him information as he seemed to desire it. Another one in five planned to tell the child some day that he was Indian but thought they would minimize the amount of information they would give

him.   Their orientation suggested they were fearful that emphasis about the Indian background would tend to create a
barrier between the child and the family.

When the adoptive mothers were asked about the reaction of close relatives to their decision to adopt an Indian
child, only one adoptive mother indicated that her family had
been against the idea; 11 other research subjects indicated
that their relatives were formerly nonsupportive but were
now accepting the idea.   Another 12 mothers spoke of mixed
reactions, with some relatives being supportive and some opposed.   About a third of the mothers stated that their relatives had been generally supportive, that there may have been
minor doubts but the child was now fully accepted.   Thirty-
six percent of the sample reported that the relatives had been
very supportive and enthusiastic throughout.

With respect to friends, fully two-thirds of the friends
of the subjects had been very supportive and enthusiastic and
the remainder were generally supportive after having initial
minor doubts.

When the adoptive mothers were asked if there was
any kind of advice they would give an agency in selecting
adoptive parents for American Indian children, based upon
their own experience thus far, there was a wide range of
responses.   About one in five thought the agency should be
sure that the parents either specifically wanted an Indian
child or that they were people who loved children to the
point of finding ethnic background unimportant.   A substantial number felt that the agency did not need to approach
potential adoptive parents looking for any particular kind of
ingredients, and tended to minimize problems that would be
particularly present because of the child's Indian background.

> Mother: Any family that loves and wants a child
> and has security within its own members can, with
> some exposure to the idea, become interested in
> an Indian adoption.   They should be exposed to
> such children.   The agencies should allow prospec-
> tive parents to see such children in their homes.

>   *   *   *

> Mother: People should have sufficient time to
> think through whether this is what they really

want. People who are sure they want an Indian
child not just a child. For us, it was a question
of adopting this child immediately or perhaps not
having a child available to us for several years.

Security of Adoptive Mothers

I was interested in determining how secure the adoptive mothers were in their general orientation for the future
for their children. Two items were taken from an index
developed by Ruderman: they dealt with the age the parent
felt a boy should be able to take care of himself after school,
and the age at which a girl should be able to take care of
herself.[4] A third question dealt with whether the adoptive
mother anticipated that the Indian child would experience any
discomfort because of his background. The Index of Security
of Adoptive Mothers' Parental Outlook appears to be a relatively stable scale, showing a Cronbach's Alpha Coefficient
of .90. It taps an orientation dealing with the optimism or
pessimism of the adoptive mothers. The mothers who scored
in the direction of being more cautious in their outlook tended
to be those whose children were subsequently found to be
relatively symptom-free during the Series Four interviews
($r = -.24$), and whose children received overall adjustment
ratings at the end of the complete series of interviews which
indicated that they were relatively well-adjusted ($r = -.32$).
Evidently, the cautionary note was not an element in dealing
with the child which seemed to create problematic behavior
in the youngsters.

Child Rearing Orientations

To develop some sense of the adoptive mother's overall orientation to child rearing, a series of questions taken
from the well-known study, Patterns of Child Rearing by
Sears, Maccoby and Levin, were included in the interviewing
schedule.[5] These questions dealt with the adoptive mothers'
expectations regarding table manners, the observation of
family rules, the expectations of neatness, and so forth.
The eight-item Index of Strict vs. Permissive Child Rearing
Orientation turned out to be normally distributed and quite
stable, showing a Cronbach's Alpha of .74.

The index proved to be significantly related to the
age of the child at placement ($r = -.36$), indicating that
(cont. pg. 139)

Table V-10

INDEX OF SECURITY OF
ADOPTIVE MOTHERS' PARENTAL OUTLOOKS
(N= 97)

Question	Response Categories	Percent Response
1. At what age do you feel a boy should be able to take care of himself after school?	Under 7 years	3.5
	8 or 9 years	18.4
	10 or 11 years	32.2
	12 or 13 years	32.2
	14 or 15 years	10.3
	16 or over	3.5
		100.0
2. At what age do you feel a girl should be able to take care of herself after school?	Under 7 years	4.6
	8 or 9 years	20.7
	10 or 11 years	29.9
	12 or 13 years	31.0
	14 or 15 years	10.3
	16 or over	3.5
		100.0
3. Do you anticipate that your child will experience any discomfort because of his Indian background?	No	64.9
	Yes, but to limited degree	27.7
	Yes	7.4
		100.0

Intercorrelation Among Items				
	1	2	3	Total Score
1	1.00	.85	.26	.62
2		1.00	.25	.60
3			1.00	.91

Cronbach
Alpha= .90

Low
Score $\longleftarrow$ $\longrightarrow$ High
Score

OPTIMISTIC OUTLOOK   CAUTIOUS OUTLOOK

Table V-11

INDEX OF
STRICT VS. PERMISSIVE CHILD REARING ORIENTATION
(N= 97)

Question	Response Categories	Percent Response
1. What table manners do you expect of your child?	Basic manners expected	54.2
	Some expectations of observance of amenities	30.1
	Little or no such expectations	15.7
		100.0
2. What is done if child fails to observe family rules for behavior at the table?	Physical punishment employed	19.1
	Non-physical punishment employed: scolding, withdrawal of love or approval	51.2
	Very permissive	29.7
		100.0
3. What do you expect of your child as far as neatness is concerned?	Very high standards	25.8
	Relatively high standards	13.5
	Moderate standards	24.7
	Very relaxed standards	36.0
		100.0
4. What rules are expected of your child with respect to marking walls?	Very high standards	60.0
	Relatively high standards	14.4
	Moderate standards	18.9
	Very relaxed standards	6.7
		100.0
5. What is done if child marks walls?	Physical punishment employed	19.5
	Non-physical punishment employed: scolding, withdrawal of love or approval	39.1
	Moderate disapproval	20.7
	Very permissive	20.7
		100.0

INDEX OF
STRICT VS. PERMISSIVE CHILD REARING ORIENTATION
(N= 97)

Question	Response Categories	Percent Response
6. How much noise is allowed in the house?	Very strict about having no noise	8.8
	Quite strict	23.1
	Moderately strict	35.1
	A few restrictions or hardly any	33.0
		100.0
7. How quickly is the child expected to obey?	Expect instant obedience	30.1
	Generally expect obedience	38.7
	Expect some delay	16.1
	Does not expect immediate obedience	15.1
		100.0
8. How often do you spank your child?	Very often	8.6
	Moderately often	11.8
	Occasionally	44.1
	Hardly at all	35.5
		100.0

	1	2	3	4	5	6	7	8	Total Score
	Intercorrelation Among Items								
1	1.00	.24	.55	.38	.19	.37	.42	.12	.74
2		1.00	.15	.02	.11	.11	.10	.15	.42
3			1.00	.40	.16	.38	.42	.25	.70
4				1.00	.23	.31	.28	.24	.59
5					1.00	.32	.19	.12	.46
6						1.00	.45	.15	.66
7							1.00	.15	.64
8								1.00	.46

Cronbach Alpha= .74

Low Score $\longleftarrow$ High Score

STRICT   PERMISSIVE

mothers were increasingly apt to show strictness in behavior
as their children got older and were more prone to be active. This makes sense--parents are less apt to be strict
with infants and young toddlers than they are with older
youngsters.

The index was not significantly correlated with the
socioeconomic status of the adoptive families (r = .10).
There was a significant association, however, with an index,
Adoptive Mothers' Life Style, to be discussed shortly (r = .29).
Mothers who scored high on this index were apt to give more
permissive responses. They were mothers whose origins
were more likely to be urban than rural, who tended to visit
with friends more frequently, and who tended to have husbands who were more prone to share chores with them involving the children.

The Index of Strict vs. Permissive Child Rearing will
also be subsequently shown to be significantly associated with
the overall adjustment of the adoptees.

Social Orientations and Life Styles
of the Adoptive Mothers

As I have previously observed, the decision to adopt
an Indian child can be seen as a social decision as well as
a personal one. The addition of a racially different child
to a family has the connotation that the family is presenting
itself to the community as a racially diverse unit. Within
the context of a society in which race is a charged matter,
this is a decision which can have implications for the adoptive family. It can influence the kind of relationships the
family will have with neighbors, with significant persons in
the community, and with close friends. The decision to absorb a child who is racially different might signify that the
adoptive family's social orientations are somewhat different
than those of many Americans. This seemed to me to be a
matter worth investigating.

Religiosity

Two items from the interview with the adoptive mothers were combined to form an Index of Their Religiosity.
One dealt with the frequency of their activity in church work,
the other with their expressed interest in participating in re-

ligious activities. Fifty-two percent of the adoptive mothers
reported fairly regular church activity and 30 percent reported occasional involvement. About 18 percent indicated
they never participated in any religious activities. A similar
distribution was reported with respect to their interest in
participating in church activities. The correlation between

Table V-12

INDEX OF RELIGIOSITY OF ADOPTIVE MOTHERS
(N= 97)

	Question	Response Categories	Percent Response
1.	Degree of frequency respondent expressed in engaging in reli-gious activities, such as church work.	Never Occasionally Fairly regularly	17.7 30.2 52.1 100.0
2.	Interest respondent expressed in partici-pating in religious activities.	Little or no interest Moderate interest Strong interest	20.8 32.3 46.9 100.0

Correlation Between Items = .91

---

the two items was .91. Of interest is the finding that a
higher degree of religiosity was related to lower class status.
The correlation with the socioeconomic status was -.31.
There was a significant relationship between the expression
of religiosity and the expressed willingness to adopt handicapped children (r = .27).

Political Orientations

        It might be expected that individuals who would be in-
terested in adopting children across racial lines would of
liberal political persuasion. We tend to assume that those

Table V-13

INDEX OF ADOPTIVE MOTHERS'
LIBERAL VS. CONSERVATIVE POLITICAL ORIENTATION

Question	Response Categories	Percent Response
1. Are you concerned with the following problems of our times: Possibility of atomic war?	Hardly concerned Somewhat concerned Very concerned	17.7 47.9 34.4 100.0
2. Concern with discrimination against minority groups?	Hardly concerned Somewhat concerned Very concerned	7.3 32.3 60.4 100.0
3. Concern re: general economic conditions?	Hardly concerned Somewhat concerned Very concerned	20.8 50.0 29.2 100.0
4. Concern re: crowded schools?	Hardly concerned Somewhat concerned Very concerned	9.4 37.5 53.1 100.0
5. Concern re: problems of old folks?	Hardly concerned Somewhat concerned Very concerned	8.3 58.4 33.3 100.0
6. Considering your views on social and political questions, how would you describe yourself?	Very or somewhat conservative Somewhat liberal Very liberal or radical	42.2 28.9 28.9 100.0
7. Would you mind telling me who you voted for in the 1960 presidential election? *	Kennedy Nixon	51.8 48.2 100.0

INDEX OF ADOPTIVE MOTHERS'
LIBERAL VS. CONSERVATIVE POLITICAL ORIENTATION

Question	Response Categories	Percent Response
8. Would you mind telling me who you voted for in 1956? **	Eisenhower Stevenson	63.5 36.5 100.0

*85 respondents voted in 1960
**82 respondents voted in 1956

Intercorrelation Among Items								
								Total
1	2	3	4	5	6	7	8	Score
1 1.00	.20	.27	.16	.21	.19	.31	.18	.57
2	1.00	.01	.17	.16	.32	.24	.28	.54
3		1.00	.16	.30	.03	.05	.09	.42
4			1.00	.33	.14	.04	.12	.48
5				1.00	.14	.19	.17	.57
6					1.00	.39	.46	.59
7						1.00	.48	.61
8							1.00	.63

Cronbach Alpha= .77

Low Score ← → High Score

CONSERVATIVE   LIBERAL

who are strongly interested in civil rights and equal treatment of racial minorities tend to be those who assume an
overall liberal political stance. Our interview material, however, would lead us to believe that, rather than our study
subjects being skewed to the liberal side, they reflect a
cross-section of political attitudes in the United States.

For example, the adoptive mothers were asked about
their voting choice in the 1956 election between Dwight D.
Eisenhower and Adlai E. Stevenson. Of the 82 adoptive

mothers who were old enough to vote at the time and had used the option of voting, 63.4 percent reported that they had voted for Eisenhower and 36.6 percent had voted for Stevenson.   The actual vote of the American people in 1956 was distributed 57.8 percent for President Eisenhower and 42.2 percent for Mr. Stevenson.   In the 1960 election between John F. Kennedy and Richard M. Nixon, of the 85 adoptive mothers who had participated in the elections 51.8 percent reported they had voted for President Kennedy and 48.2 percent had voted for Mr. Nixon.   The actual breakdown in the voting of the American people was 50.1 percent for John F. Kennedy and 49.9 percent for Mr. Nixon.   Thus the adoptive parents report voting behavior which is close to the national pattern.

This finding supports the view that the recruitment of adoptive parents for these Indian children was not restricted to one side of the political spectrum.   Further, when the adoptive mothers were asked: "Considering your views on social and political questions, would you describe yourself as conservative, somewhat conservative, somewhat liberal, very liberal?" some 42 percent described themselves as conservative or somewhat conservative, while 29 percent thought they were somewhat liberal and another 29 percent very liberal.

When the items on voting behavior and related items were combined into an Index of Liberal vs. Conservative Political Orientation, it was possible to further assess the potential meaning of the political orientations of the adoptive mothers.   The index showed a fairly high degree of reliability with an Alpha Coefficient of .77.   A high score would indicate a liberal-minded mother and a low score reflect a conservative political orientation.   These orientations were significantly associated with the socioeconomic status of the families ($r = .22$); the higher the status of the mother, the more apt she was to espouse liberal attitudes.   There was also a significant association between the political orientations of the adoptive mothers and their expressed religiosity ($r = .-29$).   This is not a surprising association.   That the measure has validity is indicated by the fact that it correlated with a similar measure of political orientation developed from the Series Three interviews with the adoptive fathers ($r = .46$).

Table V-14

INDEX OF TRADITIONAL VS. MODERN FEMALE IDEOLOGY
(N= 97)

Question	Response Categories	Percent Response
1. Maintaining an interest in national and world affairs*	Little or no interest Moderate interest Strong interest	7.3 53.1 39.6 100.0
2. Engaging in sports activity**	Never Occasionally Fairly regularly	39.6 39.6 20.8 100.0
3. How do you feel about taking care of the house--would you say you like it very much, pretty much, or not at all.	Very much Pretty much Not at all	29.5 59.0 11.6 100.0
4. Engaging in political discussions**	Never Occasionally Fairly regularly	28.1 43.8 28.1 100.0
5. Going to concerts**	Never Occasionally Fairly regularly	56.3 38.5 5.2 100.0
6. Reading magazines	Never Occasionally Fairly regularly	5.2 22.9 71.9 100.0
7. Being able to get away from housework and the children sometimes during the day***	Can be happy without this Must have this to be happy	74.0 26.0 100.0

	Question	Response Categories	Percent Response
8.	Going out occasionally in the evening***	Can be happy without this	59.4
		Must have this to be happy	40.6
			100.0

*Respondent was told: "Thinking of the kind of person you are, would you say that you have a special interest in the following aspects of living."

**Respondent was told: "We know that raising children is a hard job. We are interested in what parents to to relax. Which of the following activities do you do fairly regularly, occasionally, not at all."

***Respondent was asked: "In your experience, which of these things do you feel you must have in order to be happy?"

Intercorrelation Among Items								
	1	2	3	4	5	6	7	8	Total Score
1	1.00	.07	.13	.26	-.20	.07	.11	.11	.44
2		1.00	.02	.09	.10	-.04	.11	-.02	.38
3			1.00	.15	-.12	.01	.32	.17	.48
4				1.00	.09	.08	.15	-.01	.52
5					1.00	.01	-.04	-.02	.24
6						1.00	.03	.01	.34
7							1.00	.42	.60
8								1.00	.48

Cronbach Alpha= .39

Low Score ⟵————————————⟶ High Score

TRADITIONAL   MODERN

Traditional vs. Modern Female Orientation

The factor analysis of the social attitude questions administered to the adoptive mothers, appeared to define a dimension of traditional vs. modern orientation with respect to feminine interests and activities. An index was created called the Index of Traditional vs. Modern Female Ideology, based upon seven items. These included such things as maintaining an interest in national and world affairs, engaging in sports activities, the respondents' feelings about housework, engaging in political discussions, and so forth. In general, the index was designed to measure the degree to which the adoptive mothers tended to confine their interests to the home as opposed to having interests related to larger issues and outside activities. While the index did not show a strong Alpha Coefficient, it did seem to coincide with other orientations of the adoptive mothers. For example, the correlation between this measure of female orientation and the index assessing the liberal vs. conservative attitudes of the adoptive mothers was quite firm ($r = .37$). The association indicated that the more traditional females were also those who were more conservative in their outlook. Also, those adoptive mothers whose interests were more external than homebound tended to be of higher socioeconomic status ($r = .27$).

A somewhat similar measure, called the Index of Adoptive Mother Life Style, is based upon items which deal with a restricted, fairly conservative view of the female role as opposed to one that is more expansive. Included in the item is information about where the respondent's father lived as a boy (thus the rural background of the adoptive mother is a part of the index). By and large, the reliability of the index appears quite weak (Alpha= .15). This measure, too, seems to be associated with political attitudes: the more restricted mothers tend to be those who are also very much on the conservative side in their political attitudes ($r = -.35$). Also, those adoptive mothers who scored high on this index, indicating a more expanded view of the female role, appeared somewhat more optimistic about the outlook for their children as they got older, as measured by the Index of Security of Adoptive Mothers' Parental Outlook ($r = .30$).

Deprivation in Mothers' Background

In order to obtain an estimate of the degree of dep-

Table V-15

INDEX OF ADOPTIVE MOTHERS' LIFE STYLES
(N= 97)

Question	Response Categories	Percent Response
1. Where did respondent's father live as a boy?	Rural area	40.9
	Small town	31.2
	Small city	1.1
	Middle-sized city	5.4
	In or near large city	21.4
		100.0
2. Visiting with friends*	Never	3.1
	Occasionally	32.3
	Fairly regularly	64.6
		100.0
3. What is pattern in respondent's family about getting up at night to take care of children?	Respondent usually	55.2
	Husband or both together	44.8
		100.0
4. Degree to which respondent is concerned that she can't give her children the time and attention she would like to give them	Never feels this way	56.8
	Sometimes or often feels this way	43.2
		100.0

Intercorrelation Among Items					
	1	2	3	4	Total Score
1	1.00	.11	.12	.17	.87
2		1.00	.23	.22	.43
3			1.00	.09	.42
4				1.00	.46

Cronbach Alpha= .15

Low Score $\longleftarrow$ $\longrightarrow$ High Score

RESTRICTED FEMALE ROLE   EXPANDED FEMALE ROLE

*Respondents were told: "We know that raising of children is a hard job. We are interested in what parents do to relax. Which of the following activities do you do fairly regularly, occasionally, or not at all?

rivation the adoptive mothers had experienced--as one approach to assessing their strengths as people--a number of questions were developed which related to their view of some of their past experiences. For example, they were asked if their families had suffered an unusual amount of tragedy. Two-thirds of the group reported that they had suffered little tragedy. They were also asked to make estimates about their parents' marriage; again, the larger group reported their parents' marriage as being happy or very happy. With respect to the general economic conditions of their families, about one-third reported that they had grown up in families where the conditions were meager or poor.

When the adoptive mother was asked whether there was anything about her own mother which had upset her when she was growing up, 47 percent of the sample recited negative items such as poor housekeeping, the bad temper of the mother, the mother's treatment of the respondent, etc. To the same question about the respondent's father, 53 percent reported negative items such as alcoholism, physical brutality, unemployment and absences of the fathers.

These items were compiled in an Index of Deprivation in the Adoptive Mothers' Background although there was no factorial basis for this construction. The Cronbach's Alpha indicates that this, too, is not a strong index. There is no significant association between this summary measure of deprivation in the adoptive mother's background and the summated score developed for the Series Four interviews dealing with the presence of problems in the adoptee's adjustment, and there is a similar absence of significant association with the Series Five score and with the Overall Adjustment Rating. This would either indicate that the weakness of the index has mitigated against finding such an association or that, whatever deprivation the adoptive mothers experienced, they have been overcome in the adult years.

Religious Differences

When the index scores of the adoptive mothers were compared on the basis of their religious identifications, there were significant differences between the scores of Jewish mothers on three indexes and those of the Catholic and Protestant mothers. The latter two groups were essentially undifferentiated from each other. The Jewish mothers were significantly more liberal in their political views, a finding

Table V-16

INDEX OF
DEPRIVATION IN ADOPTIVE MOTHERS' BACKGROUNDS

Question	Response Categories	Percent Response
1. Would you say your family suffered an unusual amount of tragedy during your childhood?	Suffered little tragedy Suffered average amount Suffered much	65.2 27.4 7.4 100.0
2. What is your estimate of your parent's marriage?	Very happy Happy Average Unhappy Very unhappy	33.3 27.6 20.7 11.5 6.9 100.0
3. What was your family's economic situation during your childhood?	Comfortable or better Meager or poor	68.9 31.1 100.0
4. Was there anything about your mother which upset you while growing up?	No negative item cited Yes (e.g., alcoholism, physical brutality, unemployment, absences, etc.)	52.6 47.4 100.0
5. Was there anything about your father which upset you while growing up?	No negative item cited Yes (e.g., alcoholism, physical brutality, unemployment, absences, etc.)	47.3 52.7 100.0

Intercorrelation Among Items					Total Score
	1	2	3	4	5	Total Score
1	1.00	.01	-.06	.10	-.08	.39
2		1.00	.17	.09	.16	.59
3			1.00	.01	.13	.52
4				1.00	-.05	.47
5					1.00	.47

Cronbach Alpha= .20

Low Score ←——————→ High Score
LOW DEPRIVATION   HIGH DEPRIVATION

Table V-17

MEAN INDEX SCORES FOR ADOPTIVE MOTHERS BY RELIGION

Index		Jewish (13)	Catholic (10)	Protestant (67)	F-test for significant differences in group means
Index of deprivation in adoptive mothers' background	$\overline{X}$	18.57	18.95	18.54	0.126 N.S.
	S.D.	1.58	2.50	2.48	
Index of adoptive mothers' liberal vs. conservative political orientation	$\overline{X}$	28.18	23.69	23.20	8.820***
	S.D.	4.27	2.86	3.98	
Index of adoptive mothers' life style	$\overline{X}$	7.53	8.50	8.68	1.987 N.S.
	S.D.	2.37	2.37	1.71	
Index of traditional vs. modern female ideology	$\overline{X}$	27.32	24.31	25.13	2.696 (p=.073)
	S.D.	4.87	1.97	3.29	
Index of adoptive mothers' orientation to the adoption of handicapped children	$\overline{X}$	19.84	22.20	21.28	0.984 N.S.
	S.D.	3.84	2.96	4.36	

Index of adoptive mothers' orientation to the adoption of Negro children	$\overline{X}$ S.D.	3.88 1.63	2.23 0.99	2.63 1.61	4.124*
Index of security of adoptive mothers' parental outlook	$\overline{X}$ S.D.	11.29 3.61	13.70 1.13	11.89 2.60	2.585 (p= .081)
Index of adoptive mothers' orientation to the adoption of children with psycho-logical problems	$\overline{X}$ S.D.	11.83 3.84	14.78 2.99	13.89 3.33	2.61 (p= .079)
Index of religiosity of adoptive mothers	$\overline{X}$ S.D.	1.31 1.32	3.00 1.05	3.01 1.97	5.389***

*The coefficient is significantly greater than zero at the .05 probability level.
**The coefficient is significantly greater than zero at the .01 probability level.
***The coefficient is significantly greater than zero at the .001 probability level.

that has been replicated in many prior studies.[6] They also
tended to evidence significantly less religiosity than the other
adoptive mothers.[7] Of interest to the field of adoption is
the fact that the Jewish adoptive mothers were significantly
more prone than the other mothers to express the view that
they could have adopted a Negro child when they first approached the agency. This might be a reflection of the more
assertive liberal political stance of the Jewish mothers.

Notes

1.   The factor analysis and rotations were carried out
       through use of the Data Test System developed by
       Arthur S. Couch at Harvard University Department
       of Social Relations. This system has a program that
       performs a variety of orthogonal rotations on factor
       loadings and factor scores. The procedure used in
       the analysis of the adoptive mothers' responses was
       the Varimax method proposed by Kaiser; it attempts
       to simplify the columns of the factor loading matrix
       determined by the principal components factor anal-
       ysis so that each factor is readily identifiable by
       variables.

2.   The distribution of the responses in Table V-5 suggested
       that there might well be a unidimensional scale re-
       flecting an ordered continuum in the adoptive moth-
       ers' responses. That is, it was anticipated that as
       one went from responses where children were pop-
       ularly regarded as easy to adopt, moving on to chil-
       dren with diminishing adoptability, the well-known
       properties of Guttman scaling would be evidenced.
       However, a number of attempts to demonstrate the
       scalar model were not successful.

3.   The correlations between Series Two Index scores and
       other variables is contained in Table X-1 in Chap-
       ter X.

4.   Florence A. Ruderman, Child Care and Working Mothers,
       Child Welfare League of America, 1968.

5.   Robert R. Sears, Eleanor E. Maccoby and Harry Levin,
       Patterns of Child Rearing (Evanston, Ill.: Row,
       Peterson, and Co., 1957).

6. See: Werner Cohn, "The Politics of American Jews" in
    Marshall Sklar, The Jews: Social Patterns of an
    American Group (New York: Free Press, 1958)
    pp. 614-626; and Jacob Katz, "Judaism" in Inter-
    national Encyclopedia of the Social Sciences, Vol. 8
    (New York: The Macmillan Co. and Free Press,
    1968) pp. 272-281.

7. Given the small sample sizes on which the means of two
    of these three groups are based, the power of the
    test (the a priori probability of detecting population
    mean differences) is relatively small.

Chapter VI

SERIES THREE INTERVIEWS WITH THE ADOPTIVE FATHERS:
THE FATHERS' VIEWS CONSIDERED

Number of fathers interviewed: 94
Date of first interview in series: 11 /9 /61
Date of last interview in series: 10 /28 /66
Mean age of children: 52. 4 mos.
Mean time interval between
  interview and date of placement: 30. 9 mos.
Mean time interval
  since prior interview: 11. 8 mos.

Child Whose Adjustment Was Rated as "Well-Adjusted"
at the End of the Five Series

[Is there anything you want to tell me about your
overall experience with Cal?] No--other than that
we have experienced no problems. He is our boy--
that is all. If we had remained in the city in
which we used to live when he came into our home,
we might have encountered trouble because of his
racial background. However, in our current rural
community which is mixed in nationalities, Cal is
well-accepted and people are very friendly. He is
a happy child who smiles a lot. He is very alive--
he knows what is said and understands. He never
makes the same mistake twice. He has a good
memory and is a bright, graceful boy. [Inter-
viewer's observation: This seems to be a very
fine placement for this alert youngster who appears
well-loved and accepted by his adoptive family. He
seems to be well-integrated into this large family
with four natural children and his future seems
assured at this time.]

(Cal was three years and three months at this interview.)

154

Child Whose Adjustment Was Rated as "Average"
at the End of the Five Series

[Is there anything you want to tell me about your
overall experience with Danny?] No--he is just a
regular child in the neighborhood. He is self-
reliant and goes around the immediate neighborhood
by himself. [Since I saw you last, what progress
would you say Danny has shown?] Kindergarten
has been good for him--he is a more social crea-
ture. He is still somewhat pugnacious. He is excessively strong and needs to be helped to be obe-
dient. [How secure would you say Danny is with
you?] Fairly secure. I believe Danny may remember something from the past and any insecurity
he feels is derived from this. We lavish a great
deal of affection on him.

(Danny was five years and three months at the time of this
interview.)

Child Whose Adjustment Was Rated as "Guarded"
at the End of the Five Series

[First of all is there anything you want to tell me
about your overall experience with Gary?] Generally, I have been very well pleased with the
scheme of things. He seems well-adjusted and
gets along well with children his age. Generally
no problems are involved in caring for him. Things
have worked out somewhat better than I expected.
[Since I saw you last, what progress would you say
Gary has shown?] He has grown physically. He
tends to consider this his home more than he did
before when it appeared that he would just as soon
consider any home in the neighborhood his. He
has a somewhat better concept of what we expect
in his household, the do's and don'ts. [What problems does Gary show?] The only problem I can
think of is a minor one. Gary disregards his toys;
he'll take them out, leave them somewhere and
then later will not have the foggiest notion of where
he put them. He is also a problem in that he can
be influenced by other children in doing things that
we don't allow. On his own, he is okay--but other
kids can lead him astray.

(Gary was seven years old at the time of this interview.)

The Perspective of Adoptive Fathers

The task of interviewing the adoptive fathers proved to be as free of difficulty as the experience with the adoptive mothers in the Series Two interviews. Ninety-four adoptive fathers were interviewed. One had reconsidered the decision of the family to cooperate in the study and refused to be interviewed. This reduced the potential number of subjects to ninety-seven. The three fathers who were not interviewed could not be reached because they were not geographically available at the time of the Series Three interviews. Two fathers were out of the country and the one other potential interviewee was temporarily involved in job moves which prevented his being interviewed.

In addition to the success in securing the cooperation of the subjects in participating in the interviews, their overall attitude about the research came across as decidely positive. There was widespread recognition of the validity of a follow-up study as a way of learning more about Indian adoptions. There was very little expression of impatience with the interviewing. The adoptive fathers' reports about their experiences reflected mild to strong enthusiasm about the way things were going. There was a strong sense of pride in the adopted children. No adoptive father reported that the experience had turned out to be worse than expected and 28 percent spoke of it as being somewhat better than expected. Thirty percent considered the adoption as having turned out to be better than expected. I had a sense in reading the interviews with the adoptive fathers that their reports had an even greater euphoric cast than the adoptive mothers'. This might well be related to the fact that the major child-caring responsibilities fell upon their wives. For the same reason, it is possible that the men in the study were less reliable informants than their wives. To buttress this observation, I shall subsequently demonstrate that the adoptive mothers showed greater internal consistency in their descriptions of the children over the course of the five interviews than was the case when father and mother descriptions were compared.

The approach to creating indexes out of adoptive fathers' responses was the same used with the Series Two data. Their responses were divided into three domains: child description, adoptive parent attitudes and concerns, and their social attitudes and life styles. A factor analytic approach was again utilized to identify configurations of items that belonged together within descriptive domains being surveyed.

Child Description

The fathers were presented with the same list of fifteen descriptive adjectives which had been presented to the mothers in the previous interview. These are set forth in Table VI-1. In the main, there is a strong parallel between the reports of the fathers and the mothers. Thus, by and large, the children are described as happy, active, bright and friendly youngsters. Very few of the children were described in a manner which would be regarded as indicative of pathology. It is only on items that deal with aggressiveness and outgoingness that we see a spread in the items. Thus, about a third of the children were said to have explosive tempers and almost two-thirds were characterized as stubborn. A large group of the children were seen as mischievous, but this was not associated with other items in a way to indicate pathogenicity. This benign outlook about the children does not occasion surprise since, by and large, from the Series Two interviews, we have the impression that most of the adoptive children do fall within a normal range. One has to consider the fact that the average age of the children at the time of these interviews was a little over four years and, despite the earlier deprivation some of them had experienced, one would not expect massive pathology at this young age.

Table VI-2 presents the product-moment correlations between the descriptions of the adoptees provided by the fathers during the Series Three interviews and those eminating from the mothers. The large number of significant correlations suggests that the fathers and mothers are obviously displaying some shared perspective about their children even though the data comes from interviews that are a year apart in time. But a test of statistical significance is a somewhat limited level of expectation. It should not occasion surprise to find fathers and mothers showing this level of agreement about what their children are like. They have presumably had ample opportunity to share their views with each other and their responses are based upon substantial contact with their children. Upon reflection, my reaction to the correlations is that they reflect quite low levels of agreement. For example, the product-moment correlation between fathers and

Table VI-1

FATHERS' DESCRIPTIONS OF BEHAVIORAL DISPOSITIONS
OF ADOPTEES DURING SERIES THREE INTERVIEWS

(N=94)

Characteristic	Very Much	Somewhat	Hardly	Not at All
		(Percentaged Across)		
Happy	93.5	6.5	--	--
Active	97.8	2.2	--	--
Mischievous	32.6	48.9	12.0	6.5
Stubborn	25.0	41.3	18.5	15.2
Quiet	4.4	35.2	26.4	34.1
Explosive temper	7.7	25.3	33.0	34.0
Shy	2.2	41.3	18.5	38.0
Agile	73.8	19.6	3.3	3.3
Bright	75.6	22.2	2.2	--
Graceful	30.4	41.3	18.5	9.8
Trusting	86.5	10.1	3.4	--
Destructive	2.2	24.2	30.8	42.8
Friendly	75.8	22.0	2.2	--
Talkative	61.8	33.7	3.4	1.1
Tense	1.1	16.3	27.2	55.4

mothers regarding the behavioral trait "mischievous" is .21. While this is significant at the .05 level for the sample size

---

Table VI-2

CORRELATIONS BETWEEN SERIES TWO (ADOPTIVE MOTHER) AND SERIES THREE (ADOPTIVE FATHER) CHILD DESCRIPTIONS

Behavioral Characteristic	Correlations[a]
Happy	Not attempted[b]
Active	Not attempted
Mischievous	.21*
Stubborn	.46**
Quiet	.14
Explosive	.42**
Shy	.36**
Agile	.24*
Bright	Not attempted
Graceful	.34**
Trusting	.22*
Destructive	.28**
Friendly	Not attempted
Talkative	.17
Tense	.09

a.   Comparison based upon N of 91 matched pairs.

b.   Where distributions of responses were markedly skewed, correlations were not calculated.

*Significant: $p < .05$;   **Significant: $p < .01$

---

we have here, it only accounts for four percent of the variance in ratings if we were to attempt to predict the fathers' description on the basis of knowing those of the mothers'.

In Chapter VIII, there will be opportunity to compare the associations between Series Two and Series Three child descriptions with a repeat of the same behavioral checklist presented to the adoptive mothers during Series Five inter-

views. The question will then arise: Which of the earlier
perceptions will show the closest concordance with the final
child descriptions? The approach generally is to avoid regarding the responses of the couple as two samples, and instead to think of the data coming from one sample of pairs.
We find substantial agreement on items dealing with the presence or absence of aggressiveness in the child as revealed
by such attributes as mischievousness, stubbornness, ex-
plosiveness, destructiveness and shyness.

Based upon the factor analysis of the adoptive fathers'
behavioral descriptions of the adoptees, a cluster of attributes
emerged that apparently tapped a single dimension which I
have chosen to call the Index of Child Temperament. On the
upper range, this would describe as rambunctious a youngster who is mischievous, stubborn and somewhat explosive
in his temper, and who tends to be on the noisy side. His
counterpart on the low end of the scale would tend to be more
controlled, pliable, and even-tempered. The Alpha Coefficient indicated the reliability to be moderately high (.63).
When the difference between the boys and the girls being described was analyzed, the boys--as might be expected--were
much more likely to be described as rambunctious than the
girls. This is a finding which has been frequently reported
in the child development literature. Thus, for example,
Sears, Maccoby and Levin note: "Most studies of aggressive
behavior in Kindergarten children have shown that boys display more frequent and more intense aggression than girls."[1]
It should be further noted that the older children were more
apt to be described as being aggressive in their behavior
(r=.25). The fathers' descriptions were generally in accord
with the mothers'; the correlation between this Index of Child
Temperament and the Series Two Index of Child Activity Lev-
el--covering essentially the same behavior--was significant
(r=.49). A theoretical perspective suggested one dimension
of child description based upon two items: the degree to
which the child was seen as being "quiet" and the degree to
which he/she was characterized as being "shy." The Index
of Quiet-Shy Type of Child is one of the least robust of the
measures used in the study. The product-moment correlation
between the two items was .27.

Beyond the level of behavioral description, there was
interest in discerning how well the children were getting
along in their daily lives. In order to describe the overall
adjustment of the adoptees, five items were combined into an
Index of Child Adjustment. The first item related to the

Table VI-3

INDEX OF CHILD TEMPERAMENT*

Question	Response Categories	Percent Response
1. Mischievous	Not at all	6.5
	Hardly	12.0
	Somewhat	48.9
	Very much	32.6
		100.0
2. Stubborn	Not at all	15.2
	Hardly	18.5
	Somewhat	41.3
	Very much	25.0
		100.0
3. Quiet	Very much	4.4
	Somewhat	35.2
	Hardly	26.4
	Not at all	34.0
		100.0
4. Explosive Temper	Not at all	34.0
	Hardly	33.0
	Somewhat	25.3
	Very much	7.7
		100.0

Intercorrelation Among Items					
	1	2	3	4	Total Score
1	1.00	.44	.25	.36	.75
2		1.00	.08	.44	.71
3			1.00	.20	.56
4				1.00	.73

Cronbach Alpha= .63

Low Score ⟵——————⟶ High Score

QUIESCENT   RAMBUNCTIOUS

*All items from this index taken from following instruction to
adoptive fathers. I am going to show you a card which lists
characteristics of children. For each characteristic, please
tell me whether your child is very much like this, somewhat
like this, hardly like this, not at all like this.

Table VI-3A

INDEX OF QUIET-SHY TYPE OF CHILD*

Question	Response Categories	Percent Response
1. Quiet	Not at all	34.1
	Hardly	26.4
	Somewhat	35.1
	Very much	4.4
		100.0
2. Shy	Not at all	38.0
	Hardly	18.5
	Somewhat	41.3
	Very much	2.2
		100.0

Product-moment correlation
between items = .27

*The subjects were told the following: "I am going to show you a card which lists characteristics of children. Please tell me whether your child is like this."

kinds of problems the child was showing. Thirty percent of the adoptive fathers reported that there were no significant problems shown by the adoptee, while 40 percent referred to problems of health or mentioned character traits generally indicative of minor difficulties. Thirty percent of the respondents mentioned problems related to developmental difficulty or personality problems. The fathers were also asked about their reactions to the identified problems of the adoptees: 61 percent expressed no concern about the problems they had mentioned, the remaining 39 percent conceded some concern or worry. The other three items in the index related to characteristics from a checklist of descriptive items shown to the fathers. These concerned the degree to which the child showed behavior which could be described as tense, mischievous or destructive. A high score on this scale would be indicative of a poorer kind of child adjustment, a low score would reflect the opposite. The Alpha Coefficient is noted in Table VI-4 as .58. The association between the child's overall adjustment and the child's aggressiveness as

Table VI-4

INDEX OF CHILD ADJUSTMENT

Question	Response Categories	Percent Response
1. What problems does your child show?	No significant problems	30.4
	Physical problems or character traits	40.2
	Developmental or personality problems; or multiple problems	29.4
		100.0
2. Tense*	Not at all or hardly	84.3
	Somewhat	14.6
	Very much	1.1
		100.0
3. What are your reactions to your child's problems?	No concern or denies any problems	61.1
	Some concern or worry	38.9
		100.0
4. Mischievous*	Not at all or hardly	22.9
	Somewhat	52.1
	Very much	25.0
		100.0
5. Destructive*	Not at all or hardly	76.0
	Somewhat	16.7
	Very much	7.3
		100.0

*Respondent was told: "I am going to show you a card which lists characteristics of children. For each characteristic, please tell me whether your child is very much, somewhat, hardly or not at all like this."

INDEX OF CHILD ADJUSTMENT

Intercorrelation Among Items					
					Total
1	2	3	4	5	Score
1 1.00	.31	.50	.16	.16	.70
2	1.00	.25	.25	.20	.66
3		1.00	.14	.04	.63
4			1.00	.14	.56
5				1.00	.50

Cronbach
Alpha= .58

Low   ⟵——————————⟶   High
Score   Score

BETTER ADJUSTMENT   POORER ADJUSTMENT

---

revealed by his activity level was significant (r = .23) but
this was partially due to the fact that there was an overlap
in one item. There was no significant statistical association
with either the age or the sex of the child.

Orientations to Types of Children
Considered Adoptable

        The adoptive fathers were surveyed about the range
of possible types of children they might have considered at
the time they first approached the agency. This was an
exact replication of the questions addressed to the mothers
in Series Two. In general, the distribution of the fathers'
responses closely resembled those secured from the adoptive
mothers. Thus, there seemed to be a fairly strong degree
of readiness to consider a variety of handicapped children
whose handicaps were correctable. As was the case with
the adoptive mother, the adoption of an Oriental child seems
to be most easily considered by the adoptive fathers; two-
thirds of the respondents said they could easily have adopted
such a child. A withdrawn, shy child who was four years of
age comes next in popularity of selection, followed by an aggressive, hyperactive youngster of the same age. On the
other hand, I again point to the fact that the decision to

adopt a child of mixed Negro-white parentage was regarded
by the fathers as one of the more difficult kinds of placements to consider. Only ten percent of the respondents said
they could have easily adopted a child who was obviously Negro in appearance, and only 17.6 percent made such an as-
sertion about a child of black-white parentage who was not
obviously Negro in appearance. This again parallels the experience with the adoptive mothers.

The expressed preference of the adoptive parents for
various kinds of children was explored further by contrasting
Series Two and Series Three data in this regard. The mean
time interval between the two series of interviews was 11.8
months, and this factor might have contributed to reducing
somewhat the measure of agreement between the parents,
since their shared experience in interracial adoption over a
year's time may have influenced their common attitudes.

Table VI-6 presents information based upon mother-
father contrasts regarding the kinds of children they could
have accepted at the time they approached the agencies. In
only one of the thirteen contingency tables presented do we
find a clear-cut difference in responses. Fathers and mothers disagreed about their ability to adopt a child of mixed
Negro-white parentage, not obviously Negro in appearance.
While 46.7 percent of the mothers said that they could not
adopt such a child, only 30 percent of the fathers took such
an adamant position. It is not clear why the latter should
have been somewhat more open in their conception of an
adoptable child. As I have suggested, a possible source of
explanation for the difference in parental perspectives may
be the time difference that separated Series Two and Series
Three interviews. The additional year of living experience
with transracial adoption may have broadened the perspectives of the fathers.

Other differences between mothers and fathers I would
identify are of the following order:

-- Forty-one percent of the mothers said they could not
   consider a slightly retarded child, in contrast with 22
   percent of the fathers.

-- Twenty-six percent of the mothers could not consider
   an older, normal child, compared to nine percent of
   the fathers.

Table VI-5

FATHERS' RESPONSES TO TYPES OF CHILDREN
COUPLE MIGHT HAVE BEEN ASKED TO CONSIDER

	Adopted Easily	Minor Reservations	Major Reservations	Could Not Consider
		(Percentaged Across)		
1. Slightly retarded child	14.1	28.3	34.8	22.8
2. Normal older child (e.g., eight years old)	35.2	39.6	16.5	8.7
3. Child with mild handicap, not correctable (e.g., deaf ear)	51.6	38.5	5.5	4.4
4. Child with fairly serious handicap, correctable (e.g., cleft palate)	30.0	45.5	16.7	7.8
5. Child with serious handicap, correctable (e.g., club foot)	30.5	38.0	23.9	7.6
6. Child with serious handicap, not correctable	12.2	20.0	32.2	35.6

7.	Child of mixed Negro-white parentage (obviously Negro in skin features and skin color)	10.0	16.7	27.8	45.6
8.	Child of mixed Negro-white parentage (not obviously Negro in appearance)	17.6	28.6	24.2	29.6
9.	An Oriental child (e.g., Chinese)	67.1	25.2	4.4	3.3
10.	A child with mental illness in his immediate background	35.5	30.0	16.7	17.8
11.	A child whose appearance is somewhat marred by injury due to forceps delivery	46.6	42.2	5.6	5.6
12.	A withdrawn, shy child (4 years old)	61.1	28.9	2.2	7.8
13.	An aggressive, hyperactive child (4 years old)	56.8	33.0	5.7	4.5

*Total number of cases with responses that fall within the forced choices listed above varies from 88 to 94.

Table VI-6

COMPARISON OF SERIES TWO (ADOPTIVE MOTHER) AND
SERIES THREE (ADOPTIVE FATHER) RESPONSES
TO TYPES OF CHILDREN COUPLE MIGHT HAVE BEEN ASKED
TO CONSIDER WHEN APPROACHING AGENCY

1. Slightly Retarded Child

Father's Response	Mother's Response				Total Percent
	Could Not Consider	Major Reservation	Minor Reservation	Easily Adopted	
Could Not Consider	10	5	5	--	(20) 22.0
Major Reservation	12	6	10	4	(32) 35.2
Minor Reservation	12	4	7	3	(26) 28.6
Easily Adopted	3	1	7	2	(13) 14.3
Total	(37)	(16)	(29)	(9)	(91)
Percent	40.7	17.6	31.9	9.9	100.0

Chi square = 8.271   9 d.f.   Not significant

2. Normal Older Child

Father's Response	Mother's Response				Total Percent
	Could Not Consider	Major Reservation	Minor Reservation	Easily Adopted	
Could Not Consider	3	--	1	4	(8) 8.9
Major Reservation	6	4	1	3	(14) 15.6
Minor Reservation	9	5	5	13	(36) 40.0
Easily Adopted	5	4	9	14	(32) 35.6
Total	(23)	(13)	(20)	(34)	(90)
Percent	25.6	14.4	22.2	37.8	100.0

Chi square = 10.542   9 d.f.   p = .309

3. Child with Mild Handicap:
Not Correctable

Father's Response	Mother's Response				
	Could Not Consider	Major Reservation	Minor Reservation	Easily Adopted	Total Percent
Could Not Consider	1	--	1	2	(4) 4.4
Major Reservation	1	--	2	2	(5) 5.6
Minor Reservation	2	1	9	22	(34) 37.8
Easily Adopted	4	1	11	31	(47) 52.2
Total	(8)	(2)	(23)	(57)	(90)
Percent	8.9	2.2	25.6	63.3	100.0

Chi square = 3.605   9 d.f.   Not significant

4. Child with Fairly Serious Handicap:
Correctable

Father's Response	Mother's Response				
	Could Not Consider	Major Reservation	Minor Reservation	Easily Adopted	Total Percent
Could Not Consider	1	1	2	3	(7) 7.9
Major Reservation	4	2	5	4	(15) 16.9
Minor Reservation	9	3	9	19	(40) 44.9
Easily Adopted	5	4	5	13	(27) 30.3
Total	(19)	(10)	(21)	(39)	(89)
Percent	21.3	11.2	23.6	43.8	100.0

Chi square = 3.649   9 d.f.   Not significant

COMPARISON OF SERIES TWO (ADOPTIVE MOTHER) AND
SERIES THREE (ADOPTIVE FATHER) RESPONSES
TO TYPES OF CHILDREN COUPLE MIGHT HAVE BEEN ASKED
TO CONSIDER WHEN APPROACHING AGENCY

5. Child with Serious Handicap: Correctable

Father's Response	Mother's Response				Total Percent
	Could Not Consider	Major Reservation	Minor Reservation	Easily Adopted	
Could Not Consider	--	2	1	4	(7) 7.7
Major Reservation	6	2	5	9	(22) 24.2
Minor Reservation	10	5	6	13	(34) 37.4
Easily Adopted	3	4	7	14	(28) 30.8
Total	(19)	(13)	(19)	(40)	(91)
Percent	20.9	14.3	20.9	44.0	100.0

Chi square = 7.272   9 d.f.   Not significant

6. Child with Serious Handicap: Not Correctable

Father's Response	Mother's Response				Total Percent
	Could Not Consider	Major Reservation	Minor Reservation	Easily Adopted	
Could Not Consider	18	8	4	2	(32) 36.0
Major Reservation	10	11	5	3	(29) 32.6
Minor Reservation	6	6	2	3	(17) 19.1
Easily Adopted	3	2	3	3	(11) 12.4
Total	(37)	(27)	(14)	(11)	(89)
Percent	41.6	30.3	15.7	12.4	100.0

Chi square = 9.018   9 d.f.   Not significant

7. Child of Mixed Negro-White Parentage; Obviously Negro in Appearance

Father's Response	Mother's Response				
	Could Not Consider	Major Reservation	Minor Reservation	Easily Adopted	Total Percent
Could Not Consider	29	7	1	4	(41) 46.1
Major Reservation	12	5	3	4	(24) 27.0
Minor Reservation	6	5	2	2	(15) 16.9
Easily Adopted					(9) 10.1
Total	(51)	(18)	(6)	(14)	(89)
Percent	57.3	20.2	6.7	15.7	100.0

Chi square = 14.002   9 d.f.   Significant at 0.123 level

8. Child of Mixed Negro-White Parentage; Not Obviously Negro in Appearance

Father's Response	Mother's Response				
	Could Not Consider	Major Reservation	Minor Reservation	Easily Adopted	Total Percent
Could Not Consider	18	4	1	4	(27) 30.0
Major Reservation	12	1	3	5	(21) 23.3
Minor Reservation	10	7	4	5	(26) 28.9
Easily Adopted	2	3	5	6	(16) 17.8
Total	(42)	(15)	(13)	(20)	(90)
Percent	46.7	16.7	14.4	22.2	100.0

Chi square = 18.486   9 d.f.   Significant at .03 level

COMPARISON OF SERIES TWO (ADOPTIVE MOTHER) AND
SERIES THREE (ADOPTIVE FATHER) RESPONSES
TO TYPES OF CHILDREN COUPLE MIGHT HAVE BEEN ASKED
TO CONSIDER WHEN APPROACHING AGENCY

9. An Oriental Child

Father's Response	Mother's Response				Total Percent
	Could Not Consider	Major Reservation	Minor Reservation	Easily Adopted	
Could Not Consider	--	--	--	3	(3) 3.3
Major Reservation	--	1	1	2	(4) 4.4
Minor Reservation	2	--	8	12	(22) 24.4
Easily Adopted	4	2	8	47	(61) 67.8
Total	(6)	(3)	(17)	(64)	(90)
Percent	6.7	3.3	18.9	71.1	100.0

Chi square = 14.162   9 d.f.   Significant at 0.118 level

10. A Child with Mental Illness
in His Immediate Background

Father's Response	Mother's Response				Total Percent
	Could Not Consider	Major Reservation	Minor Reservation	Easily Adopted	
Could Not Consider	5	4	4	3	(16) 17.8
Major Reservation	2	2	6	5	(15) 16.7
Minor Reservation	4	1	10	13	(28) 31.1
Easily Adopted	3	5	8	15	(31) 34.4
Total	(14)	(12)	(28)	(36)	(90)
Percent	15.6	13.3	31.1	40.0	100.0

Chi square = 10.966   9 d.f.   Significant at 0.279 level

11. A Child Whose Appearance is Somewhat Marred

Father's Response	Mother's Response				
	Could Not Consider	Major Reservation	Minor Reservation	Easily Adopted	Total Percent
Could Not Consider	--	--	1	4	(5) 5.6
Major Reservation	--	--	2	3	(5) 5.6
Minor Reservation	2	1	7	27 ·	(37) 41.6
Easily Adopted	--	3	11	28	(42) 47.2
Total	(2)	(4)	(21)	(62)	(89)
Percent	2.2	4.5	23.6	69.7	100.0

Chi square = 5.497   9 d.f.   Not significant

12. A Withdrawn, Shy Child (Four Years Old)

Father's Response	Mother's Response				
	Could Not Consider	Major Reservation	Minor Reservation	Easily Adopted	Total Percent
Could Not Consider	--	--	1	6	(7) 7.9
Major Reservation	2	--	--	--	(2) 2.2
Minor Reservation	3	2	5	15	(25) 28.1
Easily Adopted	3	3	11	38	(55) 61.8
Total	(8)	(5)	(17)	(59)	(89)
Percent	9.0	5.6	19.1	66.3	100.0

Chi square = 23.275**   9 d.f.   Significant at 0.006 level

COMPARISON OF SERIES TWO (ADOPTIVE MOTHER) AND
SERIES THREE (ADOPTIVE FATHER) RESPONSES
TO TYPES OF CHILDREN COUPLE MIGHT HAVE BEEN ASKED
TO CONSIDER WHEN APPROACHING AGENCY

13. An Aggressive, Hyperactive Child
(Four Years Old)

Father's Response	Mother's Response				
	Could Not Consider	Major Reservation	Minor Reservation	Easily Adopted	Total Percent
Could Not Consider	--	1	--	3	(4) 4.5
Major Reservation	2	1	--	2	(5) 5.7
Minor Reservation	3	3	7	16	(29) 33.0
Easily Adopted	5	3	11	31	(50) 56.8
Total	(10)	(8)	(18)	(52)	(88)
Percent	11.4	9.1	20.5	59.1	100.0

Chi square = 9.2333   9 d.f.   Not significant

-- Forty-four percent of the fathers said they could easily
   adopt a child with a fairly serious handicap that was
   correctable, compared to 30 percent of the mothers.
   Similar differences were revealed with respect to other
   gradations of physical handicap.

-- By way of contrast with the aforesaid findings, the
   mothers were more adventuresome about a child whose
   appearance is somewhat marred by a difficult birth delivery. Seventy percent of the mothers said they could
   easily have adopted such a child, compared to 47 percent of the fathers.

   The factor analysis of the adoptive fathers' responses in
the domain of parent behavior revealed a strong factor related
to the adoption of handicapped children. A single index com-
posed of 11 items was created to measure the adoptive fathers' orientations in this regard. Whereas the responses of
(cont. p. 178)

Table VI-7

INDEX OF ADOPTIVE FATHERS' ORIENTATIONS
TO THE ADOPTION OF HANDICAPPED CHILDREN*

Question	Response Categories	Percent Response
1. A withdrawn, shy child	Could not consider	7.8
	Major reservations	2.2
	Minor reservations	28.9
	Adopted easily	61.1
		100.0
2. A child whose appearance is somewhat marred by injury due to forceps delivery	Could not consider	5.6
	Major reservations	5.6
	Minor reservations	42.2
	Adopted easily	46.6
		100.0
3. A child with fairly serious handicap, correctable (e.g., cleft palate)	Could not consider	7.8
	Major reservations	16.7
	Minor reservations	45.5
	Adopted easily	30.0
		100.0
4. An aggressive, hyperactive child (4 years old)	Could not consider	4.6
	Major reservations	5.7
	Minor reservations	33.0
	Adopted easily	56.7
		100.0
5. A child with serious handicap, not correctable	Could not consider	35.6
	Major reservations	32.2
	Minor reservations	20.0
	Adopted easily	12.2
		100.0
6. A slightly mentally retarded child	Could not consider	22.8
	Major reservations	34.8
	Minor reservations	28.3
	Adopted easily	14.1
		100.0

INDEX OF ADOPTIVE FATHERS' ORIENTATIONS
TO THE ADOPTION OF HANDICAPPED CHILDREN*

Question	Response Categories	Percent Response
7. A child with mild handicap, not correctable (e.g., deaf in one ear)	Could not consider	4.4
	Major reservations	5.5
	Minor reservations	38.5
	Adopted easily	51.6
		100.0
8. A child with serious handicap, correctable (e.g., club foot)	Could not consider	7.6
	Major reservations	23.9
	Minor reservations	38.0
	Adopted easily	30.5
		100.0
9. A normal older child (e.g., eight years old)	Could not consider	8.8
	Major reservations	16.5
	Minor reservations	39.6
	Adopted easily	35.1
		100.0
10. A child with mental illness in his immediate background	Could not consider	17.8
	Major reservations	16.7
	Minor reservations	30.0
	Adopted easily	35.5
		100.0
11. An Oriental child (e.g., Chinese)	Could not consider	3.3
	Major reservations	4.4
	Minor reservations	25.3
	Adopted easily	67.0
		100.0

*The subjects were told the following: "As you may know, the agency has many kinds of children to place for adoption. Now, I would like you to think back to the time you first came to the agency to apply for adoption. Suppose children of the following types had been offered to you for consideration. I would like you to tell me whether you might easily have adopted such a child, would have had some reservations about adopting, had major reservations, or would not have been able to take such a child under any circumstances."

Cronbach Alpha= .63

Intercorrelation Among Items

	1	2	3	4	5	6	7	8	9	10	11	Total Score
1	1.00	.54	.36	.79	.32	.33	.42	.35	.38	.26	.27	.72
2		1.00	.40	.47	.44	.48	.46	.39	.33	.44	.37	.76
3			1.00	.30	.41	.44	.31	.83	.42	.19	.05	.68
4				1.00	.29	.21	.26	.27	.29	.33	.36	.66
5					1.00	.55	.35	.36	.40	.31	.18	.66
6						1.00	.46	.40	.37	.13	.10	.64
7							1.00	.27	.34	.27	.22	.63
8								1.00	.33	.17	.06	.64
9									1.00	.22	.12	.60
10										1.00	.36	.53
11											1.00	.44

High Score
↑
EASILY ADOPTED

Low Score
↓
MAJOR RESERVATIONS

the mothers was differentiated into two clear-cut factors, handicapped children and children with psychological problems, the fathers' responses identified one major factor accounting for both.   Table VI-7 contains the items included in the index and their intercorrelations.   As can be seen, the index has a high degree of reliability with an Alpha Coefficient of .84.

The readiness to consider the adoption of handicapped children was correlated in negative fashion with the socioeconomic status of the families, that is, lower class adoptive parents could more easily consider the adoption of handicapped children.   This is in accord with the previously reported finding of Maas and Engler that lower class people are more adventuresome in their approach to adoption.[2]   Of additional interest is the fact that this index is significantly correlated with the measure developed from the Series Two responses of the adoptive mothers called Index of Adoptive Mothers' Orientation to the Adoption of Handicapped Children $(r = .21)$.

A two-item index was created to tap the expressed readiness of the adoptive fathers to consider, albeit on a hypothetical basis, the adoption of Negro children.   One item dealt with the readiness to consider a child of mixed Negro-white parentage who was obviously Negro in features and skin color while the second item referred to a child who was not obviously Negro in appearance.   The product-moment correlation between the two items was .78.   Contrary to the previous finding about handicapped children, those adoptive fathers who were among the minority to respond that they could have adopted a Negro child easily, or that they had only minor reservations about such a child, tended to be individuals of higher socioeconomic status $(r = .30)$.

Security of Outlook

There were a number of questions where the responses of the fathers seemed cautious rather than optimistic. For example, the fathers were asked whether they anticipated that their child might experience some discomfort about his being Indian as he grew up.   A third were quite affirmative in stating that they did expect some discomfort would be experienced while another fourth of the sample expected some slight discomfort.   Forty percent responded that they did not expect any difficulties.   Later in the interview, the fathers

Table VI-8

INDEX OF ADOPTIVE FATHERS' ORIENTATIONS
TO THE ADOPTION OF NEGRO CHILDREN*

Question	Response Categories	Percent Response
1. Child of mixed Negro-white parentage (obviously Negro in features and in skin color)	Could not consider	45.5
	Major reservations	27.8
	Minor reservations	16.7
	Adopted easily	10.0
		100.0
2. Child of mixed Negro-white parentage (not obviously Negro in appearance)	Could not consider	29.7
	Major reservations	24.2
	Minor reservations	28.6
	Adopted easily	17.5
		100.0

Product-moment correlation
between items = .78

*The subjects were told the following: "As you may know,
the agency has many kinds of children to place for adoption.
Now I would like you to think back to the time when you
first came to the agency to apply for adoption. Suppose
children of the following types had been offered to you for
consideration. I would like you to tell me whether you
might easily have adopted such a child, would have had
some reservations about adopting, had major reservations,
or would not have been able to take such a child under any
circumstances."

_____

were again asked whether there were any particular kind of
difficulties that they expected their child would experience;
almost fifty percent expressed fear that their children would
encounter various kinds of discriminatory behavior. In addition to these two items, the parents were asked items tak-
en from Ruderman's study of parents' attitude toward the use
of day care.[3] Inquiry was made as to when the fathers felt
a boy should be able to take care of himself and when he
felt a girl should be able to take care of herself.

Table VI-9

INDEX OF SECURITY OF PARENTAL OUTLOOK

Question	Response Categories	Percent Response
1. Do you anticipate that your child may experience some discomfort about his being of Indian background as he grows up?	Yes, will experience some discomfort	33.7
	Yes, but to slight degree	26.3
	No, does not anticipate child will experience any discomfort	40.0
		100.0
2. Are there any particular kinds of difficulties you anticipate that your child will encounter?	Fears child will encounter various kinds of discriminatory behaviors	48.8
	Does not expect any difficulties	51.2
		100.0
3. At what age do you feel a boy should be able to take care of himself?	Age 16 years or over	7.7
	Age 14 or 15 years	9.7
	Age 12 or 13 years	17.4
	Age 10 or 11 years	31.5
	Age 8 or 9 years	14.1
	Age 6 or 7 years	4.4
	Age 5 years or under	--
	Don't know, depends	14.1
	Other	1.1
		100.0
4. At what age do you feel a girl should be able to take care of herself?	Age 16 years or over	9.8
	Age 14 or 15 years	9.8
	Age 12 or 13 years	21.8
	Age 10 or 11 years	25.0
	Age 8 or 9 years	13.0
	Age 6 or 7 years	3.3
	Age 5 years or under	--
	Don't know, depends	15.2
	Other	2.1
		100.0

Intercorrelation Among Items				
	1	2	3	4	Total Score
1	1.00	.17	.23	.11	.40
2		1.00	.27	.23	.40
3			1.00	.87	.95
4				1.00	.92

Cronbach
Alpha= .94

Low
Score $\longleftarrow\!\!\!\!\!\longrightarrow$ High
Score

CAUTIOUS OUTLOOK   OPTIMISTIC OUTLOOK

The four items were revealed in the factor analysis as constituting a distinct cluster of items and when they were formed into an index, the reliability as assessed by Cronbach's Alpha was substantial (.94). This index subsequently proved to be significantly correlated with the adjustment scores achieved by the children in the Series Four interviews. Of interest is that there also were significant correlations with two other indexes developed from the Series Three interviews with the fathers, the Index of Deprivation in Adoptive Fathers' Background and the Index of the Child's Indian Appearance. The adoptive fathers who had the more deprived backgrounds tended to be quite cautious in their orientations to the future. On the other hand, those who tended to deal openly with their child's physical appearance, were more optimistic in their outlook.

Support for Indian Adoption

The reports of the adoptive fathers indicated that more than half had encountered mixed reactions from their closest relatives when they revealed their plans to adopt an Indian child. While most cases involved relatively mild, negative responses, in a few instances more serious family rifts developed. One father's parents broke off with the couple because they could not tolerate the notion of transracial adoption. The adoptive fathers also indicated in 45 percent of the cases that some friends reacted negatively--mostly

Table VI-10

INDEX OF BACKGROUND SUPPORT FOR INDIAN ADOPTION

Question	Response Categories	Percent Response
1. Generally, what has been the reaction of your closest relatives with respect to your decision to adopt an American Indian child?	Some negative reaction ranging from strong antagonism to minor doubts	57.5
	Relatives have been completely supportive	42.5
		100.0
2. How have your friends reacted?	Some negative reaction ranging from strong antagonism to minor doubts	45.6
	Friends have been completely supportive	54.4
		100.0
3. Could you tell me whether you had any opportunity to come into contact with Indians before you adopted your child?	No prior contact	50.0
	Slight contact	18.2
	Had fairly significant prior contact	31.8
		100.0
4. Were you ever particularly interested in the American Indian?	No particular interest	39.5
	Slight interest	23.3
	Had fairly strong interest	37.2
		100.0

Intercorrelation Among Items					
	1	2	3	4	Total Score
1	1.00	.52	.14	.15	.70
2		1.00	.09	.23	.71
3			1.00	.25	.57
4				1.00	.63

Cronbach Alpha= .54

Low Score $\longleftarrow$ $\longrightarrow$ High Score

LOW SUPPORT   HIGH SUPPORT

mildly.   Linked to these items were two others related to
prior contact with and interest in American Indians.   The
Index of Background Support for Indian Adoption showed modest reliability (Alpha = .54).   The fathers who scored high
on the index tended to be of lower socioeconomic status
(r = -.28).

Child's Appearance

Three items were identified by the factor analysis of
the characteristics of the children: they concerned the adoptive father's sense of the distinctiveness of the child's Indian
appearance, and his awareness of the general public's reaction to the child being that of curiosity and awareness of
his Indian appearance.   When asked whether the adoptee's
Indian characteristics made him strikingly different from the
father, 42 percent responded that they indeed felt the child
looked different from themselves and the rest of the family.
Another 27 percent felt the child looked different but not
strikingly so.   Almost a third of the respondents felt that
the child did not look different from the members of the
family.

The adoptive fathers were also asked whether people
ever commented to them about the child's appearance or his
looking different.   About a third said people never commented about this and another 29 percent observed that such
comments occurred rarely.   About 26 percent spoke of people commenting frequently or fairly often about the child's
appearance.

The third item dealing with the matter of appearance
was related to the fathers' awareness of being stared at in
public when he was out with the child.   Forty-six percent
reported being aware of staring while almost 52 percent de-
nied experiencing such a phenomenon.   The three items were
pooled to form the Index of Child's Indian Appearance.   This
index correlated quite firmly with a similar index created
from the Series Two interviews with the adoptive mothers
(r = .51), indicating a fairly good degree of agreement between fathers and mothers in this area.

Child Rearing Orientation

The adoptive fathers were interviewed about their child
(cont. p. 186)

Table VI-11

INDEX OF CHILD'S INDIAN APPEARANCE
(Series 3)

Question	Response Categories	Percent Response
1. In general, would you say that your child's Indian characteristics make him strikingly different from you in appearance?	Feels child does not look different from self and family	30.6
	Feels child looks different but not strikingly so	27.3
	Feels child looks different from self and rest of family	42.1
		100.0
2. Do people ever comment to you about your child's appearance (or his looking different from you)? How often?	People never comment about it	35.6
	Such comments occur rarely	28.7
	Used to get such comments, less so now	9.2
	People comment fairly often, perhaps two or three times a month	17.3
	People comment frequently about it	9.2
		100.0
3. Do you ever get the feeling when you are in public places that people stare at you and the child?	No, not aware of staring	51.7
	Yes, but feels it happens less now than it used to	2.3
	Yes, aware of staring	46.0
		100.0

Intercorrelation Among Items			
	1	2	3	Total Score
1	1.00	.32	.50	.80
2		1.00	.22	.68
3			1.00	.76

Cronbach
Alpha= .60

Low Score ⟵——————————⟶ High Score

DOES NOT LOOK DIFFERENT   LOOKS DIFFERENT

Table VI-12

INDEX OF
STRICT VS. PERMISSIVE CHILD REARING ORIENTATION

Question	Response Categories	Percent Response
1. What do you expect of your child regarding obeying you?	Strong expectation of immediate obedience	6. 8
	Fairly strong expectation of immediate obedience	38. 7
	Wants obedience but tolerates delay	26. 1
	Tolerant towards noncompliance	28. 4
		100. 0
2. What do you expect of your child regarding neatness?	Very high standards	2. 5
	Fairly high standards	25. 3
	Neither strict nor lenient	26. 6
	Fairly lenient	27. 9
	Very lenient	17. 7
		100. 0
3. What is expected with regard to child's treatment of home's walls and furniture?	Many restrictions	10. 6
	Fairly strict	47. 2
	Neither strict nor lenient	18. 8
	Few restrictions	23. 4
		100. 0
4. What is expected of child with regard to putting toys away?	Always expected to do so	20. 7
	Usually expected to do so	32. 2
	Sometimes expected to do so	33. 3
	Generally quite lenient	13. 8
		100. 0
5. What is expected of child with regard to restrictions on noise in the home?	Quite strict in limiting noise	10. 6
	Moderately strict	23. 5
	A few restrictions set	37. 7
	Not at all strict	28. 2
		100. 0

INDEX OF
STRICT VS. PERMISSIVE CHILD REARING ORIENTATION

Question	Response Categories	Percent Response
6. What do you expect of child regarding table manners?	Basic manners expected	78.7
	Try for basic manners but do not insist	18.0
	Little effort made to develop table manners	3.3
		100.0

Intercorrelation Among Items							
	1	2	3	4	5	6	Total Score
1	1.00	.20	.31	.12	.19	.14	.54
2		1.00	.20	.48	.25	.27	.66
3			1.00	.36	.29	.16	.64
4				1.00	.31	.17	.68
5					1.00	.09	.59
6						1.00	.50

Cronbach Alpha= .65

Low Score ⟵——————————————⟶ High Score

STRICT   PERMISSIVE

---

rearing orientations just as their wives had been in Series
Two.   The items were taken from the Sears, Maccoby and
Levin study. [4]   The factor analysis of parent role items
identified a distinct domain dealing with child rearing and a
six-item index was created.   Essentially, it is based upon
the responses of the fathers regarding their strictness or
permissiveness with respect to such things as expecting obedience from their children, their attitudes about neatness,
marking furniture, putting toys away and general restrictions
about noise in the home.   The parenting disposition of the
adoptive fathers was measured by the Index of Strict vs.
Permissive Child Rearing Orientation.   The index showed an
Alpha Coefficient of .65.   It significantly correlated with the
measure of the child rearing orientations of their wives

(r = .35). It also correlated significantly with the assessment of the fathers' traditional versus modern male ideology. Of further interest is the fact that, by and large, the most permissive fathers were those whose children were adopted at younger ages and who were consequently younger during the Series Three interviews (r = -.29). Thus the permissiveness may be related to unwillingness to inflict more severe child rearing techniques upon very young children.

As might be expected, the father's tendency to be permissive in his child rearing orientation was significantly correlated with his tendency to be liberal in his political outlook (r= .21). There was no significant association between the socioeconomic status of the fathers and their expressed permissiveness.

I will subsequently show that the fathers who had the most permissive orientation were also those whose adoptees tended to score higher on the Overall Adjustment Rating developed for the adoptees at the end of the series of interviews.

Social Perspectives of Adoptive Fathers

As was the case with the Series Two interviews with the adoptive mothers, the interviewing schedules used to survey the attitudes of the adoptive fathers contained a number of dimensions which were calculated to assess various social attitudinal orientations of the adoptive fathers. As indicated previously, the adoption of an Indian child was seen as an act on the part of the parents which had social implications. Implicit in the adoption was the statement that the race or ethnicity of a child would not be an important barrier to integrating him within the family. Thus a number of social viewpoints were tapped in the interview which later emerged as identifiable attitudinal domains in the factor analytic exploration of the responses of the subjects.

The first index created was the Index of Lower Class-Rural Background, a nine-item index which proved to have a high degree of reliability (Cronbach's Alpha Coefficient = .91). On the lower end of the continuum, the index describes adoptive fathers of middle class backgrounds with an urban orientation. On the opposite end were adoptive fathers who tended to be lower class and rural in their orientations. As can be seen in Table VI-13, almost 55 percent of the adoptive fa-

Table VI-13

INDEX OF LOWER CLASS-RURAL BACKGROUND

Question	Response Categories	Percent Response
1. What general social class would you say your family was in?	Upper middle class	27.7
	Lower middle class	16.9
	Upper working class	41.0
	Lower working class	14.4
		100.0
2. How much schooling did your father have?	Graduate or professional school	8.6
	Completed college	4.9
	Some college	8.6
	Completed high school	13.6
	Some high school	21.0
	Completed grade school	19.8
	Some grade school	23.5
		100.0
3. Where did your father live as a boy?	Middle-sized or large city	25.3
	Small town or small city	29.9
	Rural area	44.8
		100.0
4. How many children were there in your family?	One or two	38.4
	Three or four	24.2
	Five or six	17.6
	Seven or eight	9.9
	Nine or more	9.9
		100.0
5. Was your father very strict?	Hardly, not at all	46.5
	Somewhat strict	19.8
	Strict	33.7
		100.0

Question	Response Categories	Percent Response
6. How much schooling did your mother have?	Graduate or professional school	3.6
	Completed college	7.2
	Some college	7.2
	Completed high school	21.7
	Some high school	24.1
	Completed grade school	19.3
	Some grade school	14.5
	No education	2.4
		100.0
7. How far was the closest large city during your childhood?	Lived in large city	35.6
	Lived within 5 miles	10.3
	Lived within 10 miles	18.4
	Lived within 25 miles	16.1
	Lived within 50 miles	14.9
	Lived more than 50 miles away	4.7
		100.0
8. What was the general economic situation of your family throughout most of your childhood?	Comfortable or better	66.7
	Meager or poor	33.3
		100.0
9. Was your mother very strict?	Hardly, not at all	51.7
	Somewhat strict	25.8
	Strict	22.5
		100.0

INDEX OF LOWER CLASS-RURAL BACKGROUND

Intercorrelation Among Items

	1	2	3	4	5	6	7	8	9	Total Score
1	1.00	.44	.30	.26	.38	.40	.09	.38	.13	.65
2		1.00	.21	.19	.27	.51	.07	.19	.20	.52
3			1.00	.48	.21	.23	.19	.25	.11	.65
4				1.00	.22	.12	.25	.06	.02	.45
5					1.00	.13	.19	.32	.33	.65
6						1.00	-.02	.40	.16	.50
7							1.00	.20	.12	.38
8								1.00	.28	.69
9									1.00	.39

Cronbach Alpha= .91

Low Score ⇕ High Score

MIDDLE CLASS-CITY ORIENTATION   LOWER CLASS-RURAL ORIENTATION

thers described themselves as coming from upper working
class or lower working class families and somewhat more
than two out of five had fathers who had less than a grade
school education. Forty-five percent of the fathers said their
own fathers had lived in rural areas. These same fathers
tended to come from families where there were many children, their parents strict, and the economic circumstances
of the family meager. A third of the sample described the
economic stiuation of their families through most of their
childhood as being meager or poor. As might be expected,
the correlation between this index and the socioeconomic status of the adoptive families was inversely associated in significant fashion (r = -.33). It is of interest, however, that
the index scores were not significantly correlated with the
political or religious attitudes of the subjects or their propen-
sities to adopt children with varying kinds of handicaps.

Religiosity

An eight-item index, developed from the questions related to the religious attitudes and practices of the adoptive
fathers, proved to be quite reliable (Alpha Coefficient = .83).
Examination of Table VI-14 reveals that most of the adoptive
fathers saw religion playing some place in their lives. Fully
55 percent indicated it was at least very important and another 27 percent reported it as being important. It is noteworthy that 51 percent of the adoptive fathers indicated they
attended religious services at least once a week. Only 18
percent said that religion was of minor importance or of no
importance at all. These views were similar to those reported by their wives. The sample was fairly split between
those who reported active involvement in other church activities and those who reported no significant involvement. Fifty-
four percent of the subjects reported that their own fathers
were not religious or hardly so; this was true of only 26 percent of their mothers.

As might be expected, there was a quite firm correlation between the adoptive fathers' expression of religiosity
and the adoptive mothers' (r = -.53).[5] It is also no surprise
to find that a high degree of religiosity is firmly correlated
with political conservatism on the fathers' part (r = .45).
The fathers' religiosity was also correlated significantly with
the adoptive mothers' political orientation (r = .40). We note
further that the more religious adoptive fathers indicated a
greater readiness to become involved in the adoption of hand-
(cont. p. 194)

Table VI-14

INDEX OF RELIGIOSITY OF ADOPTIVE FAMILIES*

Question	Response Categories	Percent Response
1. How important is religion in your life?	Most important thing in life	23.3
	Very important	32.2
	Important	26.7
	Not so important	8.9
	Of no importance	8.9
		100.0
2. How important is religion to your wife?	Most important thing in life	25.3
	Very important	37.4
	Important	22.0
	Not so important	9.8
	Of no importance	5.5
		100.0
3. How often do you attend religious services?	At least once a week	51.1
	Two or three times a month	8.7
	At least once a month	8.7
	Three or four times a year	10.9
	Only holidays	4.3
	Rarely/never	16.3
		100.0
4. To what extent is religion included in home activities of your family? For example, family prayers, reading the Bible, saying Grace at meals and so forth.	A great deal	12.5
	More than average	22.7
	Average	39.8
	A little	14.8
	Not at all	10.2
		100.0

*Based upon Series Three Interviews with the adoptive fathers.

Question	Response Categories	Percent Response
5. Aside from religious services, what other church activities do you take part in?	Significant involvement in church activities (e.g., holds office in Men's Club, teaches Sunday School, active in committee(s), etc.)	52.3
	No significant involvement in church activities	47.7
		100.0
6. Aside from religious services, what other church activities does your wife take part in?	Significant involvement in church activities (e.g., holds office in Sisterhood, teaches Sunday School, active in committee(s), etc.)	56.3
	No significant involvement in church activities	43.7
		100.0
7. Was your father very religious?	Yes (response unqualified)	26.4
	Yes, somewhat to moderately so	19.5
	No, father was not religious or hardly so	54.1
		100.0
8. Was your mother very religious?	Yes (response unqualified)	52.7
	Yes, somewhat to moderately so	20.9
	No, mother was not religious or hardly so	26.4
		100.0

INDEX OF RELIGIOSITY OF ADOPTIVE FAMILIES

Intercorrelations Among Items

	1	2	3	4	5	6	7	8	Total Score
1	1.00	.80	.58	.69	.40	.45	.28	.27	.83
2		1.00	.62	.57	.47	.38	.20	.16	.78
3			1.00	.57	.49	.42	.14	.17	.74
4				1.00	.39	.47	.23	.17	.76
5					1.00	.65	.14	.05	.67
6						1.00	.11	.03	.65
7							1.00	.50	.48
8								1.00	.44

Cronbach Alpha= .83

Low Score $\longleftarrow$ $\longrightarrow$ High Score

RELIGIOUS   NOT RELIGIOUS

---

icapped children than was true of the less religious subjects $(r = -.37)$. The religious fathers also were parents in larger-sized family units than the less religious parents.

Since the religious orientation of the families was not infrequently mentioned in the initial interviews as being related to the feeling that all children were essentially equal and deprived children especially ought to be placed in adoptive homes, it was anticipated that religiosity would be related to other aspects of the adoptive experience. Aside from the stronger inclination of religious adoptive parents to adopt handicapped children, however, religiosity did not seem to be significant with respect to the overall adjustment of the adopted children, although some association was found with a count of child symptoms in Series Five. This will be amplified further in Chapter X when the correlates of the major outcome variables are examined.

Political Orientation

As might be expected from the analysis of the adop-

Table VI-15

INDEX OF ADOPTIVE FATHERS'
LIBERAL VS. CONSERVATIVE POLITICAL ORIENTATION

Question	Response Categories	Percent Response
1. Considering your views on social and political questions, how would you describe yourself?	Very conservative	4.6
	Somewhat conservative	41.4
	Somewhat liberal	28.7
	Very liberal	25.3
		100.0
2. Would you mind telling me who you voted for in the 1960 presidential election?	Richard Nixon	36.6
	John Kennedy	63.4
		100.0*
3. In the 1956 election?	Dwight Eisenhower	61.3
	Adlai Stevenson	38.7
		100.0**
4. Are you concerned with the following problems of our times: alleged general decline in morality?	Very concerned	42.4
	Somewhat concerned	32.6
	Not at all concerned	25.0
		100.0
5. Concern with struggle against Communism?	Very concerned	47.3
	Somewhat concerned	37.4
	Not at all concerned	15.3
		100.0

*Percentage based upon 82 respondents: 10 fathers did not vote in 1960.

**Percentage based upon 80 respondents: 12 fathers did not vote in 1956.

INDEX OF ADOPTIVE FATHERS'
LIBERAL VS. CONSERVATIVE POLITICAL ORIENTATION

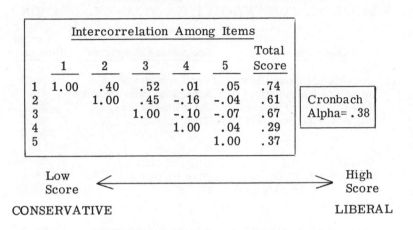

	Intercorrelation Among Items					
	1	2	3	4	5	Total Score
1	1.00	.40	.52	.01	.05	.74
2		1.00	.45	-.16	-.04	.61
3			1.00	-.10	-.07	.67
4				1.00	.04	.29
5					1.00	.37

Cronbach
Alpha= .38

Low   High
Score ←—————————————————————————————→ Score

CONSERVATIVE   LIBERAL

---

tive mothers' responses, the social attitudes of the adoptive fathers--when subjected to factor analysis procedures--revealed a domain of political orientation.   Table VI-15 is an Index of Adoptive Fathers' Liberal vs. Conservative Political Orientation.   The adoptive fathers were generally divided between conservatives and liberals, with about five percent describing themselves as very conservative and 41 percent as somewhat conservative.   About 29 percent of the fathers described themselves as somewhat liberal and another 25 percent as very liberal.   In the 1956 national election, 61 percent of the adoptive fathers who voted cast their votes for Dwight Eisenhower; this compared to 57.8 percent of the national voters.   In the 1960 election, the adoptive fathers deviated somewhat from the national pattern, 63 percent voting for John Kennedy, compared with only 50.08 percent of the nation's voters.   The five-item index created from these responses shows only modest reliability estimate (Cronbach's Alpha = .38).

The scores achieved by the adoptive fathers on this index were significant associated with those of their wives (the correlation between Series Two and Series Three indexes measuring political attitudes was .46).   As observed previously, fathers who espoused more liberal ideas also tended

to be less religious in their observance and attitudes.   The
correlation between the two measures was quite firm (r = .45).
The more liberal orientations also tended to be voiced by
fathers whose socioeconomic status was higher (r = .23).
Examination of the relationship between our various measures
also indicated overlap between political orientations and general parental orientations.   Thus, the more liberal adoptive
fathers also tended to be those who were more permissive
in their child rearing orientations (r = .21).   As was the case
with religiosity, expression of a conservative outlook was associated with the ability to adopt handicapped children.   Since
these indexes are highly intercorrelated, we will analyze
their significance for our outcome variables in Chapter X in
a multiple correlation procedure where the predictive power
of the indexes can be tested as a group.

Social Problem Orientation

The factor analysis of the adoptive fathers' social attitudes revealed a dimension of social perspective distinct
from the issue of liberal vs. conservative orientation.   A
group of items related to an overall interest in social problems was used to test the adoptive fathers' concerns about
such problems as the possibility of an atomic war, discrimination against minority groups, general economic conditions
in the country, and problems of old folks.   There were several questions also designed to tap their interest in international affairs, in reading about social problems, and their
tendency to belong to organizations.   Almost two out of five
adoptive fathers reported belonging to at least two organizations.

In the main, the concerns of the fathers were fairly
well distributed and the Index of Social Problem Orientation
of Adoptive Fathers as displayed in Table VI-16 proved to
be fairly reliable (Alpha Coefficient = .62).   Examination of
the index showed that it was not significantly correlated with
the index measuring the liberal vs. conservative orientation
of the adoptive fathers although the liberal fathers tended to
be more social problem oriented.   The only index with which
this social problem orientation was significantly correlated
dealt with the adoptive fathers' orientation to the adoption of
Negro children.   Paradoxically, it turns out that the stronger
the social problem orientation, the less ready was the adoptive father to consider the adoption of a Negro child.

Table VI-16

INDEX OF SOCIAL PROBLEM ORIENTATION
OF ADOPTIVE FATHERS

Question	Response Categories	Percent Response
1. Possibility of an atomic war*	Hardly concerned	32.6
	Somewhat concerned	34.8
	Very concerned	32.6
		100.0
2. Discrimination against minority groups*	Hardly concerned	12.0
	Somewhat concerned	33.7
	Very concerned	54.3
		100.0
3. General economic conditions in the country*	Hardly concerned	8.7
	Somewhat concerned	52.2
	Very concerned	39.1
		100.0
4. Problems of old folks*	Hardly concerned	9.8
	Somewhat concerned	54.4
	Very concerned	35.8
		100.0
5. Thinking of the kind of person you are, would you say that you have a special interest in the following aspects of living: (3) Keeping up with international affairs	Little or no interest	2.3
	Moderate interest	39.3
	Strong interest	58.4
		100.0
6. Thinking of the kind of person you are, would you say that you have a special interest in the following aspects of living: (6) Reading interest	Little or no interest	7.8
	Moderate interest	36.0
	Strong interest	56.2
		100.0

*Respondent was asked: "Do you tend to be concerned about the following social problems of our times? Would you say you are very concerned, somewhat concerned, or hardly concerned about these problems?

Question	Response Categories	Percent Response
7. Do you belong to any organizations? How many?	No organizations	27.8
	One organization	33.3
	Two organizations	16.7
	Three organizations	13.3
	Four organizations	6.7
	Five organizations	2.2
		100.0

Intercorrelation Among Items

	1	2	3	4	5	6	7	Total Score
1	1.00	.22	.42	.14	.17	.18	-.01	.55
2		1.00	.23	.23	.21	.27	.12	.59
3			1.00	.36	.04	.13	.06	.58
4				1.00	.21	.29	-.01	.58
5					1.00	.26	.17	.53
6						1.00	.26	.62
7							1.00	.42

Cronbach Alpha= .62

Low Score ⟷ High Score

LOW SOCIAL CONCERNS   HIGH SOCIAL CONCERNS

What emerges as being of even greater interest, as revealed in Chapter X, is that the social problem orientation of the adoptive fathers was significantly linked to our three major outcome measures: the symptom picture developed in Series Four, the symptom picture developed in Series Five and the Overall Adjustment Rating created at the end of the field interviewing. In all three instances, expression of high social concerns and involvement in community life were correlated with poorer adjustment on the part of the adopted children. This is a matter about which we will wish to speculate when we get into the analysis of the outcome measures in Chapter X.

Table VI-17

INDEX OF TRADITIONAL MASCULINE IDEOLOGY

Question	Response Categories	Percent Response
1. In your experience, which of these things do you feel you <u>must</u> have in order to be happy? (Item e) Having your wife keep a well-run household	Can be happy without this Don't know, not sure Must have this to be happy	47.6 1.2 51.2 100.0
2. (Item f) Having your wife at home rather than being employed outside of the home	Can be happy without this Don't know, not sure Must have this to be happy	24.7 10.6 64.7 100.0
3. Who gets up at night to take care of the children?	Father or father and mother alternately Mother exclusively	61.8 38.2 100.0

Intercorrelation Among Items			
	1	2	3	Total Score
1	1.00	.46	.10	.74
2		1.00	.17	.77
3			1.00	.60

Cronbach
Alpha= .49

Low
Score $\longleftarrow$ $\longrightarrow$ High
Score

MODERN   TRADITIONAL

Masculine Ideology

A three-item index (Table VI-17) was designed to differentiate between traditional and more egalitarian views of the relationship between men and women. The first item dealt with the degree to which the adoptive father required to have his wife keep a well run household in order to be happy. The sample was fairly evenly split on this. The adoptive father was also asked whether he had to have his wife at home rather than being employed outside of the home. Twenty-five percent indicated they could be happy without this and about 11 percent were not sure of their response. Almost two-thirds of the adoptive fathers indicated that they preferred having their wife at home. Finally, the third item in the index dealt with the sharing of household tasks. The item selected dealt with who got up at night to take care of the children; the findings showed that 62 percent of the fathers shared this task with the mothers; in 38 percent of the cases, this was exclusively the mother's job. The reliability of the index was modest (Alpha Coefficient = .49). The index is significantly correlated with the religiosity of the mother, a traditional male outlook being associated with high religiosity. However, the index does not show a significant association with the index measuring the fathers' religiosity, nor with the index measuring the traditional female ideology of the adoptive mothers. The adoptive fathers who espoused a traditional conception of the male role also tended to report child rearing behaviors which would be considered nonpermissive.

I also attempted to assess the adoptive fathers' satisfaction with their work situation. The Index of Adoptive Fathers' Work Satisfaction is a three-item index of quite low reliability, and is not presented here. About 50 percent of the adoptive fathers reported they had achieved as much success in their work as they aspired to, and two-thirds said they did not prefer any other kind of work. Further, about 29 percent were very satisfied with their current income and about 62 percent were fairly satisfied. There were only two indexes significantly correlated with this measure of work satisfaction. Adoptive fathers who expressed a low degree of work satisfaction were linked to wives who in Series Two reported rather constricted notions of the female role ($r = -.28$). The basis for the relationship between the two measures is not clear and may well be due to chance factors. The other linkage to work satisfaction was the expressed ability to adopt handicapped children: the more dissatisfied fathers were evidently more open to the adoption of handicapped children. Interestingly, there was no significant association between work satisfaction and the socioeconomic status of the family (r = .01).

Deprivation

As with the adoptive mothers, there was interest in determining how much deprivation the adoptive fathers had experienced in growing up. This was seen as one link to their potential performance as parents, the assumption being that those who had had extremely deprived lives would be more apt to encounter difficulty as parents. A five-item index was created on the basis of the factor analysis of the fathers' responses.

The first item concerned the fathers' reports as to whether there was anything about their own fathers that had upset them. Forty-three percent of the respondents answered positively, indicating such items as alcoholism, physical brutality, unemployment and absence of their fathers while they grew up. When asked whether their fathers had been affectionate to them, 38 percent of the respondents indicated that they had experienced less than fully affectionate behavior from their fathers. With respect to the general economic conditions of their families, a third reported poor economic conditions.

The fourth item consisted of an estimate by the adoptive father of his own parents' marriage. Only 13 percent reported unhappy marriages and 29 percent reported average marriages. The final item dealt with the adoptive fathers' perspective on the amount of tragedy the family had experienced while he grew up. Sixty-two percent reported little tragedy, 23 percent reported an average amount, and 15 percent reported having suffered considerable tragedy in their childhood.

The Alpha Coefficient for this index was modest, being .47. Surprisingly the index was significantly correlated with the Index of Security of Parental Outlook, indicating that those with background deprivation tend to be somewhat more optimistic. This incongruous finding may be related to the fact that two of the items dealing with the parental outlook referred to the age at which a child should be able to fend for himself. The more deprived parents tended to push this

Table VI-18

INDEX OF DEPRIVATION IN
ADOPTIVE FATHERS' BACKGROUNDS

Question	Response Categories	Percent Response
1. Was there anything about your father that upset you?	No negative item cited	57.1
	Yes, negative items cited (alcoholism, physical brutality, unemployment, absences, etc.)	42.9
		100.0
2. Was your father affectionate to you?	Unqualified positive response	61.9
	Less than fully affectionate	38.1
		100.0
3. What was the general economic situation of your family throughout most of your childhood?	Good economic situation (well-to-do to comfortable)	66.7
	Poor economic situation	33.3
		100.0
4. What is your estimate of your parents' marriage?	Very happy	25.8
	Happy	31.5
	Average	29.2
	Unhappy	9.0
	Very unhappy	4.5
		100.0
5. Would you say that your family suffered an unusual amount of tragedy during your childhood?	Suffered little tragedy	61.6
	Suffered average amount of tragedy	23.3
	Suffered considerable tragedy	15.1
		100.0

INDEX OF DEPRIVATION IN
ADOPTIVE FATHERS' BACKGROUNDS

	Intercorrelation Among Items					Total Score
	1	2	3	4	5	
1	1.00	.35	.25	.34	-.12	.56
2		1.00	.09	.26	-.02	.51
3			1.00	.15	-.13	.37
4				1.00	.18	.83
5					1.00	.42

Cronbach
Alpha= .47

Low
Score $\longleftarrow$ ————————— $\longrightarrow$ High
Score

LOW DEPRIVATION   HIGH DEPRIVATION

---

down to quite a young age. Also, the correlation may be related to the fact that the more deprived fathers appeared to
have taken on a kind of stoicism and seemed less concerned
about discomforts their children might encounter because of
their Indian background. Of further interest is the positive
association between the amount of deprivation the fathers experienced and the temperament of the children: the more
deprived fathers reported child characteristics in which the
children appear to be more aggressive. The only further
lead on the meaning of this index is that adoptive fathers who
were more deprived tended to be married to women who
tended to be more homebound as measured by the Index of
Adoptive Mothers' Life Styles ($r = -.23$).

Religious Backgrounds and Parent Attitudes

Table VI-19 presents the mean index scores achieved
by the adoptive fathers, analyzed by their religious backgrounds. As was the case in the analysis of similar material for the adoptive mothers, there is significant differentiation between the Jewish adoptive parents and the Catholic and
Protestant parents, with the latter two groups again relatively undifferentiated in their index scores.[6] Thus, the Jewish

adoptive fathers were significantly higher in their expression
of liberal political orientation than the Catholic and Protestant adoptive parents.   Also, the Jewish adoptive fathers
were decidedly less religious than their Catholic and Protestant counterparts.   A higher degree of social problem orientation is also found among the Jewish adoptive fathers than
in the other two groups.   Chapter III demonstrated a further
source of differentiation among the three groups with respect
to socioeconomic status.   A replication of this is found in
Table VI-19, the Catholic and Protestant adoptive fathers
scoring higher on the Index of Lower Class-Rural Background.
Despite this, the Jewish adoptive fathers were more prone
than the other two religious groups to report having experienced some tragedy in their growing up.   All in all, the differentiation among the three groups is very much in line with
previous studies of the social attitudes of Jews as contrasted
with Catholics and Protestants in the United States.

Notes

1.   Robert R. Sears, Eleanor Maccoby, and Harry A. Levin,
      Patterns of Child Rearing (Evanston, Ill.:   Row, Pe-
      terson and Co., 1957), p. 264.

2.   Henry S. Maas and Richard Engler, Jr., Children in
      Need of Parents (New York: Columbia University
      Press, 1959), p. 375.

3.   Florence Ruderman, Child Care and Working Mothers
      (New York: Child Welfare League of America, 1968).

4.   Robert R. Sears, et al., Patterns of Child Rearing,
      op. cit.

5.   The negative sign for the correlation sign for the cor-
      relation is due to the reverse direction of the two
      indexes.

6.   See Footnote 7, Chapter V.

Table VI-19

MEAN INDEX SCORES FOR ADOPTIVE FATHERS BY RELIGION

Index		Jewish (13)	Catholic (10)	Protestant (67)	F-test for significant differences in group means
Index of adoptive fathers' liberal vs. conservative political orientation	$\overline{X}$	21.62	18.93	18.96	6.137**
	S.D.	1.65	3.76	2.46	
Index of religiosity of adoptive families	$\overline{X}$	24.69	17.62	17.61	12.453***
	S.D.	4.25	3.25	4.98	
Index of traditional masculine ideology	$\overline{X}$	15.51	15.39	15.53	0.027 N.S.
	S.D.	1.45	1.03	2.12	
Index of adoptive fathers' work satisfaction	$\overline{X}$	9.51	9.13	8.49	1.956 N.S.
	S.D.	2.07	1.88	1.78	
Index of background support for Indian adoption	$\overline{X}$	8.97	10.04	10.49	2.054 N.S.
	S.D.	2.20	3.14	2.44	

Index					Coefficient
Index of adoptive fathers' orientation to the adoption of handicapped children	$\overline{X}$ S.D.	35.85 8.05	39.55 4.89	38.34 6.81	0.969 N.S.
Index of security of parental outlook	$\overline{X}$ S.D.	11.31 3.79	12.20 3.74	11.12 3.54	0.392 N.S.
Index of strict vs. permissive child rearing orientation	$\overline{X}$ S.D.	2.54 0.93	2.13 0.61	2.51 1.05	0.659 N.S.
Index of deprivation in adoptive fathers' backgrounds	$\overline{X}$ S.D.	10.00 1.58	8.10 2.18	8.73 1.79	3.648*
Index of adoptive fathers' orientation to the adoption of Negro children	$\overline{X}$ S.D.	2.90 1.86	3.70 1.94	3.50 1.86	0.677 N.S.
Index of social problem orientation of adoptive fathers	$\overline{X}$ S.D.	23.29 3.28	18.76 4.08	20.40 3.91	4.396*
Index of lower-class rural background	$\overline{X}$ S.D.	37.19 6.01	41.69 4.44	42.76 7.29	3.579*

*The coefficient is significantly greater than zero at the .05 probability level.
**The coefficient is significantly greater than zero at the .01 probability level.
***The coefficient is significantly greater than zero at the .001 probability level.

Chapter VII

SERIES FOUR INTERVIEWS
WITH ADOPTIVE MOTHERS AND FATHERS:
HOW FARE THE CHILDREN?

Number of couples interviewed: 88
Date of first interview in series: 3/16/64
Date of last interview in series: 6/27/67
Mean age of children: 61.9 mos.
Mean time interval between
interview and date of placement: 42.5 mos.
Mean time interval
since prior interview: 12.2 mos.

Child Whose Adjustment Was Rated as "Well-Adjusted"
at the End of the Five Series

> [Interviewer's observation: An apparently happy,
> well-adjusted family in which child is loved and
> well accepted for himself by each member of the
> family. He is developing well--appears to be hap-
> py and secure and is described by adoptive parents
> as being very bright and a great source of happi-
> ness to them. From everything they say in this
> interview, it is to be expected that Cal's welfare
> will be fostered to the maximum his adoptive par-
> ents can provide and a good life seems assured for
> him. Although the adoptive parents indicate that
> they are not planning to initiate discussion of the
> child's adoptive status with respect to his Indian
> background until he finds out, they imply that they
> feel he is so secure within the family that their
> telling him the facts as they know them when he
> asks will suffice.]

(Cal was four years and five months old at the time of this
interview.)

208

Child Whose Adjustment Was Rated as "Average"
at the End of the Five Series

[Interviewer's observation: The family seemed re-
luctant to estimate Danny's intelligence but finally
they both agreed that he was of about average intelligence. I sensed that there was disappointment
which they were controlling. The parents described
the child as highly energetic and sometimes difficult to control. Both parents spoke of the fact that
Danny was beginning to become conscious of being
Indian and adopted. His teacher made a point of
this in school and the adoptive mother spoke to her
to put a stop to this. There was nothing negative
in this but there seemed to be some discomfort
with making a point about his being different. While
the parents described Danny as being generally happy, he is also frequently moody; he gets sullen and
pulls away from them and withdraws. They had
had a good deal of problem with his aggression towards children which was made worse because he
was so strong. But now he is getting along with
them better. At another point in the discussion,
the parents pointed out that some children don't
like Danny because he is so big and strong for his
age. He comes across as a child who was never
gentle but rather agressive and pushy. I felt there
is an identification they are making with him. They
spoke of community thinking that they are odd balls
because they have different values and in the next
breath they spoke of his being odd ball because of
his size and strength. They noted also that he is
fearful of being alone in his room with the door
shut and the adoptive mother stays with Danny when
he is going to bed. In describing his overall personality traits, the parents described him as friendly and outgoing but he can turn surly very quickly
particularly when he gets tired at play. He is easily excited and when tired, resorts to tears and
tantrums. He is also very affectionate.

Seeing the parents together, I had the impression
of the adoptive mother as the dominant partner, although this position was not held by aggressiveness.
If anything, she is the "strong mother" and there
is a strong feeling of togetherness between them.
The mother seems like an overly conscientious

mother and lacks spontaneity with the children, as
she does in her general manner of speech. She
did most of the talking but her husband joined in.
The denial of the difference of the children by the
father continues to be very strong and may endan-
ger the children's ability to work out this problem.
Both parents deny their anxiety about the children.
Yet they are concerned about Danny because of his
slowness in picking up reading and although they
minimized it with me, they have had concern about
his agressive behavior. Both are warm with children. The children tend to be very active physically.]

(Danny was six years and six months at the time of this interview.)

Child Whose Adjustment Was Rated as "Guarded" at the End of the Five Series

[Interviewer's observation: From the interview
with the adoptive mother, one gets the impression
of a troubled youngster with problems referred to
earlier persisting. While she may be more sensitive to the child's many needs of which she speaks,
one is inclined to wonder if the adoptive father is
not more basically accepting of this child than is
the adoptive mother. Earlier impression has been
that adoption of this child was more the adoptive
father's conviction than the adoptive mother's.

While child will undoubtedly be provided for mate-
rially in this home, the question remains as to
whether his emotional needs are and will be met
as he grows. The fact that the couple indicate that
their own older child has problems with which they
seem unable to cope may be an indicator of their
handling of adoptee who apparently came into home
with problems.]

Symptoms:
  Speech--could not say "R's" and "S's"--is out-
    growing this
  Toilet training--soiling, using out of doors for
    toilet--these events seem to happen in spells
  Chronic colds--very often

Stomach or intestinal disorders--somewhat often
General disposition--has his ups and downs, can
get quite moody, somewhat excitable, has
many wants, is restless. "He is not an easy
child."
Problems:
Sleep disturbance--very severe
Phobias--very severe
Restlessness--very severe
Excessive fears or anxiety--very severe

He has been quite restless throughout stay in
home--continuously wants to go some place....
He reacts to loud noises--getting less severe.

(Gary was eight years old at the time of this interview.)

The Series Four Interview

This interview was designed to be conducted with the
adoptive mother and adoptive father available as a pair.
Since the previous two interviews had been conducted with
each individually, this gave an opportunity for the interviewer
to interact with the parents together and to see them respond
in terms of their joint interactions. The interview further
deviated from the previous two by being designed to lie somewhere between the flexible and unstandardized type of interview characteristic of clinical interviewing and the completely
structured interviews which were conducted in Series Two
and Series Three. The interviewers were provided with a
topical outline which they could follow in a flexibly ordered
manner, being guided by the responses of the adoptive parent. The interview guide called for obtaining information
from the families in the following categories:

1. Developmental progress: Child's development with
respect to physical growth, weight and height, walking, talking, toilet training, intelligence, reading
readiness, eating, and so forth.

2. Health status: Child's general health, impairments
in functioning, ailments suffered, and general energy
level.

3. Child's Indian background: Child's appearance,
changes in appearance since he's been in the home,

discussion within the home about his Indian background, nature of child's interest in his Indian background.

4. Child's personality and general disposition: Degree of moodiness, general emotional state, signs of tension or strain, general personality characteristics, personality problems (speech, sleep, phobias, restlessness, aggressive behavior, fears or anxiety, enuresis, others), unusual sensitivity, child's mannerisms and temperament and overall personality traits.

5. Child's social relationships: Degree to which child is gregarious, self-isolating, relationships with peers, relationships with adults, nature of general social situation in which child finds himself.

6. Problems of child attributable to his Indian or adoptive status: Frequency of discussion about adoption, frequency of discussion about child's Indian background, degree of child's curiosity about his background, degree to which child seems anxious about being different from others around him, special information given child about his biological parents.

7. School adjustment (applicable only to children in first grade or higher): Level of child's school performance, his attitudes towards school, prevalence of problems with respect to intellectual capacity, motivation to learn, relationship problems with peers, etc.

8. Child rearing patterns: Tendency to spank, forms of discipline, degree of supervision of the child, and so forth.

9. Family climate: Problems adoptive parents are contending with (health, economic difficulties, etc.), presence of other relatives in the home, general emotional climate of the home, degree of open conflict in the family, degree of open demonstrativeness in the family, relationship between child and parents and relationship between child and siblings.

10. Future plans: Plans of adoptive parents to adopt other children.

Following the interview with the adoptive parents, the interviewers filled out a codebook in which information was

provided in categorical form. The information obtained from
the interview was codified to present the parents' viewpoints.
The caseworker-interviewers were encouraged to write summaries at the end of the interview in which their own professional impressions could be displayed.

Eighty-eight of the 96 families received Series Four
interviews. Two families were not interviewed because of
their temporary unavailability within the areas to which project staff could travel, and six families were not interviewed
because of their relative late entrance into the project.

Portraying Child Adjustment

The major focus of the Series Four interview was the
child's developmental status seen from the perspectives out-
lined above. Attempting to consolidate this information into
a summary measure of the child's adjustment poses a rather
difficult task. Generally, the approach taken here is to cover
a broad array of symptoms which would be indicative of primary behavior disorders of childhood. Thus, the interview
covered developmental problems, problems of proneness to
health disorders with emotional components, problems related to the development of personality and the development
of social relationships. In a sense, one can take the view
that a good adjustment reflects the absence of symptoms. In
other words, it is easier to enumerate conditions of pathology than to describe health in its positive terms.

The problem of classifying children according to their
behavior disorders has been well described by Anthony:

> ...It is possible to look upon the primary behavior
> disorders of childhood as a nuclear syndrome with
> internalizing, externalizing, and somatic compo-
> nents. As the child develops and the pressures
> that confront him become more specific and clas-
> sifiable, the three nuclear components, depending
> upon their preponderance in the original syndrome,
> may begin to produce differential effects so that
> more specific syndromes begin to emerge out of
> the diffuse, primary behavioral background.[1]

Anthony cites the work of Wertz (1962) who has attempted to follow behavior disorders, both primary and secondary types, through childhood into adolescence.[2] According

to Wertz, there is a constant ebb and flow of behavior disorder symptomatology until the child enters adolescence. He
indicates that whether or not the predominant type of behavior disturbance during childhood is of the habit, neurotic, or
conduct type or a mixture of all three in varying proportions,
there are often periods of quiescence and invariably an acute
exacerbation in adolescence. At this time, the condition may
settle down into a chronic character disorder or erupt further into a psychosis. He sees the secondary disorders as
having a different natural history, usually involving organic
aspects and a life-time history of maladjustment.

O'Connor and Franks have noted how unimpressed
they are with the state of the science of classifying behavior
pathology in children. "A review of our knowledge in any
field other than the field of delinquency does not support the
view that the psychology of abnormality in children has made
notable progress. In learning studies, motivation and knowledge of social behavior, evidence is accumulating, but where
neurosis and psychosis are concerned we are scarcely able
to offer a definition."[3]   As Anthony notes, "The abnormal
psychology of childhood is still far from being an experimental or a descriptive science, although it is moving gradually
toward the point when significant elements of past or present
history, taken in conjunction with test responses, might be
able to forecast the type of behavior disorders that will even-
tually develop; this has already been carried out with some
success in the case of delinquency."[4]

There appears to be almost universal agreement that
the problem of classifying behavior disorders will continue
to plague the mental health profession for a long time to
come. Robbins, for example, notes:

> ...It is unlikely that we will ever be able to de-
> velop a natural system of classification based upon
> a qualitatively unique etiology. Whatever classifi-
> cations will be developed will be somewhat artifi-
> cial, depending on the purposes for which they are
> designed and the implicit or explicit hypotheses
> which they will reflect.[5]

Table VII-1 presents 28 items selected from the codebook prepared for the Fourth Series interview. These items
are relevant to an overall assessment of the children's adjustment and cover a broad array of phenomena. The items
are included under such domains as developmental progress
(cont. p. 220)

Table VII-1

FREQUENCY OF SYMPTOMS REPORTED FOR CHILDREN
AT SERIES FOUR INTERVIEWS AND THEIR WEIGHTING
IN SUMMATED SYMPTOM SCORE (N=88)

Symptom	Weighted 1 point	Weighted 2 points	Weighted 3 points	Symptom-free Weighted 0 points
Walking impairment	Slight 5	Serious 0	XXXX	None 83
Speech impairment	Slight 19	Serious 3	XXXX	None 66
Toilet training problems	Minor 17	Serious 0	XXXX	None 71
Eating problems	Minor 28	Serious 0	XXXX	None 60
Estimate of health	Fair 7	Poor 0	XXXX	Excellent health 81

FREQUENCY OF SYMPTOMS REPORTED FOR CHILDREN
AT SERIES FOUR INTERVIEWS AND THEIR WEIGHTING
IN SUMMATED SYMPTOM SCORE (N= 88)

Symptom	Weighted 1 point	Weighted 2 points	Weighted 3 points	Symptom-free Weighted 0 points
Chronic colds	Occasional 18	Somewhat often 14	Very often 8	Rarely or never 48
Stomach disorders	Occasional 6	Somewhat often 4	Very often 2	Rarely or never 76
Allergies or skin disorders	Occasional 13	Somewhat often 6	Very often 6	Rarely or never 63
Respiratory difficulties	Occasional 5	Somewhat often 6	Very often 7	Rarely or never 70
Obesity or underweight	Occasional 4	Somewhat often 8	Very often 0	Rarely or never 76
Sleep disorders	Occasional 5	Somewhat often 7	Very often 5	Rarely or never 71

General child disposition	Moderately happy 10	Unhappy 0	XXXX	Generally happy 78
Extent of moodiness	Occasional 27	Frequent 5	XXXX	Rarely 56
Extent of tenseness	Moderate 9	Very 5	XXXX	Generally not tense 77
Reaction to child's personality	Moderately pleased 11	Displeased 1	XXXX	Highly pleased, satisfied 76
Speech problems	Mild 9	Somewhat severe 9	Very severe 0	No problem 70
Sleep disturbance	Mild 5	Somewhat severe 7	Very severe 5	No problem 71
Phobias		Somewhat severe 1	Very severe 1	No problem 86
Restlessness		Somewhat severe 5	Very severe 4	No problem 79
Aggressive behavior	Mild 2	Somewhat severe 7	Very severe 3	No problem 76

FREQUENCY OF SYMPTOMS REPORTED FOR CHILDREN
AT SERIES FOUR INTERVIEWS AND THEIR WEIGHTING
IN SUMMATED SYMPTOM SCORE (N=88)

Symptom	Weighted 1 point	Weighted 2 points	Weighted 3 points	Symptom-free Weighted 0 points
Excessive fears or anxiety	Mild 4	Somewhat severe 12	Very severe 5	No problem 67
Enuresis	Mild 3	Somewhat severe 4	Very severe 4	No problem 77
Other personality problem	Mild 3	Somewhat severe 8	Very severe 6	No problem 71
Sensitivity	Mild 6	Fairly strong 16	XXXX	None 66
Overall personality	Mild problems 18	Moderately severe problems 4	XXXX	None reported 66
Gregariousness of child	Slightly gregarious 16	Not gregarious 3	XXXX	Very gregarious 69

	Minor difficulty	Moderate difficulty	XXXX	Not shy at all
Shyness with peers	5	2	XXXX	81
Shyness with adults	10	1	XXXX	77

Summated score

Total	Frequency	Percentage	Cumulative
0	3	3.41	3.41
1	4	4.55	7.95
2	9	10.23	18.18
3	6	6.82	25.00
4	4	4.55	29.55
5	5	5.68	32.23
6	8	9.09	44.32
7	7	7.95	52.27
8	4	4.55	56.82
9	5	5.68	62.50
10	8	9.09	71.59
11	9	10.23	81.82
12	4	4.55	86.36
13	1	1.14	87.50
14	4	4.55	92.05
16	2	2.27	94.32
17	1	1.14	95.45
18	2	2.27	97.73
31	2	2.27	100.00

Mean = 7.932   Median = 7.000   SD = 5.701   Skewness = 1.507   Kurtosis = 4.127

(walking, talking, toilet training and eating), health status
(colds, stomach disorders, allergies, etc.), personality (general emotional disposition, moodiness, tenseness, sleep
disturbances, phobias, etc.) and social behavior (gregarious-
ness, shyness with peers, etc.). It can be seen that for any
given item, a large majority of the children are reported to
be symptom-free. It is rare that an item shows that even a
third of the children have problems. The codified responses
of the adoptive parents were weighted so that severe symptoms were loaded more heavily in the Summated Symptom
Score than those which were reflective of mild disturbance or
disability. The summary measure showed a mean of 7.932
points with a standard deviation of 5.7.

The distribution was slightly skewed and tended to be
flat.[6] However, it provided a summary measure which had
certain virtues: (1) it reflected the concrete reports of the
adoptive parents rather than a summary judgment of the interviewer; (2) it was broad-ranged, covering a variety of
disabilities, and reflected the lack of commitment of the investigator to a specific dimension of child personality such
as has interested other investigators (e.g., aggression, anxiety, and so forth); (3) the specific items seemed well related
to the task of describing children who tended to be about five
years old; (4) the items seemed appropriate kinds of information to gather for both boys and girls; and (5) the items
appeared to be the kind that did not compel the adoptive parents to make highly abstract judgments and were posed in descriptive terms well understandable to the layman.

These virtues do not, of course, diminish the serious
criticism that the symptom list does not reflect a unified conceptual view of the nature of the adjustment of children. A
careful examination of the literature in this field led to the
conclusion that the state of the art with respect to description
of behavior disorders in children were simply too primitive
to anticipate that a more conceptually sound nosology could
be developed for the purpose of this study. At least this was
true at the time the interviewing schedule was created in
1963. Since then, the summaries of Anthony, Robbins, and
others, previously cited, have confirmed the judgment that
the state of technology of child behavior disorder description
is still quite primitive.

It is necessary to scan Table VII-1 to get some sense
of the kinds of problems revealed by the adoptees. Thus, it
is not without significance to note that 25 percent of these

adoptees showed some speech impairment and about 20 percent showed toilet training problems. Almost a third of the
children had some kind of eating problems. Chronic colds
were frequently reported, and allergies and skin disorders
affected almost 30 percent of the adoptees.

Particularly noteworthy were the fairly frequent reports of emotional sensitivity shown by the adoptees in the
home. Some 25 percent of the adoptees showed symptoms
in this area and they were often expressed in terms of discomfort and uncertainty when they were criticized by the
adoptive parents. In a number of cases, the sensitivity of
the child seemed to be related to some lack of sureness that
he would be kept in the home when he misbehaved or did not
live up to the adoptive parents' expectations.

I shall subsequently analyze the relationship between
the symptom picture developed at Series Four and a similar,
but more elaborate portrayal of behavioral disorders shown
by the adoptees based upon interviews with the adoptive mothers in Series Five interviews. I will further analyze the relationship between these symptom pictures and an overall
summary judgment made about the children based upon professional scrutiny of all of the information gathered in the
sequence of interviews. In general, the symptom picture developed for this series is based on the assumption that poorly adjusted children will show greater prevalence of symptoms
in more domains than will better adjusted children. This
may be a debatable assumption since individuals inflicted with
one severe symptom might suffer as much disability as those
whose symptoms are more broadly spread. However, past
research in assessing adoptees reflects the conception that
the personality of the child must be seen in holistic terms
and if there is major disorder in one area, it is not apt to
be confined to that area.

Demographic Characteristics and Child Symptoms

Table VII-2 presents a correlation matrix including
the major demographic variables available for describing the
adoptees and their families. As might be anticipated, there
is a significant correlation between the child's age at the
time of his placement in the adoptive home and the frequency
of symptoms reported by his parents (r = .22). This coincides with the general notion that adoptions that take place
at later ages are more hazardous since the child has endured

Table VII-2

INTERCORRELATIONS AMONG SELECTED DEMOGRAPHIC CHARACTERISTICS OF THE ADOPTEES AND THEIR FAMILIES AND SERIES FOUR CHILD SYMPTOM SCORES

	A	B	C	D	E	F	G	H	I	J
A. Adoptee's Age at Placement in the Home	--									
B. Adoptee's Age at Series Four Interview	.87***	--								
C. Sex of Child	.01	.03	--							
D. Socioeconomic Status of Adoptive Family	-.10	-.11	-.06	--						
E. Biological Mother's Disability Index	.22*	.22*	-.03	-.03	--					
F. Adoptive Father's Age at Placement	.18	.21*	.21*	.10	-.03	--				
G. Adoptive Mother's Age at Placement	.11	.12	.13	.21	-.07	.82***	--			
H. Ordinal Position of the Adoptee in the Adoptive Family	-.01	.01	.22*	.08	-.21	.20	.22*	--		
I. Number of Indian Children Adopted by Family	.30**	.17	-.10	.00	.24*	-.07	-.15	-.24*	--	
J. Series Four Child Symptom Score	.22*	.15	-.12	.04	.16	.00	.14	-.08	-.06	--

NOTE: For demographic variables N=96; for Series Four scores N=88. Sex of child coded 1=boy, 2=girl. *Significant: $p < .05$; **Significant: $p < .01$; ***Significant: $p < .001$.

living experiences that are often quite unstable. The table,
indeed, lends support to such a view since the correlation
between the adoptee's age when he was placed in the home
and the index measuring the disability of the biological mother is significantly correlated (r = .22). However, caution
must be used in linking age at placement with subsequent adjustment of adoptees because of our understanding that symptoms of children tend to increase over time as a function of
the greater mobility of the children and their capacity to interact more negatively with those around them as they get
older. However, the correlation between the adoptee's age
at the Series Four interview and the symptom score is somewhat diminished when contrasted with the adoptee's age at
placement. This suggests that, over a period, the age dif-
ferentials among the adoptees tend to be less important.
When adoptee's age at placement is correlated with the Series
Four Child Symptom Score, partialing out the child's current
age, we see that the correlation becomes somewhat diminished ($r_{12.3}$ = .18). This suggests that part of the linkage
between age at placement and symptoms appearing during the
Series Four interviews is related to the fact that the children
placed late were somewhat older during the Series Four interviews, and were more likely to display the symptoms as
part of the proneness of older children to have more symptoms.[7]

No significant association was found between any of
the other demographic variables included in the table and the
Series Four Child Symptom Score. It may be observed, for
example, that while the association between the Biological
Mothers' Disability Index and the Series Four Child Symptom
Score is in a direction which suggests linkage between the
two, the correlation does not achieve significance (r = .16).
A similar lack of significant association characterizes such
variables as the sex of the child, the socioeconomic status
of the adoptive family, the adoptive parents' ages at placement, the ordinal position of the child, and the number of
Indian children adopted by the family. Aside from the age
at placement, therefore, it would appear that the demographic variables do not markedly differentiate among the adoptees
with respect to the frequency of symptoms they show.

Table VII-3 presents a multiple correlation analysis
of the demographic characteristics of the adoptees in which
the contribution of eight demographic variables to the explained variance in the Series Four Child Symptom Scores
are examined. The computer program used for this analysis

Table VII-3

MULTIPLE CORRELATION ANALYSIS OF SERIES FOUR CHILD SYMPTOM SCORES
USING SELECTED DEMOGRAPHIC CHARACTERISTICS OF
THE ADOPTEES AND THEIR FAMILIES AS INDEPENDENT VARIABLES

Step Number[a]	Demographic Variable	Cumulative Multiple R	Cumulative Multiple R^2	F-test[b]	ΔR^2	t-test
1	Adoptee's Age at Placement in the Home	.2210	.0489	4.366 *	.0489	2.09*
2	Adoptee's Age at Last Interview	.2728	.0744	3.3763*	.0255	1.52
3	Number of Indian Children Adopted by Family	.3081	.0949	2.9016*	.0205	1.37
4	Sex of Child	.3435	.1180	2.7417*	.0231	1.46
5	Biological Mother's Disability Index	.3672	.1348	2.5244*	.0168	1.26
6	Adoptive Mother's Age at Placement	.3841	.1475	2.3076*	.0127	1.09

7	Ordinal Position of the Adoptee in the Adoptive Family	.3926	.1541	2.0563	.0066	0.78
8	Socioeconomic Status of the Adoptive Family	.3927	.1543 [#]	1.7783	.0002	0.11

[a]The computer regression program used in this analysis has a number of options which may be invoked to order the computations for the variables in the variable specification. In this analysis, the "best prediction" criterion was used in selecting the next independent variable to be entered into the equation. The first variable selected is the one with the highest correlation with the dependent variable. The next variable selected is the variable with the maximum partial correlation with the dependent variable, relative to the independent variable that is in the equation, and so forth. This produces a solution which is "stepwise" in the usual sense, meaning that the best variable was entered at each step.

[b]Percent of variance explained by each variable when added.

*Significant: $p < .05$.

[#] R^2 corrected for degrees of freedom = .0688.

allowed the option of "best prediction" so that variables were entered into the analysis which had the maximum partial correlations with the sumptom scores after other variables had been entered. All in all, the cumulative multiple correlation is modest (multiple R = .43). From the perspective of predicting symptom scores based on demographic information known at the time the children were placed in the homes, I can say that our predictive capacity is quite limited. There are evidently many other factors operating in the lives of the children which determine the frequency of symptoms displayed by them.

Series Two Attitude Scores

Table VII-4 presents a correlation matrix containing seven of the attitudinal indexes created from the responses of the adoptive mothers during the Series Two interviews. One of the important emphases of that interview was the development of a profile of the social attitudes of the adoptive mothers in various domains. The indexes included in the table would seem to tap rather important dimensions of life style and general value orientation as well as aspects of the adoptive parent role that might have relevance for how the adoptive mothers conducted themselves as parents.

Only one measure is significantly correlated with the Series Four Child Symptom Score: a significant negative correlation prevails between the index assessing the orientation of the subjects to the adoption of Negro children and the frequency of child symptoms. In other words, women who indicated they were disposed to consider the adoption of Negro children were more apt to have children who had less symptomatic difficulties (r = -.21). No other attitudinal measure was significantly associated with the summary adjustment measure.

It is not easy to explain why this significant, albeit modest, association exists. I do not, for example, find such a relationship with liberal political orientation or with the adoptive mothers' stance with respect to female ideology. It is also noteworthy that there is no significant association between the index measuring the permissiveness of the adoptive mother and the symptom picture, although the more permissive mothers had children with fewer symptoms. What makes the measure even more problematic is that there is no such significant association with the adoptive fathers' ori-
(cont. p. 234)

Table VII-4

INTERCORRELATIONS AMONG ADOPTIVE MOTHER SERIES TWO
ATTITUDINAL INDEXES AND SERIES FOUR CHILD SYMPTOM SCORES

Index	A	B	C	D	E	F	G	H	I
A. Liberal vs. Conservative Political Orientation	--								
B. Adoptive Mothers' Life Style	-.35**	--							
C. Traditional vs. Modern Female Ideology	.37**	-.22*	--						
D. Orientation to the Adoption of Handicapped Children	-.19	.08	-.09	--					
E. Orientation to the Adoption of Negro Children	.08	-.11	.17	.21*	--				
F. Orientation to the Adoption of Children with Psychological Problems	-.21*	-.02	-.08	.47**	.05	--			
G. Religiosity of Adoptive Mother	-.29**	.03	-.10	.27**	.07	.17	--		
H. Strict vs. Permissive Child Rearing	-.12	.29**	.06	.10	.44**	-.06	.02	--	
I. Series Four Child Symptom Score	.14	.08	.06	.04	-.21*	.08	-.10	-.09	--

NOTE: For attitudinal indexes, N= 96; for Series Four scores, N= 88.
*Significant: p < .05;   **Significant: p < .01.

Table VII-5

MULTIPLE CORRELATION ANALYSIS OF SERIES FOUR CHILD SYMPTOM SCORES
USING ADOPTIVE MOTHER SERIES TWO ATTITUDINAL INDEXES AS INDEPENDENT VARIABLES

Step Number[a]	Attitudinal Index	Cumulative Multiple R	Cumulative Multiple R^2	F-test	$\triangle R^2$	t-test
1	Orientation to the adoption of Negro children	.2110	.0445	3.9594*	.0445	1.99*
2	Liberal vs. conservative political orientation	.2630	.0692	3.1206*	.0247	1.49
3	Orientation to the adoption of children with psychological problems	.2933	.0860	2.6040	.0168	1.24
4	Adoptive mother life style	.3230	.1043	2.3872	.0183	1.29

5	Orientation to the adoption of handicapped children	.3292	.1083	1.9684	.0040	0.61
6	Traditional vs. modern female ideology	.3346	.1120	1.6814	.0037	0.57
7	Religiosity of adoptive mothers	.3392	.1151	1.4675	.0031	0.52
8	Strict vs. permissive child rearing	.3392	.1151[#]	1.2679	.0000	0.03

[a]The computer option for determining step order is same as cited in Table VII-3.

*Significant: $p < .05$.

[#]R^2 corrected for degrees of freedom = .0245.

Table VII-6

INTERCORRELATIONS AMONG ADOPTIVE FATHER SERIES THREE
ATTITUDINAL INDEXES AND SERIES FOUR CHILD SYMPTOM SCORES

Index	A	B	C	D	E	F	G	H	I	J	K
A. Liberal vs. Conservative Political Orientation	--										
B. Religiosity of Adoptive Family	.45**	--									
C. Traditional Masculine Ideology	-.03	-.01	--								
D. Work Satisfaction	-.03	-.03	.15	--							
E. Background Support for Indian Adoption	-.09	-.03	.28**	.12	--						
F. Orientation to the Adoption of Handicapped Children	-.29**	-.25	.14	.21*	.21*	--					

	A	B	C	D	E	F	G	H	I	J
G. Strict vs. Permissive Child Rearing Orientation	.21*	.10	-.21*	-.04	-.02	-.01	--			
H. Orientation to the Adoption of Negro Children	-.11	-.01	.13	-.12	.03	-.18	-.04	--		
I. Social Problem Orientation	.18	-.07	-.06	.04	-.09	-.18	.01	-.21*	--	
J. Lower Class-Rural Background	-.07	-.07	-.06	-.15	.11	-.05	.07	-.01	.00	--
Outcome										
K. Series Four Child Symptom Score	.04	.11	-.03	-.15	.08	-.07	.02	.04	.23*	-.06

*Significant: $p < .05$; **Significant: $p < .01$.

Table VII-7

MULTIPLE CORRELATION ANALYSIS OF SERIES FOUR CHILD SYMPTOM SCORES USING ADOPTIVE FATHER SERIES THREE ATTITUDINAL INDEXES AS INDEPENDENT VARIABLES

Step Number[a]	Attitudinal Index	Cumulative Multiple R	Cumulative Multiple R^2	F-test	$\triangle R^2$	t-test
1	Social problem orientation	.2254	.0508	4.5475*	.0508	2.13*
2	Work satisfaction	.2754	.0758	3.4464	.0250	1.51
3	Background support for Indian adoption	.3016	.0910	2.7686	.0152	1.18
4	Lower class-rural background	.3196	.1021	2.3321	.0111	1.01
5	Religiosity of adoptive family	.3283	.1078	1.9564	.0057	0.71
6	Orientation to the adoption of Negro children	.3352	.1124	1.6877	.0046	0.64

| 7 | Traditional masculine ideology | .3384 | .1145 | 1.4591 | .0021 | 0.44 |
| 8 | Liberal vs. conservative political orientation | .3407 | .1161# | 1.2806 | .0016 | 0.38 |

a The computer option for determining step order is same as cited in Table VII-3.

*Significant: $p < .05$.

R^2 corrected for degrees of freedom = .0266.

entation to the adoption of Negro children. My inclination would
be to view the finding with interest while being mindful of the
fact that the association could be a result of random factors not
under my control.

Table VII-5 presents a multiple correlation analysis
in which the eight attitudinal indexes from Series Two were
entered step-wise into an analysis of the Series Four Child
Symptom Scores. In the main, the analysis yields modest
results with a multiple correlation of . 34. Only one variable
made a significant contribution to the cumulative variance and
that was the previously cited index involving the adoption of
Negro children.

Series Three Attitudinal Indexes

Table VII-6 shows the intercorrelations of ten attitudinal indexes derived from the Series Three interviews with
the adoptive fathers and the Series Four Child Symptom
Scores. It is again found that only one index is significantly
correlated with the frequency of symptoms. As already noted,
the index of the fathers' Orientation to the Adoption of Negro
Children does not show a significant association (r = . 04) with
the symptom score. On the other hand, an index called Social Problem Orientation turns out to be significantly associated with the frequency of symptoms (r = . 23).

The more oriented the adoptive fathers were to concerns about social problems and being involved in organizations, the more symptoms their children appeared to display.
Again, this does not seem to be a matter of political persuasion since the index measuring liberal versus conservative
orientations is not significantly associated with either the social problem orientation or the outcome measure. What
makes the Index of Social Problem Orientation of some interest is the fact that it perseveres in its significance and
is manifest when we examine the symptom score developed
from the Series Five interviews. It is also prominent when
we subsequently analyze the Overall Adjustment Scores developed for the adoptees by use of a rating procedure. Thus,
the finding does seem firm and whets one's interest.

Why are people who are more socially aware and socially active apt to have children who have more problematic
symptoms? We have no ready answer for this, particularly
since the social problem orientation is significantly corre-

lated with only one other attitudinal index, the Orientation to
the Adoption of Negro Children (r= -.21).   This is a matter
which will warrant further investigation in Chapter X in the
summary analyses of the outcome measures pooling all independent variables as potential contributors to the regression analysis.

Table VII-7 presents the multiple correlation analysis
of the Series Four outcome scores, using the "best criterion"
as a step-wise procedure for entering into the regression
equation the attitudinal indexes created from the adoptive father interviews.   The cumulative multiple correlation is again
found to be modest (R= .34).   The index measuring social
problem orientation is the only attitudinal index contributing
in significant fashion to the variance in symptoms reported
for the children.

Notes

1. E. James Anthony, "Behavior Disorders," Chapter 28
   in Paul H. Mussen, Editor, Carmichael's Manual of
   Child Psychology, Third Edition, Vol. II (New York:
   John Wiley and Sons, 1970), p. 732.

2. F. J. Wertz, "The Fate of Behavior Disorders in
   Adolescence," American Journal of Orthopsychiatry,
   Vol. 32, No. 3 (1962), pp. 423-433.

3. N. O'Connor and C. Franks, "Childhood Upbringing and
   Other Environmental Factors," Chapter 10 in H. J.
   Eyesenck, Handbook of Abnormal Psychology (New
   York: Basic Books, 1961), p. 393.

4. E. James Anthony, "Behavior Disorders," op. cit.,
   p. 752.

5. Lewis L. Robbins, "A Historical Review of Classification
   of Behavior Disorders and One Current Perspective,"
   in Leonard D. Eron, Editor, The Classification of
   Behavior Disorders (Chicago: Aldine Press, 1966),
   p. 35.

6. The measure of skewness (g_1) is derived from the
   formula:

$$g_1 = \sum_{i=1}^{N} \left(\frac{X_i - \overline{X}}{S}\right)^3 \Big/ N \ .$$

The measure of kurtosis (g_2) is derived from the formula:

$$g_2 = \sum_{i=1}^{N} \left(\frac{X_i - \overline{X}}{S}\right)^4 \Big/ N - 3 \ .$$

In general, the greater the skewness, the larger the difference between the mean and the median.

7.   Benson Jaffee and David Fanshel, How They Fared in Adoption: A Follow-Up Study (New York: Columbia University Press, 1970).

Chapter VIII

SERIES FIVE INTERVIEWS WITH ADOPTIVE MOTHERS:
THE LAST OF THE SERIES

Number of mothers interviewed: 60
Date of first interview in series: 2/17/65
Date of last interview in series: 3/8/68
Mean age of children: 73.5 mos.
Mean time interval between
interview and date of placement: 52.9 mos.
Mean time interval
since prior interview: 12.4 mos.

Child Whose Adjustment Was Rated as "Well-Adjusted"
at the End of the Five Series

[In what way has Cal changed since I saw you last?]
Actually, he has not really changed but he seems
to be more aware of his being Indian and it seems
to have more meaning for him. To a degree, he
has always been aware of this. He does not talk
about it, but I have noticed he is doing Indian draw-
ings and seems to enjoy his Indian books. Nevertheless, he seems happy to undertake the role of
either cowboy or Indian. [What is the nature of
Cal's relationship with his siblings?] He gets along
with them very well. They all love each other.
[Does he demand an unusual amount of attention
from you?] No, the reverse. He is able to do
everything that he needs to do for himself such as
dressing himself, bathing himself, etc. He is very
independent. [Does Cal show any of the fears encountered by other children his age?] Only fear
of thunderstorms. He has always been afraid of
storms but this is declining considerably. When
he was smaller, I used to hold him and rock him.
Since he has been a little older, he likes to sit
near someone. Last summer, if it stormed at

237

night, I would delay the bedtime, and if it happened
during the night, I would just talk it out with him.
I consider this to be natural because electric storms
can be frightening. Otherwise, he eats and sleeps
very soundly. He is very unself-conscious. He
seems to be very active and a happy youngster. He
has terrific stamina and he is obviously very bright
and agile. He seems to trust us a great deal and
has no trouble making friends. His health has been
excellent and he has had virtually no illness. He
is never moody and generally doesn't seem to be
under any sort of strain. [In general, would you
say that Cal has been an easy or difficult child to
raise?] He has been very easy. This is because
of his exceptional personality. I regard him as
unusually talented and one of the most flexible children I have ever seen and he seems to know and
understand how to get along with everyone. [What
sort of things do you enjoy in Cal?] His exuber-
ant nature, his love of life, and his generally happy attitude. [In what way do you get on each other's nerves?] Cal is not the kind of youngster who
gets on anybody's nerves. He is very demonstra-
tive and I enjoy playing with him everyday. He is
very rarely moody or unhappy. [Parents want their
children to behave differently or change their habits and attitudes in some respects. What changes
have you tried to have Cal make in the way he be-
haves in his habits or personality?] I would not
want to interfere with his personality and I have
the attitude of "hands off" about changing habits
and personality. Sometimes I need to get after
him to blow his nose when he has a cold but that's
not important enough to mention. [What kind of
things made Cal angry?] Angry is a strong word.
If I do not let him finish soda left over from a
picnic, for example, he expresses himself and may
cry out and if his daddy is around, he may go to
him. If it is important enough, I hold to "No."

[Interviewer's observation: Unquestionably, this
child has a genuine sense of belonging in this family in which he is accepted and loved. He appears
to be an exceedingly appealing and well-adjusted
child who, according to the adoptive mother, has
considerable inner resources and flexibility of personality.]

(Cal was five years and five months at the time of this interview.)

Child Whose Adjustment Was Rated as "Average" at the End of the Five Series

[To start with, please tell me about Danny's progress since I last saw you. In general, what has his development been like?] Danny has learned to read. His study habits have improved. He is happier and more settled. There is less display of temper. His health has been good and he seems to have more stamina. I am very enthused about his developmental progress. [Have you during the past year had to tell Danny to stop "acting like a baby"?] Yes, he is extremely slow about doing things and careless about finishing work. But he is improving. For example, within the last year he has stopped asking to have his bottom wiped after going to the toilet. [How does Danny get along with his brother?] They are good friends. They play well at physical things. They have the usual scraps. [Have there been any of the following behaviors that have caused you concern?] Just his nail biting. We try to get Danny to stop biting his nails by promising him a new bicycle when he grows nails. He tries and stops for a few days but then reverts back. Otherwise, the only difficulties we have is that he occasionally has trouble falling asleep or he has upset stomach disorders. He also sometimes gets upset when he is scolded and we think he overdoes it. [In general, is there a single problem about Danny that concerns you most?] Yes, his school difficulties. I am very concerned about this and have been seeing the teacher to improve her attitudes towards him. He has difficulty adjusting to a new group and to a new experience. He tends to freeze and does not learn well. In addition, he does best in a one-to-one relationship. The way the school functions sometimes has created difficulties for him. The kindergarten teacher gave him a glowing report but the first grade teacher was telling her that Danny might be uneducable. In January there was a change of teachers and the new teacher understood him better and he responded to her. This year, the class is on a departmental

system which is somewhat difficult for Danny. The
teacher feels that Danny is not doing well and his
report card has not been good in respect to his
work. He is very well-behaved and retiring in
class. Although I don't like doing it, I finally began helping him myself and he has made tremen-
dous strides as a result.

[Interviewer's observation: I wonder whether Danny's present problem may not be related to his
separation experience at age two. The protection
of himself against the onslaught of new experiences
may be related to this. Danny appears to be a
child whose hostility is pushed inward with occasional outbursts and whose reaction is one of neg-
ativism and withdrawal when threatened. This may
be a repetition of his reaction to the threat of separation. I do feel the parents work very hard with
him and that in the long run, he will be helped to
overcome this.]

(Danny was seven years and three months at the time of this
interview.)

Child Whose Adjustment Was Rated as "Guarded"
at the End of the Five Series

[To start with, please tell me about Gary's progress since I last saw you?] His progress has been
rocky. There have been good periods and some
not good.... He has given quite a bit of trouble;
he has been a bit of a behavior problem. At times
I have been discouraged. We recently have been
getting help at the local family agency. [Is there
any area of behavior shown by Gary which you consider particularly immature for his age?] Yes. He
cries and whines more than a nine year old should.
He is not able to or does not want to follow direc-
tions or do what he is told to do. He is also baby-
ish in a lot of ways. [What is the nature of Gary's
play pattern?] He plays beautifully with children.
They like him and he manages very well in his play.
[Has Gary during the past year seemed to demand
an unusual amount of attention from you?] Yes. He
goes out of his way to tease, make a fuss and to
do things he is not supposed to do, all of which I

feel is his way of trying to get my goat. He does
not openly ask for affection and these things seem
to be a funny way of his asking for it. [Does Gary
show unusual sensitivity when he is scolded or corrected?] Sometimes. He gets real blue. I am a
little concerned about this reaction which is especially noticeable if he becomes too fatigued. I
have been trying to be more understanding and not
to spank him when he reacts this way. [In general,
is there a single problem about Gary that concerns
you most?] His lying and his stealing which for a
while was a big problem but this has gotten to be
less of a problem lately. [How secure would you
say Gary is with you?] Quite insecure. I am trying to pull myself out of the idea that it is "all my
fault" because I know his early childhood was a
hard one--he was probably rejected by three mothers before he got to me. [To what extent has he
been under a strain?] He has very much been under a strain--he shows it by his behavior. I think
it is related to his not really knowing whether he
is accepted or belongs in this family. [In general,
would you say Gary has been an easy or difficult
child to raise?] Quite difficult, it has not been
easy.

[Interviewer's observation: While this child has
had somewhat serious problems and the adoptive
mother considers him to be quite insecure, she and
he are having professional help and she expresses
some insight into his difficulties being related to
experience prior to placement. She does recognize
his assets and appears to be sincere and conscientious in efforts to help him gain security. Apparently he makes a very good social adjustment and
at times has a winning, outgoing personality.]

(Gary was eight years old at the time of this interview.)

The Series Five interviews represented a more limited enterprise than the prior four series. It was necessary
to bring the extended field operations of the developmental
study to a close in 1968 so that the final analysis could be
completed within reasonable time. The reader will note from
Table II-2 presented earlier, that the very first interview in
the study took place on November 11, 1960, and the last of
Series Five took place on March 8, 1968, a 7 1/2-year

spread. If the study had been allowed to run its complete
course, the last Series Five interview would have been completed in early 1970.

The reduction of the study sample from 97 to 60 adoptive families[1] creates some limitation upon my ability to gen-
eralize. However, I do not consider this a critical impairment in the overall study on three grounds: (1) A variety of
child adjustment measures have been developed from the second to the fifth series, so that there is not complete depend-
ency upon the fifth series; (2) it is possible to perform the
statistical analysis of the data with changing sample sizes;
(3) it is possible to make summary judgments on the basis
of four interviews as well as five, partialing out the effect
of the younger age of the children who were not followed a
year later; and (4) comparisons of those seen with those not
seen for the Series Five interviews showed no significant difference between the two groups on all major variables. The
sixty families are not unrepresentative of the larger study
population except for the fact that they adopted earlier.

The average age of the children at the time of the
fifth interview was about six years. Most were just entering
upon their school careers. While the school adjustment of
older children was covered in depth, I will not report on the
interviews here because 39 of the adoptees were either not
yet in school or had too recently embarked upon their student
careers for the questions about school to have consistent
meaning for all subjects. Inquiry into how the children fared
in school must await renewed research contact with the families some years hence.

Child Characteristics

In Table VIII-1, the correlations between Series Two
(mother), Series Three (father), and Series Five (mother)
child descriptions are shown. While the descriptions of the
fathers show a number of statistically significant associations
with the later descriptions of the mothers, there is a higher
degree of association when the mothers' two ratings are compared. Eight out of 12 behavioral characteristics on which
the adoptive mothers' responses were compared, Series Two
vs. Series Five, showed product-moment correlations above
.40. This magnitude of correlation is true for only one comparison when Series Three descriptions are correlated with
Series Five. It should perhaps not occasion surprise to find
(cont. p. 252)

Table VIII-1

INTERCORRELATIONS BETWEEN
PARENTS' CHILD DESCRIPTIONS FOR THREE TIME SERIES

Behavioral Description	Comparing Series 2 and Series 3 (Mother vs. Father)[a]	Comparing Series 2 and Series 5 (Mother vs. Herself)[b]	Comparing Series 3 and Series 5 (Father vs. Mother)[b]
Happy	Not attempted[c]		
Active	Not attempted		
Mischievous	.211*	.542**	.231
Stubborn	.460**	.425**	.361**
Quiet	.136	.243	.225
Explosive	.423**	.448**	.463**
Shy	.358**	.237	.383**
Agile	.240*	.443**	.277*
Bright		.408**	.309*
Graceful	.339**	.410**	.386**
Trusting	.223*	.320*	.057
Destructive	.283**	.409**	.112
Friendly	Not attempted		
Talkative	.174	.104	.122
Tense	.086	.467**	.050

a.   Comparison based upon N of 91 matched pairs.

b.   Comparison based upon N of 57 matched pairs.

c.   Where distributions of responses were markedly skewed, correlations were not calculated.

  *Significant at .05 level.

**Significant at .01 level.

Table VIII-2

FREQUENCY OF SYMPTOMS REPORTED FOR CHILDREN
AT SERIES FIVE INTERVIEWS AND THEIR WEIGHTING
IN SUMMATED SYMPTOM SCORE (N=60)

Symptom	Weighted 1 point	Weighted 2 points	Weighted 3 points	Symptom-free Weighted 0 points
Progress shown by child	XXXX	Moderate problems 14	Moderate-to-serious problems 4	No problems 42
Immature behavior	Sometimes 23	Frequent 8	XXXX	None 29
Demand for attention	Sometimes 46	XXXX	XXXX	Little 14
Thumbsucking	XXXX	Shows symptoms 15	XXXX	Symptoms not shown 45
Masturbation	XXXX	Shows symptoms 10	XXXX	Symptoms not shown 50

Disturbing dreams	XXXX	Shows symptoms 16	XXXX	Symptoms not shown 44
Daytime wetting	XXXX	Shows symptoms 5	XXXX	Symptoms not shown 55
Nocturnal wetting	XXXX	Shows symptoms 12	XXXX	Symptoms not shown 48
Soiling	XXXX	Shows symptoms 4	XXXX	Symptoms not shown 56
Insufficient appetite	XXXX	Shows symptoms 11	XXXX	Symptoms not shown 49
Food finickiness	XXXX	Shows symptoms 16	XXXX	Symptoms not shown 44
Tics and mannerisms	XXXX	Shows symptoms 6	XXXX	Symptoms not shown 54
Nail biting	XXXX	Shows symptoms 9	XXXX	Symptoms not shown 51
Speech problems	XXXX	Shows symptoms 12	XXXX	Symptoms not shown 48

FREQUENCY OF SYMPTOMS REPORTED FOR CHILDREN
AT SERIES FIVE INTERVIEWS AND THEIR WEIGHTING
IN SUMMATED SYMPTOM SCORE (N= 60)

Symptom	Weighted 1 point	Weighted 2 points	Weighted 3 points	Symptom-free Weighted 0 points
Other behaviors	XXXX	Shows symptoms 35	XXXX	Symptoms not shown 25
Difficulty falling asleep	Sometimes 16	Often 7	XXXX	Hardly ever or never 37
Stuttering or stammering	Sometimes 6	Often 5	XXXX	Hardly ever or never 49
Upset stomach	Sometimes 6	Often 2	XXXX	Hardly ever or never 52
Fear of strangers	Sometimes 4	Often 4	XXXX	Hardly ever or never 52
Fear of thunderstorms	Sometimes 10	Often 10	XXXX	Hardly ever or never 40

Fear of high places	Sometimes 1	Often 1	XXXX	Hardly ever or never 58
Fear of animals	Sometimes 6	Often 3	XXXX	Hardly ever or never 51
Discomfort in other homes	Sometimes 2	Often 2	XXXX	Hardly ever or never 54
Sensitive to scolding	Sometimes 21	Often 17	XXXX	Hardly ever or never 22
Other fears	Sometimes 4	Often 0	XXXX	Hardly ever or never 56
Sleeping pattern	Somewhat soundly 17	Somewhat unsoundly 2	XXXX	Soundly 41
Overactive	Somewhat 19	Very much 1	XXXX	Not at all 40
Telling lies	Sometimes 27	Fairly often 2	XXXX	Never 31
Being destructive	Sometimes 11	Fairly often 5	XXXX	Never 44

FREQUENCY OF SYMPTOMS REPORTED FOR CHILDREN
AT SERIES FIVE INTERVIEWS AND THEIR WEIGHTING
IN SUMMATED SYMPTOM SCORE (N= 60)

Symptom	Weighted 1 point	Weighted 2 points	Weighted 3 points	Symptom-free Weighted 0 points
Being overly dependent	Sometimes 16	Often 6	XXXX	Rarely 38
Child problem which worries parent	Slight concern 27	Moderate or major concern 5	XXXX	No problem of concern 28
Security of child	Fairly secure 6	Somewhat secure 2	Quite insecure 1	Very secure 51
Child attribute: shy	Somewhat 26	Very much 3	XXXX	Not at all/hardly 31
Child attribute: trusting	Somewhat 13	Not at all/hardly 4	XXXX	Very much 43
Child attribute: destructive	Somewhat 8	Very much 1	XXXX	Not at all/hardly 51

Child attribute: tense	Somewhat 15	Very much 2	XXXX	Not at all/hardly 43
Personality problem identified	Problem identified 6	XXXX	XXXX	No problem identified 54
Health status	Occasional minor illness 18	Fair health 3	Poor health 1	Excellent health / no illness 38
Effect of illness on functioning	Slight impairment 2	Moderate impairment 1		No impairments 57
Chronic colds	Occasional 4	Somewhat often 2	XXXX	Rarely or never 54
Stomach disorders	Occasional 3	Somewhat often 1	XXXX	Rarely or never 56
Allergies or skin disorders	Occasional 9	Somewhat often 0	XXXX	Rarely or never 51
Respiratory difficulties	Occasional 3	Somewhat often 2	XXXX	Rarely or never 55

FREQUENCY OF SYMPTOMS REPORTED FOR CHILDREN
AT SERIES FIVE INTERVIEWS AND THEIR WEIGHTING
IN SUMMATED SYMPTOM SCORE (N= 60)

Symptom	Weighted 1 point	Weighted 2 points	Weighted 3 points	Symptom-free Weighted 0 points
Obesity or underweight	Occasional 2	Somewhat often 3	XXXX	Never a problem 55
General disposition	Moderately happy 7	Generally unhappy 0	XXXX	Generally happy 53
Moodiness	Occasional 15	Frequent 2	XXXX	Rare or never 43
Extent child under strain	Somewhat 22	Very much 3	XXXX	Not at all 35
Avoided by other children	XXXX	Avoided 2	XXXX	Not avoided by children 58
Shy of children	XXXX	Shy 6	XXX	Not shy of children 54

Aggressive with children	Aggressive 8	XXXX	Not aggressive with children 52
Too serious for play	Too serious 3	XXXX	Not too serious for play 57
Too sensitive-- easily hurt by children	Too sensitive 13	XXXX	Not too sensitive / not easily hurt 47
Ease of raising child	Very difficult 2	Somewhat difficult 10	XXXX	Very easy /easy to raise 48

Summated Score

	0-5	6-10	11-15	16-20	21-25	26-30	31-35	36-40
Total Frequency	1	12	14	10	10	7	5	1
Percentage	1.67	20.00	23.33	16.67	16.67	11.66	8.33	1.67
Cumulative	1.67	21.67	45.00	61.67	78.34	90.00	98.33	100.00

Mean = 18.017   Median = 16.00

S. D. = 8.274
Skewness = 0.376
Kurtosis = -0.822

more stability in intra-rater as opposed to inter-rater comparisons on repeated inquiries. From the perspective of the Series Five interviews it would seem that the adoptive mothers have a fairly consistent view of the adoptees and this coincides with my impression that, except for a few cases, there were few "surprises" in the portraits of the children. Most reports of the mothers were consistent with earlier reports in most domains.

Child Symptoms

In analyzing Series Four interviews, items were culled from the codebook filled in by the interviewers after an interview with both parents and these were included in a summated symptom score. The Series Five interview was more highly structured and involved a large number of fixed-alternative responses. In Table VIII-2, a substantial number of symptoms embedded in the interviews with the adoptive mothers are set forth with the frequency distributions for each item. I have again used the procedure of simply summating the items, employing an arbitrary weighting procedure which assigns increasing values to gradation of symptoms according to the disturbance suggested. The symptoms are descriptive of problems in developmental progress, health status, personality development, behavioral characteristics and social relationships.

Scanning the elaborate array of items, the reader will note that for almost all categories of problems only a minority of the children were described by the adoptive mothers as showing symptoms. Among the more frequently reported slight and moderately severe symptoms are:

-- Thumbsucking (15 children)
-- Disturbing dreams and sleep difficulty (16 children)
-- Nocturnal wetting (12 children)
-- Food finickiness (16 children)
-- Speech problems (12 children)
-- Fear of thunderstorms (20 children)
-- Sensitivity to scolding (38 children)
-- Excessive activity (20 children)
-- Telling lies (29 children)
-- Being under a strain (25 children)

When the symptoms were summated, the distribution scores tended to show a fairly good approximation of a nor-

Table VIII-3

CORRELATIONS BETWEEN
SELECTED DEMOGRAPHIC CHARACTERISTICS
OF THE ADOPTEES AND THEIR FAMILIES
AND SERIES FIVE CHILD SYMPTOM SCORES

(N= 60)

	Correlation with Series Five Child Symptom Scores
Adoptee's age at placement in the home	-.01
Adoptee's age at Series Five interview	-.04
Sex of child	.00
Socioeconomic status of adoptive family	.17
Biological mother's disability index	-.04
Adoptive father's age at placement	.06
Adoptive mother's age at placement	.17
Ordinal position of the adoptee in the adoptive family	-.08
Number of Indian children adopted by family	-.09

mal distribution with little skewness and only moderate kurtosis. This score becomes the important measure derived
from the Series Five interviews.

Analysis of Series Five Child Symptom Scores

In Table VIII-3, the correlations between various demographic variables and the Series Five Child Symptom
Scores are displayed. Not one of the independent variables
shows a significant relationship to this summary measure.
Thus the age of the children at the time of the Series Five
interviews shows no association with the score $(r = -.01)$.
This contrasts with the finding that the age of the children
was significantly related to the Series Four Child Symptom
Scores $(r = .22)$. As with the Series Four interview, the sex
of the child, the socioeconomic status of the adoptive family,
and the adoptive father's age when the child was placed do
not show significant associations with the summated symptom
scores. Also, the Biological Mother's Disability Index is
not linked to symptoms $(r = -.04)$. The same lack of significant association holds true for such independent variables as
the ordinal position of the adoptee in the adoptive family and
the number of American Indian children placed with the family.

A multiple correlation was calculated analyzing the
contribution of demographic variables to the Series Five Child
Symptom Scores. The cumulative multiple correlation of .29
is exceedingly modest, more so than the multiple correlation
of .42 found in analyzing the contribution of demographic variables to the variance in Series Four Child Symptom Scores.
Whether the Series Five summary measure is a less sensitive indicator of the child's adjustment than for the previous
series will be examined in Chapter X when all of the child
adjustment measures used in this study will be brought together for a summary analysis. At this point, it is worth
noting the surprising failure of the symptom score to show
a firmer correlation with the age of the child at placement.

When the index scores created from the Series Two
interviews with the adoptive mothers were correlated with
the Series Five Child Symptom Scores, only one index was
almost significantly correlated with the summary measure.
The Index of Religiosity of the Adoptive Mother showed the
largest degree of association $(r = -.21)$, the implication being
that children in more religious homes tended to show less

Table VIII-4

MULTIPLE CORRELATION ANALYSIS OF SERIES FIVE CHILD SYMPTOM SCORES USING SELECTED DEMOGRAPHIC CHARACTERISTICS OF THE ADOPTEES AND THEIR FAMILIES AS INDEPENDENT VARIABLES

Step Number[a]	Demographic Variable	Cumulative Multiple R	Cumulative Multiple R^2	F-test	ΔR^2	t-test
1	Adoptive mother's age at placement	.1681	.0282	1.6858	.0282	1.30
2	Socioeconomic status of adoptive family	.2150	.0462	1.3813	.0180	1.04
3	Ordinal position of the adoptee in the adoptive family	.2510	.0630	1.2554	.0168	1.00
4	Adoptive father's age at placement	.2754	.0758	1.1284	.0128	0.87
5	No. of Indian children adopted by family	.2913	.0848	1.0013	.0090	0.73
6	Sex of child	.2931	.0859	0.8299	.0011	0.25
7	Adoptee's age at placement in the home	.2945	.0867 #	0.7056	.0008	0.22

[a]The computer option for determining step order is same as cited in Table VII-3.
#When degrees of freedom are corrected for, R^2 approaches zero.

Table VIII-5

CORRELATIONS BETWEEN
ADOPTIVE MOTHER SERIES TWO ATTITUDINAL INDEXES
AND SERIES FIVE CHILD SYMPTOM SCORES

(N= 60)

Series Two Index	Correlation with Series Five Child Symptom Scores
Liberal vs. conservative political orientation	.13
Adoptive mother lifestyle	.02
Traditional vs. modern female ideology	.18
Orientation to the adoption of handicapped children	-.18
Orientation to the adoption of Negro children	-.02
Orientation to the adoption of children with psychological problems	-.17
Religiosity of adoptive mother	-.21
Strict vs. permissive child rearing	-.08

adjustment problems at Series Five. In the previous chapter, only one Series Two index was significantly correlated with the Series Four Child Symptom Scores, that is, the Index of the Orientation to the Adoption of Negro Children ($r = -.21$), showing that the greater the propensity of the adoptive mother to characterize Negro children as adoptable by the family, the fewer symptoms shown by the adoptees. Thus we have an overall picture of the Series Two indexes as not being markedly or consistently linked to the two summary measures of the adoptees' reported symptoms.

A multiple correlation analysis of the contribution of Series Two Index Scores to the variance in Series Five Child Symptom Scores showed a quite modest cumulative multiple correlation ($R = .33$), similar to the cumulative multiple correlation between these same index scores and the earlier Series Four Child Symptom Scores.

When the index scores created from Series Three interviews with the adoptive fathers were correlated with the Series Five Child Symptom Scores, three indexes showed significant associations. The Index of Religiosity of Adoptive Family revealed--as was the case with the Series Two Index of Religiosity of the Adoptive Mother--that children in highly religious homes tended to show fewer symptoms at the time of the Series Five interviews ($r = .25$).[2] An even firmer association is found between the Index of the Orientation to the Adoption of Handicapped Children and the Series Five summary symptom measure ($r = -.31$), suggesting that fathers who could positively contemplate adopting a handicapped child had adoptees who tended to have fewer symptoms at the time of the last interview. One further significant correlation was found between the Index of Social Problem Orientation and the symptom score ($r = .27$). The tendency to be concerned about social problems and to be involved in community organizations was linked to a greater number of child symptoms at the time of the Series Five interview. The particular rationale for the associations is not clear. One possible explanation is that children seem to thrive better in homes under firm control, where the fathers are internally oriented to their families. The linkage of the symptom score to low communal involvement, high religiosity, and strict child rearing ($r = .17$) is consistent with the picture of a setting in which the "old fashioned" virtues predominate.

The multiple correlation analysis of the contribution of the fathers' Series Three index scores as independent var-

Table VIII-6

MULTIPLE CORRELATION ANALYSIS OF SERIES FIVE CHILD SYMPTOM SCORES USING ADOPTIVE MOTHER SERIES TWO ATTITUDINAL INDEXES AS INDEPENDENT VARIABLES

Step Number[a]	Attitudinal Index	Cumulative Multiple R	Cumulative Multiple R^2	F-test	$\triangle R^2$	t-test
1	Religiosity of adoptive mothers	.2137	.0457	2.7747	.0457	1.67
2	Traditional vs. modern female ideology	.2668	.0712	2.1845	.0255	1.25
3	Orientation to the adoption of children with psychological problems	.2942	.0865	1.7682	.0153	0.97
4	Strict vs. permissive child rearing	.3081	.0949	1.4422	.0084	0.71
5	Adoptive mother life style	.3220	.1037	1.2490	.0088	0.73
6	Orientation to the adoption of handicapped children	.3281	.1076	1.0654	.0039	0.49

| 7 | Orientation to the adoption of Negro children | .3314 | .1098 | 0.9164 | .0022 | 0.36 |
| 8 | Liberal vs. conservative political orientation | .3314 | .1098[#] | 0.7864 | .0000 | 0.00 |

[a]The computer option for determining step order is same as cited in Table VII-3.

[#] When degrees of freedom are corrected for, R^2 approaches zero.

Table VIII-7

CORRELATIONS BETWEEN
ADOPTIVE FATHER SERIES THREE ATTITUDINAL INDEXES
AND SERIES FIVE CHILD SYMPTOM SCORES

Series Three Index	Correlation with Series Five Child Symptom Scores
Liberal vs. conservative political orientation	.08
Religiosity of adoptive family	.25*
Traditional masculine ideology	-.22
Work satisfaction	-.03
Background support for Indian adoption	-.20
Orientation to the adoption of handicapped children	-.31*
Strict vs. permissive child rearing orientation	.17
Orientation to the adoption of Negro children	-.07
Social problem orientation	.27*
Lower class-rural background	.02

*Significant: p < .05.

iables to explain the variance in Series Five Child Symptom
Scores turns out to be more substantial than was the case
with the mothers' attitude scores.   The cumulative multiple
correlation of seven of the fathers' index scores as shown in
Table VIII-8 was .51 with the corrected R^2 equal to 16 percent.   That the social attitudes of adoptive fathers should
have more explanatory potential than those of adoptive mothers in accounting for symptoms of children involved in transracial findings is a provocative finding.   I am not able to illuminate this phenomenon any further, since my other findings do not help to explain the dynamics involved.   This is
a lead which might be followed by other investigators.

Future Orientations to the Research

Since this was the last contact with the adoptive mothers in the series, they were asked to share their reactions
to the research experience.   How had the experience struck
them?   As shown in Table VIII-9, about three-fourths of the
respondents were positive in their assessments.   An additional twenty percent were neutral in their comments.   Only sev-
en percent were cool or slightly negative about the research.
The range of their comments were as follows:

> We have been very happy to cooperate.   We'd be
> interested in knowing what the experiences of other
> parents have been like.

*   *   *

> I have found it to be interesting and I have enjoyed
> having an opportunity to talk about my child.

*   *   *

> I am not certain of how useful it is going to be.
> The interviews take a good deal of time and it
> seems the same questions are covered repeatedly.
> My husband's feelings are stronger than mine; he
> is sorry we began participating in the research
> because of the time required.

*   *   *

> If it's just going to be facts and figures stored away

Table VIII-8

MULTIPLE CORRELATION ANALYSIS OF SERIES FIVE CHILD SYMPTOM SCORES USING ADOPTIVE FATHER SERIES THREE ATTITUDINAL INDEX SCORES AS INDEPENDENT VARIABLES

Step Number[a]	Attitudinal Index	Cumulative Multiple R	Cumulative Multiple R^2	F-test	R^2	t-test
1	Orientation to the adoption of handicapped children	.3070	.0943	6.0362*	.0943	2.46*
2	Social problem orientation	.3748	.1405	4.6579*	.0462	1.75
3	Traditional masculine ideology	.4124	.1701	3.8261*	.0296	1.41
4	Religiosity of adoptive family	.4457	.1987	3.4087	.0286	1.40
5	Strict vs. permissive child rearing	.4710	.2219	3.0792	.0232	1.27
6	Background support for Indian adoption	.4933	.2433	2.8403	.0214	1.23
7	Liberal vs. conservative political orientation	.5100	.2601[#]	2.6109	.0168	1.10

[a]The computer option for determing step order is same as cited in Table VII-3.

*Significant: $p < .05$.

[#]R^2 corrected for degrees of freedom = .1605.

I'll feel cheated, but it's okay if it's useful in getting children placed.

                    *   *   *

I rather enjoyed it--some of the questions I don't
understand. I've only had an eighth grade education. I was out of school a lot because of illness.

                    *   *   *

I don't mind at all.

                    *   *   *

I would be most interested in reading a report. I
have participated to help others.

                    *   *   *

It doesn't bother me.

                    *   *   *

We're always glad to have you. We talk about our
favorite subject. We have not been annoyed in any
way.

                    *   *   *

I have found it to be very interesting in that it has
allowed me an opportunity to examine my own attitudes as a parent which I would not otherwise do.
The interviews help you to know more about yourself. I have a real interest in the results. My
husband feels the same way and we'd be willing to
continue participation in the research at any future
date.

                    *   *   *

We are pleased it is occurring. I, more than my
husband, have been suspicious of the validity or
relevance of the questions asked--especially in the
earlier interviews but as the years have gone by,
they have seemed more relevant. I think the purposes and objectives of the research are excellent.

We have been happy to contribute and have found it
an enriching experience--a growth experience since
following each interview, my husband and I have
been prompted to sit down together and examine
what we are doing in terms of the questions asked.

The mothers were asked whether the adoptees were
aware of the visits of the interviewers. The responses indicated that the families were about evenly divided between
those whose children were aware of the visits and those where
there was no confiding about the matter. The range of the
mothers' comments is as follows:

She has been told that your visits have been made
in connection with people who are in charge of getting children like herself into homes where they
would have a better chance for a nicer life and it
is to find out if there is a good way to do it or if
changes should be made. I told her that it is almost like taking a vote to see if people are happy
in their homes and if there are ways to improve it.

*   *   *

No. He went through enough when we adopted him.
If I should mention the research, he might wonder
why all this interest in him.

*   *   *

She doesn't really understand. I tell her the lady who
helped get her is coming.

*   *   *

I told her you do research on Indian adoptions to
see if you should continue to do it and to find Mom-
mies and Daddies for babies.

The last and most important question directed to the
adoptive mothers related to their attitude toward the adoptee
being seen for a research interview several years after the
Fifth Series interview. The responses ranged widely. About
37 percent were unqualifiedly positive about such a prospect.

Table VIII-9

REPORTS OF ADOPTIVE MOTHERS
ABOUT ADOPTIVE FAMILY'S REACTION TO THE RESEARCH

1. Could you tell me what your reaction to the research has been?

Coded Responses	No.	Percent
a. Slightly negative, cool to the research	4	6.8
b. Neither positive or negative	11	18.6
c. Generally positive	17	28.8
d. Affirmatively positive	27	45.8
	59	100.0

(1 non-response)

2. Has the child been aware of the visits we have made?

Coded Responses	No.	Percent
a. Not aware of visits	28	46.7
b. Is aware of visits	30	50.0
c. Other	2	3.3
	60	100.0

3. What do you think your attitude would be about the possibility of our having an interview with your child several years from now?

Coded Responses	No.	Percent
a. Definitely opposed	1	1.7
b. Must consider answer; not ready to respond	4	6.7
c. Willing to have child seen; but response is qualified	7	11.7
d. Acceptable if child is willing and circumstances are right	25	41.6
e. Unqualified positive response	22	36.6
f. Other	1	1.7
	60	100.0

An additional 42 percent of the respondents said that such an interview was acceptable if the child's circumstances at the time were good.   They wanted to be sure that the interview wouldn't upset the child and that he/she was willing to participate.   Four mothers said they would have to give the matter further thought and one mother was strongly opposed to the idea.   In the main, the responses were on the positive side, albeit with cautious undertones.   Here are some of the comments of the mothers on this question:

> We would be willing and I think she would be willing and would know the reason why.

*   *   *

> I would not object as long as it was handled along the same lines and with the same discretion as interviews with us.   By the time you would see him, he would certainly be aware of his background and I think his reaction would be positive.   I would want the interview handled in such a way that he would not be made to feel he is an oddity or different.

*   *   *

> It would depend upon how well he is getting along at the time and how he accepts his adoptive status.

*   *   *

> If he didn't object, I wouldn't either, I believe.

*   *   *

> Okay, but I want to know what you'll talk about then.

*   *   *

> It would be fine with me.   I want to read the results when it's done.

*   *   *

I would want to know what the purpose of such an interview would be. I have not given it thought and I would wonder what repercussion it would have on my child. I think it would depend upon the child at the time and if I felt such an interview could be done without disturbing her.

*   *   *

I think my reaction would be positive but it would depend upon my child's maturity at the time. On our part we'd like to continue participating in the study since we think it is very worthwhile.

*   *   *

I think it could be worked out and see no reason why not. She would be well aware of her adoptive status by that time.

*   *   *

I would think it would be worthwhile. You won't really know what happens with the children until they are older and meet all kinds. They are sheltered now.

*   *   *

I don't think it would bother me. But if our child didn't go along with it, we wouldn't force him to see you.

*   *   *

I think it would be very good and an important part of the research.

Notes

1. The reduction from 97 to 60 families to be interviewed left 25 families who were not seen because the field operations had to be brought to a close. One mother was too ill to be seen in the last interview, another was unavailable.

2. The Index of Religiosity of Adoptive Family was con-
    structed so that a low score portrayed high religiosity.
    Hence a positive correlation between the index and the
    Series Five Child Symptom Scores means that higher
    religiosity is associated with lower symptom scores.

Chapter IX

OVERALL ASSESSMENT OF CHILD ADJUSTMENT

A major reason for maintaining contact with the adoptive parents over a five-year period was to develop a picture of how they and the children were experiencing the adoptive arrangement. Since adoption across racial lines is a comparatively rare experience in the United States, there was interest in establishing whether such placements were viable from the perspective of both parents and children.

This is not to say that it was my expectation or that of the sponsors of this research that tales of woe would be recounted to the interviewers after the adoptive placements. On the contrary, the expectation was that these adoptions would indeed result in quite positive experiences for the parents and secure placements for the children. However, it is one thing to arrange for such placements with the hope that positive outcomes will result; it is yet another to clearly establish whether the aspirations that lie behind these adoptions have been fulfilled.

Further, while there was no expectation that an unhappy portrait would emerge from the study of these adoptions, there were still areas of the adoptive experience about which little was known. For example, it was important to get the adoptive parents' perspective on whether or not the social climate in the communities in which they lived was sufficiently positive to allow the Indian child to be integrated into an essentially white environment. In addition, it was anticipated that further down the road, when the children were teenagers and older, the whole matter of interracial dating and courtship would likely arise and would pose problems relative to the child's Indian background which previously might not have seemed significant. I have earlier cautioned the reader to keep clearly in mind the limited perspective of this report on the outcome of the adoptions since I only take into account the first five years of the adoptive experience--years in which the children are still relatively young and just embarking up-

on their school careers. In a sense, this volume is an interim report on the experiences of the families and children
and it is my hope that a subsequent re-survey of the families
will illuminate further the modes of adaptation of the families
and the adjustment of the children.

Measuring the Adjustment of the Children

In this volume, several approaches to characterizing
the adjustment of the children have been used. Chapters VII
and VIII described summated scores based on the Series Four
and Series Five interviews, in which the approach was taken
of simply tabulating an array of symptoms based upon information provided by the adoptive parents. Although without
elegance with respect to the conceptual underpinnings of the
portraiture developed, such indexes of adjustment have the
virtue that they are not based upon the ratings of outsiders.
By covering a large number of symptoms in a variety of
spheres considered important to the child's adjustment, the
hazard that the values of the investigator will intrude upon
the judgment process tends to be minimized. Generally, the
more items in the symptom list, the more the risk of bias
in the creation of outcome measures is diminished. It should
be noted that the product-moment correlations between the
Series Four and Series Five scores is a significant one ($r =$
.48), although it is obvious that the two measures do not completely coincide in their assessments.

The Child Progress Scale

My approach to measuring adjustment leans heavily
upon my prior work with Benson Jaffee in conducting a follow-
up study of families who had adopted twenty to thirty years
earlier in New York City. We conceived of the outcome of
adjustment as being related to significant life-space areas,
twelve in number.[1] The major outcome variable we created
for this earlier study was based upon various kinds of information provided by the parents. In the study presented here,
the outcome measures are based upon a series of judgments
on a scale I call the Child Progress Scale.[2] The development of professional judgments on the scale required the rater
to read the interviews with the parents for whatever number
of series they had completed. The areas to be rated included
the following:

A. Physical Growth and Development: This domain covered the child's physical well being and developmental
progress. In the realm of health, focus was upon the
presence or absence of disabling health conditions.
These included illnesses which might occur episodically
as well as conditions of a long-standing and chronic
nature. The developmental conditions concern such
phenomena as physical growth, walking, speech, sleeping, eating, and elimination--all related to a perspective of the child as an emerging biological organism.

B. Intellectual and Cognitive Competence: This domain
covered the child's intelligence and intellectual potential as revealed by the parents' reports of their impression of his intelligence, his degree of alertness,
his reading readiness, and his performance in school
(if he was of school age). Any condition other than
behavior which might jeopardize the child's present or
subsequent school adjustment was included as a problem (e.g., low intelligence, thought disorder, etc.).

C. Personality Characteristics and Behavior Patterns:
This domain covered pathological elements in the
child's personality including psychotic, prepsychotic
and neurotic status, as well as disturbances of character (character disorders). The presence of phobias,
deep anxiety states, antisocial behavior, extreme aggressiveness, extreme withdrawal, and like behavior
was to be noted as problems. Characterological traits
were to be considered problems only if they became
problematic and dysfunctional for the child in terms
of his emotional equilibrium, his sense of well-being,
and his ability to carry out tasks appropriate for his
age and sex.

D. Social Relationships: This domain covered the child's
ability to develop satisfying social ties with other children as well as with adults. The presence of self-
isolating tendencies, the selection of inappropriate playmates, insecurity in social situations, excessive conformity, etc., were to be regarded as problems.

E. Family Relationships: This domain covered the ability
of the adopted child to become integrated within the
adopted family. It referred to tendencies within him
rather than the family's attitude towards him, although
these were seen as difficult orientations to separate.

An adopted child might have problems if he felt the
home was not permanently his, if he felt he had a
second-class status, or if he was painfully aware of
the contrast in ethnicity between himself and his parents. Problems in relating to either parent or siblings or in accepting parental authority were to be
noted.

The rating task called for culling from the interview
schedules, information provided by the parents relative to each
of these five domains. In addition, comments by the case-
worker-interviewers about these topics were also abstracted.
The rating task required that a judgment be made as to
whether or not a problematic condition (or conditions) had
been identified. In the event of such identification, a rating
was required designating the problem as serious, moderate,
or mild. In addition, where a problem was identified, a
judgment was required as to whether the problem was apt to
become more serious, apt to remain stable in its present
form, or apt to decline in severity (or disappear /or had already disappeared). Following this, the rating task required
that an overall adjustment rating be made, taking into account
the accumulated information that had been gathered about the
child. An effort was made to keep this judgment independent
of the assessment of the parents. An Overall Adjustment
Rating scale with seven levels was created as follows:

Level One.   Child is making an excellent adjustment in all
spheres of his life--the outlook for his future adjustment
is seen as excellent.

Level Two.

Level Three.   Child is making an adequate adjustment--
his strengths outweigh the weaknesses he shows--the outlook for his future adjustment is seen as hopeful.

Level Four.

Level Five.   Child is making a mixed adjustment--gener-
ally the problems he faces are serious and the outlook for
his future adjustment is somewhat guarded.

Level Six.

Level Seven. Child is making an extremely poor adjust-
ment--the outlook for his future adjustment is seen as un-
promising.

An additional rating was required, assessing the quality of the adoptive home using the rating scale developed by
Witmer, et al. in their study of independent adoptions in the
state of Florida.[3] The rating task required that an attempt
be made to keep the judgment of the family independent from
the assessment of the child. This judgment was based upon
the interview materials contained in the various interviewing
schedules as well as the summaries prepared by the case-
worker-interviewers who provided written impressions of the
parents following each research interview. The rating is a
five-point scale and has the following anchoring points:

A.   Considering all the information secured in the home
     interviews, this seems to be the kind of home situa-
     tion one would want a child to have; the kind in which
     a child would have the best opportunity for healthy de-
     velopment.

B.

C.   This relates to the kind of home situation in which
     some factors are not as one would like them to be
     but not the kind that seem likely to be seriously harm-
     ful to the child.

D.

E.   Considering all the information secured in the home
     interviews, this seems to be the kind of home situa-
     tion from which one would like to protect a child; the
     kind likely to interfere with his happiness and healthy
     development.

Assignment of Ratings and Reliability Check

Ideally, it would have been preferable to have a team
of raters read the materials and to use a combined judgment
for each case. It was not deemed possible to do this because
of the limitation of resources. Therefore, I made the decision to undertake the primary judgment task myself. Over a

six-month period, every set of research materials of the 96
families was thoroughly read by me, all indicators relevant
to the rating task were abstracted, and the judgments previously described were made. This procedure has advantages
and disadvantages that are quite obvious. The use of a single judge meant that all families were being viewed from the
same perspective. Being well acquainted with the research
literature on the making of professional judgments, I made
considerable effort to guard against a variety of sources of
bias in the assignment of ratings.

The deficit of the rating procedure is that, of course,
any idiosyncrasies peculiar to the single rater might serve
to mitigate against certain types of children in families or
in favor of others. This hazard made it important to arrange
for a thorough reliability check of these ratings and this was
built into the rating procedure. Before going into this, it
should be pointed out that the following sources of bias were
seen as hazards in the enterprise:

1. Contextual bias. If a record has been read in which
    some pathology is evident, the next case of a middle-
    range child may be rated more positively than normal
    because it is contrasted with the first. An effort was
    made to consider cases with reference to criteria and
    anchoring illustrations rather than relative to other
    cases.[4]

2. "Halo effect." Ratings in a given domain tend to re-
    flect an overall gestalt created about a child. An ef-
    fort was made to make judgments as if each area
    being rated was discrete. Thus a child might show
    great maturity in his relationship with his peers even
    though his mother reported him to be very difficult in
    other areas of living.

3. Response set. There are hazards that a judge may
    be so taken with the adoptive parents that he will be
    uncomfortable in making negative ratings. Or con-
    versely, he may be so oriented to psychopathology,
    that he will tend to be fixed or invariant in finding
    such behavior. An attempt was made to avoid such
    central tendencies as well as to avoid introducing var-
    iation for its own sake.

Orientation to Assessment

   The approach used here in evaluating the adjustment
of the child is to specify areas in which he may reveal problems. The reader might well ask: "How is a 'problem' defined?" From the perspective developed, a problem is viewed
as reflecting evidence given by the child of an internalized
tendency to operate in such a manner as to threaten the quality of his personal and social adjustment. Put another way,
it is a problem he carries within him and reflects a tendency
to function in less than adequate fashion--as defined by his
parents and significant others. It does not reflect merely the
presence of limitations in his environment. For example, a
child who lives in a rather isolated rural area where there
are few playmates available is not necessarily rated as having
a problem in social functioning. If he is extremely shy of
other children and engages in avoidant behavior, he is then
considered to have a problem for the purposes of the study.

   Rating a child as having a problem does not imply anything about the cause of the problem. If a mother reports
herself as a "worrier" who has kept the child tied to her, to
the point where he is extremely dependent upon her, this child,
if he avoids other children, is considered showing problems
of adjustment even though the source of his difficulty origi-
nates outside of himself.

   Since there have been a series of interviews with each
family, the question arose as to whether the rating of the
child's adjustment would be based upon any single interview
or on the accumulated interviews. My decision was to consider the evidence of problems as a cumulative process, giving major emphasis to those problems which were identified
and which persisted until the last interview. The seriousness
of the problem would be judged by whether it increased or
declined intensity.

   Part of the difficulty in making the judgment about the
children's adjustment was related to the variability in age.
Ratings were undertaken with the general notion that the children's behavior had to be seen within the context of their
ages. It is generally known that the younger the child is,
the less time there has been for problems to arise. We also know from the data in this study that such elements of behavior as aggressiveness or resistance to socialization may
not be evident when a child is a toddler but may emerge as
he becomes more mobile and vocal.

All in all, the approach I have employed to the assessment of the children have a commonsense orientation and is
most consonant with my experience in prior studies and with
the resources available for this investigation. Yet it is obviously not fool-proof and, no doubt, is vulnerable to some
elements of subjective error.

The rating of a problem as serious, moderate or mild
was one that required a judgment based upon all of the information available in the interview. An important feature
of the child's problem would be the seriousness with which
the parents viewed it. If it was a source of concern, which
greatly worried the parent, this was seen as part of the picture. However, the professional judgment might not coincide
exactly with that of the parent since the frames of reference
might not match. For example, an adoptive mother might
indicate that she was worried about the child's food finickiness while at the same time informing the interviewer that
her pediatrician did not think it was a matter of serious concern. The interviewers who saw the adoptive families were
graduate caseworkers with considerable experience in child
welfare. Their evaluative comments were also part of the
informational picture that helped shape the judgment.

Prevalence of Problems

Table IX-1 sets forth the five domains covered by the
Child Progress Rating Scale and constitutes the judgments
made by the single rater, myself, on the prevalence of problems and the prediction for their future course. With respect
to health and physical growth and development, 56 percent of
the adoptees were seen as demonstrating no problems. Another 29 percent displayed only mild problems. The group
displaying moderate problems or serious problems was less
than 15 percent--only one child showed what was considered
a serious problem. Most of the health problems identified
had either disappeared or the expectation was that they would
decline. Only eight percent of the conditions identified were
seen as fairly stable and not apt to change and none were
seen as problems that could be expected to become worse.

With respect to intellectual and cognitive competence,
two-thirds of the adoptees were seen as having no problems
based upon the reports of the parents. An additional 18 percent appeared to have mild problems and 10 percent were
said to have moderate problems. Only three percent were

considered to show serious problems in this domain. Of those displaying problems, most had either already overcome them or it was expected that they would decline in significance. Twelve percent of the adoptees had problems that were believed to be static and none had problems that were expected to become worse.

The domain of personality and behavior patterns was one in which the problems were much more prevalent than in any other area. Only 28 percent of the children were rated as having no personality or behavior problems to speak of. Another 46 percent demonstrated mild problems, in most cases characterological in nature. Nineteen percent of the children were seen as having moderate problems and almost 13 percent were seen as having serious problems. For two-thirds of the children, the future course seemed to be that there would be no problems of any significance. Another 26 percent had problems that did not appear to be subject to change, and for two percent it was predicted that the problems would worsen.

With respect to social relationships, fully three-quarters of the children were rated as not displaying problems. An additional 14 percent were seen to have only mild problems while ten percent showed moderate problems. Only one child was judged as showing serious problems in this area. In the main, the children were either without problems or had problems that were apt to decline.

The area of family relationships proved to be a rather difficult domain in which to make judgments--particularly since the interviews were largely focused upon young children whose reactions to family life were more difficult to discern. The interview data was judged to show that there were problems in only one out of five situations, eight percent showing mild problems and about 12 percent showing moderate problems. In the main, these family problems were expected to decline, and only five percent of the children were judged to have fairly permanent family relationship problems. In only one case was this judged likely to become worse.

The Overall Adjustment of the Child

This rating is the most important measure of how well the adoption appears to be working out. That is, it is an attempt to summarize all that has been learned about the child's

Table IX-1

PROBLEMS ATTRIBUTED TO ADOPTEES ON CHILD PROGRESS RATING SCALE
AND PREDICTIONS OF THEIR FUTURE COURSE

(N=96)

Domain	No Problem	Mild Problem	Moderate Problem	Serious Problem	Future Course	
	(Percentaged Across)					
Health and physical growth and development	56.3	29.2	13.5	1.0	No problem	56.3
					Apt to decline	35.5
					Apt to be stable	8.2
					Apt to worsen	--
						100.0
Intellectual and cognitive competence	68.8	17.7	10.4	3.1	No problem	68.8
					Apt to decline	18.8
					Apt to be stable	12.4
					Apt to worsen	--
						100.0

Personality and behavior patterns	28.1	45.8	18.8	12.5	No problem	28.1
					Apt to decline	43.8
					Apt to be stable	26.0
					Apt to worsen	2.1
						100.0
Social relationships	75.0	13.6	10.4	1.0	No problem	75.0
					Apt to decline	13.6
					Apt to be stable	11.4
					Apt to worsen	--
						100.0
Family relationships	80.2	8.3	11.5	--	No problem	80.3
					Apt to decline	13.5
					Apt to be stable	5.2
					Apt to worsen	1.0
						100.0

adjustment up to the point of the last contact. It is important to bear in mind in considering the total study population
that we are dealing with a relatively young group, most of
whom, when the parents were last seen, were just entering
school. We know that at such a young age most children will
appear to be adjusting within a relatively normal range.
Greater differentiation can be expected when the children are
older and well along in their school careers. The judgments
made about the children on the scale designed to measure
their overall adjustment showed the following distribution within the seven levels available:

No.	Percent	
10	10	Level One. (Child is making an excellent adjustment in all spheres--the outlook for his future adjustment is excellent.)
41	43	Level Two.
24	25	Level Three. (Child is making an adequate adjustment--his strengths outweigh the weaknesses he shows--the outlook for his future adjustment is hopeful.)
10	10	Level Four.
10	10	Level Five. (Child is making a mixed adjustment--generally the problem he faces are serious and the outlook for his future adjustment is guarded.)
1	1	Level Six.
None		Level Seven. (Child is making an extremely poor adjustment--the outlook for his future adjustment is unpromising.)

More than fifty percent of the children were rated as
showing relatively problem-free adjustments (Levels One and
Two) and another 25 percent were rated as showing adequate
adjustments with strengths outweighing weaknesses (Level
Three). Another ten percent of the children were rated at
Level Four--located midway between adjustments regarded as
adequate and those viewed as guarded. Only ten percent were
judged to be in Level Five because they were showing serious
problems and the outlook for their futures was guarded. Only

a single child was seen as being at Level Six where the outlook for his future adjustment looked dim, and none of the
children were judged to be at Level Seven. In the main, then,
the distribution of the children along the seven levels provides
a positive view of the progress of adoptions thus far. Eight
out of ten children are doing quite well and thus far do not
reveal problems in sufficient volume and intensity to cause
alarm. Only one child in ten has shown problems which
makes his future adjustment appear uncertain. This should
be a source of some assurance for those who have been par-
ty to these placements--particularly the social workers on
the reservations who helped identify the children for placement.

Home Ratings

There may also be interest in the distribution of ratings made about the adoptive home itself, using the scale developed by Witmer and her associates in the Florida study.
The task was to consider the problems the parents had to
face in caring for the child and to make a judgment about the
quality of the care given and the general strengths and weaknesses of the parents. An effort was made to try to keep
the judgments independent from those made of the child, although, as shown by the Florida study, this is a condition
more easily desired than carried out.

The distribution of judgments was as follows:

No.	Percent	
18	19	Level One. (This seems to be the kind of home situation one would want a child to have; the kind in which a child would have the best opportunity for healthy de- velopment.)
48	50	Level Two.
20	21	Level Three. (This relates to the kind of home situation in which some factors are not as one would like them to be, but not the kind that seem likely to be seriously harmful to the child.)
8	8	Level Four.

<u>No.</u>   <u>Percent</u>

No.	Percent	
2	2	Level Five. (This seems to be the kind of home situation from which one would like to protect a child; the kind likely to interfere with his happiness and healthy development.)

By and large, then, most of the homes were judged to be of good quality, 90 percent falling in the top three categories. This compares with 71 percent for the Florida study. One must bear in mind that this earlier study dealt with parents of children who were older than the ones considered here--on the average five years older. It may be assumed that parental qualities are brought more to the test as children get older.

The product-moment correlation between the Overall Adjustment Rating of the child and the summary rating of the qualities of the home was .67. This is significant and indicates that the ratings are not independent. However, that the correlation is not even larger reflects, I believe, the account taken in the judgment process of the fact that a number of families adopted children at older ages who revealed problems which they brought into the family situation at the time of arrival, and that these difficulties did not seem to reflect parental mishandling.

Reliability of Judgments

In order to test the reliability of the judgments made on the Child Progress Rating Scale, volunteers were recruited to read research materials on randomly selected research subjects. It was possible to undertake an inter-rater reliability test for 53 adoptive families in the study. Thirty-two independent ratings were undertaken by Dr. Ervin Varga, a psychiatrist, and his wife, Dr. Vera Varga, a pediatrician.[5] Both were European-trained, with a wealth of experience including practice in Hungary, England and other countries. They were limited, however, by lack of exposure to American children at the time of their contribution to this study. This husband-wife professional couple approached the rating task by individually reading the research interviews and then jointly filling out the Child Progress Rating Scale.

An additional 21 sets of research protocols were read

by social caseworkers employed at three adoption agencies in New York City: the Louise Wise Services, the Spence Chapin Adoption Service and the Talbot Perkins Adoption Service.

Table IX-2 shows the correlations between the ratings of the second raters and myself as well as the matrix of intercorrelations among the ratings. In the diagonal, there is presented the inter-rater reliability measure for the 53 cases that were rated a second time. On the whole, the reliabilities within each domain are quite modest, the strongest emerging for the rating of intellectual competence (r = .68). The ratings dealing with physical growth and development, personality and behavioral characteristics, and social relationships showed correlations that ranged from .52 to .57. The reliability of the rating of family relationships was the lowest achieved (r = .32). While the size of correlations does not show great strength, it is not unsimilar to the experience of Witmer, et al. who found a reliability coefficient of .42 in testing the rating of adoptive parents.[6]

The Overall Child Adjustment Rating shows considerably higher reliability than the ratings of the individual domains. The correlation between the pairs of raters for this important rating was .82. The home rating reliability was less impressive (r = .51). The disparity between the reliability of the overall rating and the reliabilities of the individual domains may perhaps be explained by the fact that in no single problem area, other than personality and behavior, was there much spread in the prevalence of problems. Thus the means of four of the five ratings tended to be skewed in the direction of the absence of problems for both the original ratings and the second set of ratings. This would tend to undermine the correlational procedure. The judgments with respect to personality and behavior and overall child adjustment ratings were not markedly skewed.

One internal check on the Overall Child Adjustment Rating is set forth in Table IX-2. For each of the five domains rated by the writer, a scoring system was developed so that the most points were assigned to problems which were rated as serious and apt to become more serious, while no points were assigned if there were no problems present. This ad hoc procedure made it possible to create a Summated Child Problem Index ranging from a potentially perfect adjustment of 0 to the most difficult adjustment of 25 points if a child suffered problems in all five areas and the prob-
(cont. p. 286)

Table IX-2

OUTCOME RATINGS: MEANS, STANDARD DEVIATIONS
INTERCORRELATIONS AND RELIABILITY*

Rating Description	1	2	3	4	5	6	7	8	Mean	S.D.
Child problems (1-5)										
1. Physical growth and development	.54	.27	.27	.38	-.00	.34	.29	.54	0.68	0.88
2. Intellectual competence		.68	.44	.37	.19	.60	.25	.68	0.61	1.05
3. Personality and behavioral characteristics			.52	.56	.49	.77	.61	.84	1.35	1.20
4. Social relationships				.57	.29	.59	.53	.76	0.49	0.96
5. Family relationships					.32	.51	.44	.57	0.39	0.88
6. Overall Child Adjustment Rating						.82	.67	.84	2.71	1.18

	.51	.63	2.25	0.93
7. Home rating				
8. Summated Child Problem Index**			3.51	3.43

*Reliability measure is the intercorrelation of ratings for 58 cases by two raters and is presented underlined in the diagonal.

**Each problem area was scored as follows:

Column 1

Problem is rated as:

3. Serious
2. Moderate
1. Mild
0. No problem manifested

Column 2

Prediction for future course:

3. Apt to become more serious
2. Apt to remain stable in present form
1. Apt to decline in severity or has already disappeared
0. No problem

OUTCOME RATINGS: MEANS, STANDARD DEVIATIONS,
INTERCORRELATIONS AND RELIABILITY

Combining the two ratings into a two-digit figure, problem
area is assigned following values:

= 5 if variable = 33 (i.e., serious problem apt to become
                       more serious)
= 4 if variable = 32
= 3 if variable = 31
= 3 if variable = 30
= 4 if variable = 23 (i.e., moderate problem apt to be-
                       come more serious)
= 3 if variable = 22
= 2 if variable = 21
= 2 if variable = 20
= 3 if variable = 13
= 2 if variable = 12
= 1 if variable = 11
= 1 if variable = 10
= 0 if variable = 00 (i.e., no problem manifested)

Summated index represents the sum of the values assigned
to each of the five problem areas.

---

lem was predicted to become worse in each area.   The correlation between this summated score and the Overall Child
Adjustment Rating was .84, indicating that the latter rating
could be viewed as a summation of information known about
the children in the five domains.

Notes

1.   Benson Jaffee and David Fanshel, How They Fared in
     Adoption (New York: Columbia University Press,
     1970) pp. 220-244.

2.   The Child Progress Scale is displayed in the Appendix.

3.   Helen Witmer, et al., Independent Adoptions: A Follow-
     Up Study (New York: Russell Sage Foundation, 1963).

4. Ben A. Orcutt, "A Study of Anchoring Effects in Clinical Judgment," Social Service Review (December 1964), pp. 408-17.

5. Dr. Ervin Varga is now a research psychiatrist at Rockland State Hospital and Dr. Vera Varga is a psychiatric resident in the same institution. At the time they had undertaken the rating tasks, they were living in Rome, Italy and had not yet experienced living in the United States. The reliability of the ratings, therefore, must be seen as conservative estimates since lack of exposure to American children may well have created a cultural bias in the ratings.

6. Witmer, et al., Independent Adoptions: A Follow-Up Study, op. cit., p. 142.

Chapter X

ANALYSIS OF ADJUSTMENT

In this chapter the adjustment of the adoptees are considered from several perspectives. Using multiple correlational techniques of analysis, an attempt is made to "understand" the major outcome measure, Overall Adjustment of the Child, in terms of the contributions of three sets of independent variables: (1) demographic characteristics of the child and his adoptive family; (2) Series Two indexes based upon structured interviews with the adoptive mothers; and (3) indexes from structured Series Three interviews with the adoptive fathers.

Demographic Variables

Table X-1 presents the product-moment correlations between a selected number of demographic variables and the Overall Child Adjustment Ratings. Three variables are significantly correlated with the adjustment rating. As might be expected, older children were rated as showing less satisfactory adjustment than younger ones ($r = .21$).[1] In order to determine whether the association was influenced by the age of the child at the time of the last interview with the family, a partial correlation was carried out to assess the relationship between the adoptee's age at the time of placement and the Overall Child Adjustment Rating controlling for the child's age at the time of the last interview with the family. This analysis deals with, for example, the matter of whether a rating tends to be a function of a child's being older when adopted or whether a Series Five interview had been completed. If the child was older when last seen, he might show more propensity for getting into trouble because of his age. The partial correlation turns out to be significant ($r_{12.3} = .21$).[2] Thus, the finding suggests that the children who were adopted when older experienced more difficulties in their adjustment over the period covered by this research. How might one explain this? My data on the number of place-

Table X-1

CORRELATIONS BETWEEN SELECTED DEMOGRAPHIC
CHARACTERISTICS OF THE ADOPTEES AND THEIR FAMILIES
AND OVERALL CHILD ADJUSTMENT RATINGS

(N = 96)

	Correlation with Overall Child Adjustment Ratings
Adoptee's age at placement in the home	.21*
Adoptee's age at last interview with family	.05
Sex of child	-.19
Socioeconomic status of adoptive family	.22*
Biological mother's disability index	.26*
Adoptive father's age at placement	-.12
Adoptive mother's age at placement	.09
Ordinal position of adoptee	-.04
Number of Indian children adopted by family	.03

*Significant: $p < .05$.

ments experienced by the children is derived from the referral summaries sent to the Indian Adoption Project and, while
not complete, suggests that the older children suffered more
turnover in foster placements. This may provide a partial
explanation of their generally poorer adjustment.

An intriguing finding links the Child Overall Adjustment Rating with the index developed to summate the disabilities of the biological mothers. The correlation between the
two measures suggests that the more disabled the biological
mother, the more poorly adjusted is the adoptee likely to be
(r = .26). Since the ratings of the children were generally
made without any awareness of the afflictions of their biological mothers, the finding can be assumed to be related to
factors other than the rating procedure. An examination of
the correlation matrix developed for the demographic and
background variables shows that the biological mothers' disability index was significantly correlated with the age of the
child (r = .22), the number of American Indian children adopted by the family (r = .24), and the ordinal position of the
child (r = -.21). These factors offer explanatory leads in our
effort to understand the linkage identified between the children
and their biological mothers.

The third demographic variable found to be significantly associated with the Overall Child Adjustment Rating is the
socioeconomic status of the adoptive family. The higher the
status of the family, the poorer is the child's Overall Adjustment Rating likely to be (r = .22). This finding is contrary
to the finding of Witmer, et al., who report, in their study of
independent adoptions in the state of Florida, small but statistically significant associations between socioeconomic status and their ratings of adoptive homes, as well as with some
of the individual measurements of the children's performance
in school. The differences they found favored children in
adoptive homes of higher socioeconomic status.[3] However,
in the follow-up study of adoptive families in New York City,
conducted by Benson Jaffee and myself, we found that children in adopted families of higher socioeconomic status tended to show more problems over the years.[4]

As a possible source of explanation of the association
between high socioeconomic status and poorer adjustment,
one can look at the association between the SES measure and
a number of the attitudinal indexes created for Series Two
and Series Three data:

Series Two Indexes:

Liberal vs. Conservative Political
Orientation $(r = .22)$

Traditional vs. Modern Female Ideology $(r = .27)$

Orientation to the Adoption
of Negro Children $(r = .31)$

Orientation to the Adoption of
Children with Psychological Problems $(r = -.22)$

Religiosity of Adoptive Mother $(r = -.31)$

Series Three Indexes:

Liberal vs. Conservative Political
Orientation $(r = .23)$

Background Support for Indian Adoptions $(r = -.30)$

Orientation to the Adoption
of Handicapped Children $(r = -.21)$

Social Problem Orientation $(r = .27)$

Lower Class-Rural Background $(r = -.33)$

The significant correlations between a number of social attitudinal indexes and the index measuring socioeconomic
status does suggest that rather diverse life styles and social
orientations were linked to the status measure. This is not
surprising since it fits in with our common sense notion of
the meaning of socioeconomic status. We shall subsequently
see that some of the attitudinal indexes linked to socioeconomic status are themselves significantly associated with outcome even with the effect of socioeconomic status controlled
in the analysis.

In Table X-2 there is set forth a multiple correlation
analysis of the Overall Child Adjustment Ratings using demographic and background characteristics as independent variables. A multiple regression computer program permitted the
option of "best" criterion for choosing variables to be entered
into the regression equation on a step-wise basis, variables
being chosen because of their potential for maximum contri-

Table X-2

MULTIPLE CORRELATION ANALYSIS OF OVERALL CHILD ADJUSTMENT RATINGS
USING SELECTED DEMOGRAPHIC CHARACTERISTICS OF THE ADOPTEES
AND THEIR FAMILIES AS INDEPENDENT VARIABLES

Step Number[a]	Demographic Variable	Cumulative Multiple R	Cumulative Multiple R^2	F-test	$\triangle R^2$	t-test
1	Biological Mother's Disability Index	.2552	.0651	6.5485**	.0651	2.56**
2	Socioeconomic Status of Adoptive Family	.3381	.1143	6.0004***	.0492	2.27*
3	Adoptee's Age at Placement	.3806	.1449	5.1963***	.0306	1.81
4	Sex of Child	.4185	.1751	4.8303***	.0302	1.83
5	Number of Indian Children Adopted by Family	.4292	.1842	4.0650**	.0091	1.00
6	Mother's Age at Placement	.4322	.1868	3.4072**	.0026	0.53

7	Adoptee's Age at Last Interview	.4327	.1873	2.8966**	.0005	0.23
8	Ordinal Position of Adoptee	.4328	.1873#	2.5069*	.0000	0.09

aThe computer option for determining step order is same as cited in Table VII-3.

#R^2 corrected for degrees of freedom = .1023.

***Significant: $p < .001$.

**Significant: $p < .01$.

*Significant: $p < .05$.

bution to the explained variance. Under this program, the
Biological Mothers' Disability Index was entered first, followed by the Socioeconomic Status Index of the family, and
then by the adoptee's age at placement; these are the three
background variables significantly correlated with the adjustment rating. The cumulative multiple correlation for the
eight demographic and background characteristics was statistically significant ($R = .43$) and accounted for 19 percent of
the variance (ten percent when corrected for degrees of freedom).

Series Two Indexes

When the attitudinal indexes created from the Series
Two interviews with the adoptive mothers were correlated
with the Overall Child Adjustment Ratings, two indexes proved
to be significantly associated with this major adjustment variable. Adoptees whose mothers scored high in their expressed
capacity to consider the adoption of Negro children were rated
as showing better adjustment ($r = -.21$). In addition, adoptees
whose mothers showed more permissive attitudes as measured
by the Strict vs. Permissive Child Rearing Index were also
rated as showing a better adjustment ($r = -.29$). Taken together, the two indexes suggest a maternal climate of permissiveness and relative openness regarding matters of race.
Interestingly, the two indexes are significantly correlated
($r = .44$).

Of perhaps equal importance is the failure of other
indexes to show significant correlations with the Overall Child
Adjustment Rating. For example, the mothers' political orientation is not significantly linked to the outcome measure
($r = .13$); neither is her degree of religiosity ($r = -.06$).

In Table X-4, I present the results of a multiple correlational analysis of the Overall Child Adjustment Ratings,
using the adoptive mothers' Series Two indexes as the independent variables. The cumulative multiple correlation is
modest (Multiple $R = .38$). The Strict vs. Permissive Child
Rearing Index makes the heaviest contribution to the variance
in the adjustment rating as the first variable entered into the
regression equation. Thereafter, the other indexes make
relatively insignificant contributions to the accounted variance,
after the contribution of the child rearing index has been controlled for. The net impression is that the social attitudes
of the adoptive mothers have thus far not been impressively
(cont. p. 298)

Table X-3

CORRELATIONS BETWEEN ADOPTIVE MOTHER SERIES TWO
ATTITUDINAL INDEXES
AND OVERALL CHILD ADJUSTMENT RATINGS

(N = 96)

	Correlation with Overall Child Adjustment Ratings
Liberal vs. Conservative Political Orientation	.13
Adoptive Mother Life-Style	-.15
Traditional vs. Modern Female Ideology	.08
Orientation to the Adoption of Handicapped Children	.06
Orientation to the Adoption of Negro Children	-.21*
Orientation to the Adoption of Children with Psychological Problems	-.04
Religiosity of Adoptive Mother	-.06
Strict vs. Permissive Child Rearing	-.29*

*Significant: $p < .05$.

Table X-4

MULTIPLE CORRELATION ANALYSIS OF OVERALL CHILD ADJUSTMENT RATINGS
USING ADOPTIVE MOTHER SERIES TWO ATTITUDINAL INDEXES AS INDEPENDENT VARIABLES

Step Number[a]	Attitudinal Index	Multiple R	Multiple R^2	F-test	ΔR^2	t-test
1	Strict vs. Permissive Child Rearing	.2871	.0824	8.4423**	.0824	2.91**
2	Traditional vs. Modern Female Ideology	.3029	.0917	4.6973**	.0093	0.98
3	Orientation to the Adoption of Negro Children	.3209	.1030	3.517*	.0113	1.07
4	Orientation to the Adoption of Handicapped Children	.3434	.1179	3.0409*	.0149	1.24
5	Orientation to the Adoption of Children with Psychological Problems	.3612	.1305	2.7011*	.0126	1.14

6	Adoptive Mothers' Life Styles	.3717	.1382	2.3783*	.0077	0.89
7	Religiosity of Adoptive Mothers	.3775	.1425	2.0893*	.0043	0.67
8	Liberal vs. Conservative Political Orientation	.3799	.1443[#]	1.8346	.0018	0.53

[a]The computer option for determining step order is same as cited in Table VII-3.

[#]R^2 corrected for degrees of freedom = .0548.

**Significant: $p < .01$.

*Significant: $p < .05$.

linked to the adjustment of the children.

Series Three Indexes

When the indexes created from the adoptive fathers'
Series Three interviews were correlated with the Overall
Child Adjustment Ratings, in only two indexes are the correlations statistically significant. Once again, the parent's
child rearing tendency looms as an influential factor, with
permissiveness being linked to better outcomes (r = -.24).
Since this is replicated for both fathers and mothers, it is
obviously a factor of some significance. The reader is reminded, however, that the child rearing orientations of the
adoptive parents were not significantly correlated with either
the Series Four or the Series Five Child Symptom Scores,
both important interim measures of child adjustment. The
question arises as to whether the Overall Child Adjustment
Rating, being a product of professional judgment, is perhaps
unduly influenced by the rater's knowledge of the child rearing proclivities of the parents. Since this is a plausible hazard, the findings should not be treated as grist for policy
statements or for determining programmatic action. Obviously, further research is required to clarify whether these
findings can be treated as firm.

The Index of Social Problem Orientation emerged as
the independent variable most highly correlated with the Overall Child Adjustment Rating (r = .34). The index was also
significantly correlated with the Series Four Child Symptom
Scores (r = .23) and the Series Five Child Symptom Scores
(r = .27). The emergence of this index as an important out-
come-linked measure comes as something of a surprise to
me. It was created on the basis of a factor analysis of the
many social attitude items derived from the Series Three interview with the fathers. Its emergence as the index most
consistently associated, in a statistically significant manner,
with the outcome measures has the quality of serendipity for
me. The reader may want to ponder about the items contained in the index. Most of them deal with the research
subjects' responses regarding the concern they feel about social problems: the threat of atomic war, discrimination a-
gainst minority groups, general economic conditions in the
country, and the problems of juvenile delinquency, old age,
and over-population. Fathers scoring high on the index are
also those who express strong interest in international affairs
and who tend to belong to a larger number of community or-
(cont. p. 302)

Table X-5

CORRELATIONS BETWEEN
ADOPTIVE FATHER SERIES THREE ATTITUDINAL INDEXES
AND OVERALL CHILD ADJUSTMENT RATING

(N = 94)

	Correlation with Overall Child Adjustment Ratings
Liberal vs. Conservative Political Orientation	.04
Religiosity of Adoptive Family	.04
Traditional Masculine Ideology	.10
Work Satisfaction	.01
Background Support for Indian Adoption	.00
Orientation to the Adoption of Handicapped Children	-.11
Strict vs. Permissive Child Rearing Orientation	-.24*
Orientation to the Adoption of Negro Children	.03
Social Problem Orientation	.34**
Lower Class-Rural Background	-.08

*Significant: $p < .05$;   **Significant: $p < .01$.

Table X-6

MULTIPLE CORRELATION ANALYSIS OF OVERALL CHILD ADJUSTMENT RATINGS
USING ADOPTIVE FATHER SERIES THREE ATTITUDINAL INDEXES AS INDEPENDENT VARIABLES

Step Number[a]	Attitudinal Index	Cumulative Multiple R	Cumulative Multiple R^2	F-test	$\triangle R^2$	t-test
1	Social Problem Orientation	.3393	.1151	12.2320***	.1151	3.50***
2	Strict vs. Permissive Child Rearing	.4204	.1768	9.9842***	.0617	2.64**
3	Orientation to the Adoption of Negro Children	.4317	.1864	7.0247***	.0096	1.04
4	Traditional Masculine Ideology	.4358	.1900	5.3351***	.0036	0.63
5	Lower Class-Rural Background	.4394	.1931	4.3073***	.0031	0.59

6	Orientation to the Adoption of Handicapped Children	.4415	.1949	3.5905**	.0018	0.45
7	Background Support for Indian Adoption	.4421	.1954	3.0534**	.0006	0.24
8	Liberal vs. Conservative Political Orientation	.4426	.1959#	2.6493**	.0005	0.23

[a]The computer option for determining step order is same as cited in Table VII-3.

#R^2 corrected for degrees of freedom = .1118.

***Significant: p < .001.

**Significant: p < .01.

ganizations than other subjects. It is of interest that the index was positively but not significantly correlated with the
Index of Liberal vs. Conservative Political Orientation (r=.18)
indicating that the orientation was not exclusively a phenomenon associated with a liberal political outlook.

What explains the association between the Index of Social Problem Orientation and the various outcome measures?[5]
I can only conjecture, and suggest that the meaning of the
finding requires further exploration in future research. It
may be a function of a confounding element in the research
interviews, not yet identified. For example, it may reflect
a desire on the part of some adoptive fathers to portray
themselves in the interviews in a manner designed to enhance
their image as being socially responsible. Or, if the substantive content of the responses can be considered to have
meaning, one can speculate that the index reflects differences
between fathers who are home-oriented and those who have
strong interests outside of the home. The linkage between
such attitudes and child adjustment may be explained in the
fact that some children have benefited from their father's
home-centeredness while others have suffered from their fathers' being distracted by outside interests. This is, of
course, quite speculative and I do not offer it with the least
sense of firmness. Rather, one can be teased by the finding
to explore aspects of parental behavior which have not been
identified before as being potentially significant.

As was the case with the indexes based upon the
mothers' responses, in Table X-5 there is again no significant correlation between the political orientations of the subjects and the Overall Child Adjustment Ratings (r=.04). In
Table X-6, there is presented a multiple correlational analysis of the child ratings using the Series Three indexes as
independent variables. Under the "best" criterion whereby
variables were chosen to enter the regression equation at
each step of the step-wise procedure on the basis of their
ability to explain variance in the dependent variable, the two
indexes significantly correlated with the adjustment rating
were entered first. Together, the Index of Social Problem
Orientation and the Index of Strict vs. Permissive Child Rearing account for about 18 percent of the variance in the Overall Child Adjustment Ratings. Six additional Series Three
index scores add only two percent of explained variance after
they are all entered into the regression equation. The cumulative multiple correlation is statistically significant but
modest in the variance accounted for (R=.44).

Table X-7

MULTIPLE CORRELATION ANALYSIS OF OVERALL CHILD ADJUSTMENT RATINGS
USING SELECTED BACKGROUND VARIABLES AS INDEPENDENT VARIABLES

Step Number	Background Variable	Cumulative Multiple R	Cumulative Multiple R^2	F-test	$\triangle R^2$	t-test
1	Age of Child at Time of Adoptive Placement	.1918	.0368	3.5914	.0368	1.90
2	Biological Mother's Disability	.2954	.0873	4.4462**	.0505	2.27*
3	Socioeconomic Status of Adoptive Family	.3662	.1341	4.7501**	.0468	2.23*
4	Age of Adoptive Mother at Time of Adoptive Placement	.3697	.1367	3.6016**	.0026	0.52

*Significant: p < .05.
**Significant: p < .01.

PARTIAL CORRELATIONS OF SELECTED ADDITIONAL VARIABLES
WITH OVERALL ADJUSTMENT SCORES CONTROLLING FOR THE EFFECTS
OF THE FOUR BACKGROUND VARIABLES

Ordinal Position of the Adoptee	-.02	Index of Adoptive Fathers' Liberal vs. Conservative Political Orientation	.00
Number of Indian Children Adopted by Family	-.07	Index of Religiosity (Series Three)	-.03
Index of Adoptive Mothers' Orientation to the Adoption of a Handicapped Child	.09	Index of Adoptive Fathers' Strict vs. Permissive Child Rearing	-.23*
Index of Adoptive Mothers' Orientation to Adopting a Child with Psychological Problems	-.07	Index of Adoptive Fathers' Social Problem Orientation	.29**
Index of Adoptive Mothers' Orientation to the Adoption of Negro Children	-.24*	Index of Lower-Class Rural Background	-.03
Index of Child's Indian Appearance (Series Two)	-.07	Index of Deprivation in Adoptive Fathers' Backgrounds	.07
Index of Religiosity (Series Two)	.04	Index of Traditional Male Ideology	.17

*Significant: $p < .05$.   **Significant: $p < .01$.

Table X-7 is an attempt to examine the relationship of indexes of social attitudes derived from Series Two and Series Three after first partialing out four demographic background variables: the age of the child at the time of placement, the Index of Biological Mothers' Disabilities, the socioeconomic status of the adoptive family, and the age of the adoptive mother at the time of placement. The multiple correlation for these four variables is .37. Despite the partialing out of these four variables, three social attitude indexes remain significantly correlated with the Overall Child Adjustment Rating. These include the Orientation to the Adoption of Negro Children from Series Two ($r = -.24$); the Index of Social Problem Orientation ($r = .29$), and the Index of Strict vs. Permissive Child Rearing ($r = -.23$), both taken from Series Three. These three indexes thus appear to be influential beyond the demograph and background factors just cited.

A Summary View of Adjustment

Table X-8 presents a correlation matrix which incorporates all indexes related to the child's adjustment. These were developed from the Series Two through Series Five interviews. The Overall Child Adjustment Rating is also included in the matrix.

It is of interest that a relatively simple index based upon two items from the Series Two interview, Index of Child Adjustment, correlates significantly with each of the three major adjustment variables developed for this study: Series Four Child Symptom Score ($r = .39$), Series Five Child Symptom Score ($r = .37$), and the Overall Child Adjustment Rating ($r = .40$). This shows that adoptive mothers are able to identify conditions relatively early in the adoptive placement experience that provide linkage to the adjustment picture secured two and three years later. The phenomenon reported here lends support to the view that there is a fairly high degree of stability in the portrait of the adopted child as it has emerged over the period covered by the annual research interviews.

The behavioral descriptions of the adoptees, while shown to be fairly stable in Chapter VIII, are not linked to the three important adjustment measures. This statement applies to the Index of Child's Friendliness-Outgoingness and the Index of Child Activity Level from Series Two, as well as the Index of Child Temperament and the Index of Quiet-

Table X-8

INTERCORRELATIONS AMONG MEASURES OF CHILD ADJUSTMENT
FROM SERIES TWO THROUGH FIVE AND OVERALL CHILD ADJUSTMENT RATING

Index	Index	A	B	C	D	E	F	G	H	I	J	K
Series Two												
A.	Child Adjustment	--										
B.	Child's Friendliness-Outgoingness	.08	--									
C.	Child Activity Level	-.39**	.00	--								
D.	Security of Adoptive Mother's Outlook	-.21*	-.03	.13	--							
Series Three												
E.	Child Adjustment	-.17	-.11	.23*	.15	--						
F.	Child Temperament	.05	.01	-.49**	.11	-.06	--					
G.	Quiet-Shy Child	-.05	-.28**	.06	-.15	-.04	-.38**	--				
H.	Security of Parental Outlook	.09	-.14	-.20	-.01	-.10	.08	-.07	--			

Series Four

I. Child Symptom Score	.39**	.20	-.21*	-.24*	-.32**	.05	-.07	.25*	--	

Series Five

J. Child Symptom Score	.37**	.01	-.20	-.13	-.20	-.01	.06	.04	.48**	--
K. Overall Child Adjustment Rating	.40**	.18	-.21	-.32**	-.14	.05	.05	-.02	.53**	.55**	--

NOTE: The N's upon which the correlations are based range from 60 when Series Five measures are involved to 96 when only Series Two measures are intercorrelated. Asterisks indicating significance are provided on the basis of the N's involved.

*Significant: $p < .05$;   **Significant: $p < .01$.

Shy Child from Series Three. Thus far, these indexes reflect differences among the adoptees that may be of interest
in their own right but do not seem to have implication for
the assessment of adoption outcomes.

As was the case with the Series Two interviews, a
Child Adjustment Score was created from responses secured
from the adoptive fathers in Series Three. The index was
significantly correlated with the Series Four Child Symptom
Score (r = -.32) and the correlation was almost significant
with respect to the Series Five Child Symptom Score (r = -.20).
However, the correlation with the Overall Child Adjustment
Rating was not significant (r = -.14) whereas, as has been described earlier, the mothers' Series Two Child Adjustment
Index was significantly correlated with the measure (r = .40).
On the basis of these findings, the adoptive mothers' evaluative assessments of their children's progress has substantially
greater predictive value than that of their husbands. On the
other hand, as seen earlier, the indexes reflecting the social
attitudes of the fathers show greater linkage to the measures
of adjustment than is true of the mothers.

The relationship between the Series Four and the Series Five Child Symptom Scores is fairly substantial (r = .48),
indicating some stability in the measures even though the
symptom lists were based upon two different types of interviews and the lists of items included in both were different
in some respects. The correlations of the symptom measures with the Overall Child Adjustment Rating were even more
impressive (.53 and .55) indicating that parental responses to
fairly concrete questions about the adjustment of their children, worded in terms they can understand, approximate fairly
closely the judgments of the professional based upon a larger
corpus of information.

In Table X-9, an attempt is made to summarize the
contribution of the various adjustment scores previously described in accounting for variance in the Overall Child Adjustment Ratings. The results of the multiple correlation
analysis show that the Series Five and the Series Four Child
Symptom Scores, when entered into the regression equation
sequentially, achieve a multiple correlation of .68 and account
for about forty percent of the variance in the ratings. Indeed, the four other measures added to the analysis account
for only a little more than three percent of additional variance. This argues for the potential use of symptom lists,
such as developed for the Series Four and Series Five inter-

Table X-9

MULTIPLE CORRELATION ANALYSIS OF OVERALL ADJUSTMENT RATING USING MEASURES
OF CHILD ADJUSTMENT DERIVED FROM
SERIES TWO THROUGH SERIES FIVE AS INDEPENDENT VARIABLES

Step Number[a]	Adjustment Measure	Cumulative Multiple R	Cumulative Multiple R^2	F-test	$\triangle R^2$	t-test
1	Series Five Child Symptom Score	.5529	.3057	41.3916***	.3057	6.43***
2	Series Four Child Symptom Score	.6306	.3976	30.6962***	.0939	3.77***
3	Series Two Index of Security of Adoptive Mothers' Outlook	.6584	.4334	23.4613***	.0358	2.41**
4	Series Three Index of Security of Parental Outlook	.6685	.4469	18.3781***	.0135	1.49
5	Series Two Index of Child Adjustment	.6787	.4607	15.3750***	.0138	1.52
6	Series Two Index of Child's Friendliness–Outgoingness	.6845	.4685[#]	13.0755***	.0078	1.15

[a]The computer option for determining step order is same as cited in Table VII-3.
*Significant: p < .05;   **Significant: p < .01;   ***Significant: p < .001.
[#]R^2 corrected for degrees of freedom = .4130.

Table X-10

MULTIPLE CORRELATION ANALYSIS OF OVERALL CHILD ADJUSTMENT RATINGS USING
SELECTED DEMOGRAPHIC CHARACTERISTICS OF THE ADOPTEES AND THEIR FAMILIES
AND SERIES TWO AND SERIES THREE ATTITUDINAL INDEXES AS THE POOL OF
INDEPENDENT VARIABLES FROM WHICH VARIABLES
CAN BE SELECTED ACCORDING TO THE "BEST" CRITERION[a]

Step Number[a]	Entering Independent Variable	Cumulative Multiple R	Cumulative Multiple R^2	F-test	ΔR^2	t-test
1	Series Three Index of Social Problem Orientation	.3393	.1151	12.2320***	.1151	3.50***
2	Series Two Index of Orientation to the adoption of Negro Children	.4325	.1871	10.6998***	.0720	2.87**
3	Series Three Index of Strict vs. Permissive Child Rearing	.4832	.2335	9.3419***	.0464	2.36*
4	Socioeconomic Status of the Adoptive Family	.5268	.2775	8.7398***	.0440	2.36*
5	Sex of Child	.5582	.3116	8.1459***	.0341	2.11*
6	Biological Mothers' Disability Index	.5819	.3386	7.5953***	.0270	1.91*
7	Series Two Index of Adoptive Mother Life Style	.5947	.3537	6.8798***	.0151	1.43
8	Series Two Index of Orientation to the Adoption of Handicapped Children	.6066	.3679	6.3308***	.0143	1.40
9	Adoptive Mothers' Age at Placement	.6169	.3805#	5.8703***	.0126	1.32

[a]The computer option of "best" criterion for determining step order is same as cited in Table VII-3.

*Significant: $p < .05$;   **Significant: $p < .01$;   ***Significant: $p < .001$.

NOTE: Variables other than those listed above which were included in the pool of independent variables available for selection by the "best" criterion included:

Demographic Variables	Series Two Attitudinal Indexes	Series Three Attitudinal Indexes
Adoptee's age at placement	Liberal vs. conservative political orientation	Liberal vs. conservative political orientation
Adoptee's age at last interview with the family	Traditional vs. modern female ideology	Religiosity of adoptive family
Ordinal position of the adoptee within the adoptive family	Orientation to the adoption of children with psychological problems	Traditional masculine ideology
No. of Indian children adopted by the family	Religiosity of adoptive mothers	Work satisfaction
	Strict vs. permissive child rearing	Background support for Indian adoption
		Orientation to the adoption of handicapped children
		Orientation to the adoption of Negro children
		Lower class–rural background

[#]R^2 corrected for degrees of freedom = .3158.

views, as a shortcut procedure which can be employed in assessing adoption outcomes. This is particularly useful when
the cost of obtaining professional judgments is prohibitive.

One final method of analyzing the Overall Child Adjustment Ratings was to develop a pool of independent variables which included all demographic and background variables, and the social attitude indexes created from the Series
Two and the Series Three interviews. Twenty-six independent variables identified in Table X-10 were thus candidates
for entrance into the multiple regression equation. The "best"
option of the computer program was utilized to select those
variables which could account for the most variance in the
child ratings at each step in the step-wise program. The
nine variables with the greatest contribution to make to the
prediction of the child adjustment ratings are set forth in the
table. The Index of Social Problem Orientation (Series Three)
was most strongly correlated; when its influence was partialed out, the next strongest variable was the Index of Orientation to the Adoption of Negro Children (Series Two), followed in turn by the Index of Strict vs. Permissive Child
Rearing (Series Three). The next three entering variables
were demographic or background in nature: the socioeconomic status of the family, the sex of the child, and the Biological Mothers' Disability Index. The cumulative multiple correlation for the ten variables was .62; they accounted for 38
percent of the variance in the ratings. Table X-10 summa-
rizes much of what has been learned in the study with respect to the Overall Child Adjustment Rating.[6]

Religious Background and Adjustment Measures

Table X-11 displays all of the measures that have
implications for understanding the adjustment of the adoptees
and their families over the course of the study. These are
analyzed according to the religious backgrounds of the 90
couples who could be assigned to one of the three major religious groupings. On none of the twelve measures presented
are there any significant differences in adjustment measures
for Jewish, Catholic and Protestant families. From this
perspective, religious identification does not appear to play
an important role in the adjustment of the children and families in the study.

Table X-11

MEANS OF SELECTED CHILD ADJUSTMENT MEASURES FROM SERIES TWO THROUGH FIVE,
OVERALL CHILD ADJUSTMENT RATINGS AND HOME RATINGS ANALYZED
BY RELIGIOUS AFFILIATIONS OF ADOPTIVE PARENTS

		Jewish (13)	Catholic (10)	Protestant (67)	F-test for significance of differences in group means
Series Two Index					
Child Adjustment	$\overline{X}$	15.44	15.36	15.30	0.011 N.S.
	S.D.	3.24	3.23	2.98	
Child's Friendliness-Outgoingness	$\overline{X}$	34.90	33.49	34.75	0.445 N.S.
	S.D.	4.41	4.31	3.99	
Child Activity Level	$\overline{X}$	11.23	10.93	11.30	0.084 N.S.
	S.D.	2.03	2.65	2.76	
Security of Adoptive Parent's Outlook	$\overline{X}$	11.29	13.70	11.89	2.585 N.S.
	S.D.	3.61	1.13	2.60	
Series Three Index					
Child Adjustment	$\overline{X}$	4.26	5.42	5.25	1.822 N.S.
	S.D.	1.75	1.88	1.78	
Child Temperament	$\overline{X}$	11.91	10.10	11.81	1.881 N.S.
	S.D.	2.66	2.80	2.65	

MEANS OF SELECTED CHILD ADJUSTMENT MEASURES FROM SERIES TWO THROUGH FIVE, OVERALL CHILD ADJUSTMENT RATINGS AND HOME RATINGS ANALYZED BY RELIGIOUS AFFILIATIONS OF ADOPTIVE PARENTS

		Jewish (13)	Catholic (10)	Protestant (67)	F-test for significance of differences in group means
Series Three Index					
Quiet-Shy Child	$\overline{X}$	4.28	5.04	4.36	0.909 N.S.
	S.D.	1.64	1.52	1.53	
Security of Parental Outlook	$\overline{X}$	11.31	12.20	11.12	0.392 N.S.
	S.D.	3.79	3.74	3.54	
Series Four					
Series Four Child Symptom Score	$\overline{X}$	6.41	6.10	6.36	1.424 N.S.
	S.D.	3.94	3.21	6.36	
Series Five					
Series Five Child Symptom Score	$\overline{X}$	20.40	19.00	17.07	0.692 N.S.
	S.D.	8.72	11.96	7.86	
Overall Child Adjustment Rating	$\overline{X}$	2.85	2.30	2.71	0.667 N.S.
	S.D.	1.28	0.66	1.21	
Home Rating	$\overline{X}$	2.08	2.10	2.28	0.394 N.S.
	S.D.	0.95	0.74	0.91	

Table X-12

MEANS OF SELECTED ADJUSTMENT MEASURES FROM SERIES TWO THROUGH SERIES FIVE, OVERALL ADJUSTMENT RATINGS AND HOME RATINGS ANALYZED BY FAMILY PATTERNS*

		American Indian Children Only (28)	American Indian and Other Adopted Children (22)	American Indian and Natural Children (40)	F-test for significance of differences in group means
Series Two Index					
Child Adjustment	$\overline{X}$	15.38	16.30	14.98	1.368 N.S.
	S.D.	3.21	3.46	2.66	
Child's Friendliness-Outgoingness	$\overline{X}$	35.89	33.33	34.56	2.630 (p= .078)
	S.D.	2.53	2.50	2.78	
Child Activity level	$\overline{X}$	11.80	9.87	11.42	3.748 (p= .028)
	S.D.	2.53	2.50	2.78	
Series Three Index					
Child Adjustment	$\overline{X}$	5.18	5.16	5.01	0.089 N.S.
	S.D.	1.61	1.70	1.99	
Child Temperament	$\overline{X}$	11.36	12.00	11.65	0.342 N.S.
	S.D.	2.87	2.79	2.68	
Quiet-Shy Child	$\overline{X}$	4.29	4.72	4.37	0.544 N.S.
	S.D.	1.46	1.28	1.69	

MEANS OF SELECTED ADJUSTMENT MEASURES FROM SERIES TWO THROUGH SERIES FIVE, OVERALL ADJUSTMENT RATINGS AND HOME RATINGS ANALYZED BY FAMILY PATTERNS*

		American Indian Children Only (28)	American Indian and Other Adopted Children (22)	American Indian and Natural Children (40)	F-test for significance of differences in group means
Series Four					
Series Four Child Symptom Score	X̄	6.52	9.42	8.55	1.561 N.S.
	S.D.	4.41	6.57	5.86	
Series Five					
Series Five Child Symptom Score	X̄	15.90	18.00	19.87	1.181 N.S.
	S.D.	7.66	7.54	9.31	
Overall Child Adjustment Rating	X̄	2.44	2.83	2.83	0.996 N.S.
	S.D.	1.16	1.03	1.26	
Home Rating	X̄	2.15	2.39	2.26	0.437 N.S.
	S.D.	0.86	1.08	0.89	

*Six families that contained both American Indian and other adopted children and natural children as well were not included in this analysis. This reduced the N from 96 to 90 for the total study group. For Series Four Child Symptom Score, N= 82, and for Series Five Child Symptom Score, N= 57.

Family Patterns

        In Chapter IV several distinct patterns were identified
with respect to the kinds of children present in the families:
(1) families which contained only American Indian children;
(2) families which contained only adopted children, but which
had both American Indian and other types of adopted children;
(3) families which contained natural children and American
Indian children; and (4) families which contained combinations
of the three types of children: natural, American Indian and
other adopted children. I was interested in determining
whether an analysis of adjustment measures by family patterns would show any significant differences. Table X-12
shows the means for the first three patterns; the fourth was
not included because only six families were of this pattern.

        On the significant adjustment measures, Series Four
and Series Five Symptom Scores, Overall Child Adjustment
Ratings, and the Home Ratings, the differences were not
significant. Only for two of the behavioral indexes from
Series Two, Child's Friendliness-Outgoingness and Child Activity Level, are there noteworthy differences, and only the
latter index goes beyond the .05 level of significance. In the
main, the distinct impression emerges that these different
patterns of family building have little implication for the adjustment of the adopted American Indian children. Parenthet-
ically, only one index from the Series Two and Series Three
interviews showed a significant difference among the three
patterns analyzed. The fathers in families which contained
only Indian children scored higher on the Index of Child's Indian Appearance, suggesting that agencies tended to place
full-blooded Indian children with childless families and less
than full-blooded children with families that had natural children of their own, or had adopted Caucasian children.

                              Notes

1. A high score on the Overall Child Adjustment Rating de-
    notes a poorer adjustment rating. See Appendix for a
    listing of major variables used in the study and their
    directionality.

2. The product-moment correlation between age of child at
    placement and his/her age at the time of the last in-
    terview with the family was .41.

3. Helen Witmer, et al., Independent Adoptions: A Follow-
    Up Study (New York: Russell Sage Foundation, 1963),
    pp. 299-303.

4. Benson Jaffee and David Fanshel, How They Fared in
    Adoption (New York: Columbia University Press,
    1970), p. 250.

5. It is also of interest that the Index of Social Problem Or-
    ientation was significantly correlated with the rating
    of the quality of the adoptive home ($r = .26$) and with
    the Series Two Index of Child Adjustment ($r = .32$).

6. While the F-tests displayed in the table are significant,
    the reader should be cautioned that since, at each
    step, the variable selected for inclusion is the one
    which gives the greatest increment to R^2, some cap-
    italization on chance factors invariably results and the
    F-tests and t-tests overstate the significance.

Chapter XI

SUMMARY AND COMMENTARY

The reader who has traveled this far has had to absorb a fairly substantial amount of information. Some of this may be well understood and integrated while other aspects of the study may still require clarification. This chapter reviews the major aspects of the study and focusses upon those research findings that appear to be of importance to those responsible for designing and administering programs for children in need of adoption. The device used here is to respond to a series of hypothetical questions that are bound to arise about the adoptions consummated through the Indian Adoption Project.

1. Having completed this study, what is your perspective on the strengths and weaknesses of the study design employed?

Response: This has been a descriptive study involving repeated interviewing of adoptive families and it is cast very much in the design of the longitudinal developmental study familiar to child development researchers. This type of design has the virtue of permitting the investigator to witness the child's development and the family's adjustment to the adoption experience from a time perspective which is concurrent with the events as they are unfolding. This is superior to the retrospective study in which parents are asked about things that have happened in the rearing of their children well in the past. A number of investigators have established that parents' recall of their own child rearing and the developmental progress of their children has many unreliable aspects. Further, the developmental study based upon repeated measures is less vulnerable than a one-shot study, which is more likely to be influenced by the particular set of circumstances prevailing at the time of the interview. Having had four or five interviews with the adoptive families, it is possible to spread the risk, so to speak, and get perspectives from a

319

variety of vantage points. Thus the description of the adjustment of the adoptees provides varying perspectives ranging from adjustment measures based upon the early second
interviews with the adoptive mothers to those coming three
and four years later.

The design employed here also has the advantage that
it has involved the adoptive fathers as key informants about
the progress of the children as well as the adoptive mothers.
The Series Three interviews were exclusively held with the
adoptive fathers and they were jointly interviewed with the
adoptive mothers in the Series One and the Series Four interviews. Thus, the portrait of the adoptive experience includes the viewpoints of both parents.

A weakness in the design, as with most other child
development studies of a longitudinal nature (such as those
reported by Kagan and Moss, Schaefer, and Bayley and Yarrow), is that there is no contrast or control group consisting
of adoptive families who have not crossed racial lines in
their adoptions or of biological families not at all involved
in the adoption phenomenon. Thus, it is not possible to
search for varying kinds of experiences in child rearing that
might characterize such types of families. It would have
been worthwhile to build in a design feature which permitted
access to other types of families, had the funds been available for this purpose. As it is, the only contrast available
is the report of my experience in comparing the attitudes of
other adoptive families with those who have adopted Indian
children, using the Borgatta Multi-Personality Inventory (see
Appendix D). Reliance has thus been placed primarily upon
internal analysis procedures, seeking to contrast subgroup-
ings within the study population with regard to variables that
have concerned me. Thus, it is possible to look at such
phenomena as differential adjustments of boys and girls who
have been adopted, the varying social attitudes and experiences in adoption of the Jewish, Catholic, and Protestant
families, the experiences of children according to their age
at the time of adoption, and the outcome of the adjustment
of the children according to the kinds of pathology revealed
by their biological mothers.

There is another element of the research design which
is quite unusual. A series of five field interviews consti-
tuted the basic procedure for gathering data. However, not
all of the families were interviewed at the same time. The
stretch of time between the interviewing of the first and last

families, for each designated interview, was considerable. For the first series, for example, there was a spread of about five and a half years between the time the first family was interviewed in 1960 and the last family in mid-1966. I finally had to cut off further field interviewing for Series Five early in 1968 because the final analysis could not be protracted any further. Thus, only 60 of the 96 families who constitute the basic study population were seen in the Series Five interviews.

The fact that the families were not uniform in the number of interviews completed required that, in analyzing the outcome of adoption, the effect of differences in age of the children at the time of the last interview be controlled for. However, the fact that the interviewing was protracted over such a long period--an aspect of the study made necessary because of the relatively slow accumulation of families who could be included in the study--means that there is an element which may be contaminating some of the data. The environments to which families had been exposed might have been different for those interviewed years apart. I do not see this as a major problem but one should be alert to its existence.

2. Has your research identified any special attributes of these adoptive parents which would make them stand out as being different from most Americans as social types?

Response: On the basis of the data displayed in this volume, the basic impression is that these adoptive parents represent a cross-section of attitudes of Americans rather than those of a homogeneous group. For example, the voting behavior of the adoptive parents in two national elections was not notably different from the national pattern. The study population seems evenly divided between those holding conservative and liberal political opinions.

While it might have been anticipated prior to the field interviews that transracial adoptions would most likely appeal to liberal-minded persons, this is contra-indicated by our data. Further, from the responses of the parents regarding their motivations for adopting an Indian child, it does not appear that political philosophical views were an important stimulus. This is not to gainsay the fact that there was one area in which the adoptive parents as a group seemed different from those parents who adopted within their own racial group.

The use of the Borgatta Multi-Personality Form with a sample of parents who adopted Caucasian children revealed that there was a significant difference in attitudes regarding the importance of civil liberties. The parents of Indian adoptees evidenced a stronger civil libertarian point of view than was true of parents who adopted white children. I do not know, however, whether this orientation developed after the Indian child entered the home or whether it predated the adoption. What is important to emphasize is that adoption agencies seeking to place children transracially need not treat the political orientation of the adoptive applicant as a particularly important determinant in parent selection. The experience in Indian adoption indicates that a broad range of social types can undertake such adoptions, and further, there seems to be very little relationship between the kinds of adjustment shown by the adopted children and the liberal versus conservative political orientations of the adoptive parents.

Since the data reveal much variability among the adoptive parents with respect to political and religious orientations, we might wonder about what these subjects might have as common attributes. Going beyond the formal data, let me identify what comes through to me from reading the responses of the subjects and the summary impressions of the case-worker-interviewers after some 435 interviews. Repeatedly, the element that has been most noteworthy in the self-descriptions of the subjects has been a certain independence, often self-referred to as a "stubborn streak," the impression of which has been reinforced by the way they talk of themselves, their spouses, their backgrounds, and their lives in their communities. While far from being nonconformists, they do have an independence of mind and do not appear easily led into accepting orientations which are basically alien to them. This may explain their ability to accept the child who, by entrance into their home, may place a distinctive stamp upon them and cause them to be viewed as different from other families. It is not that they would not care what their neighbors think, it is rather that they would not allow themselves to be guided in their actions by such considerations.

3. <u>What is your overall impression of how the adoptees and their parents have fared in the first four to five years since the children were placed in the homes?</u>

<u>Response:</u> My overall impression is that the children

are doing remarkably well as a group. From a physical
growth and development standpoint, they appear to be thriving,
and there are very few instances of serious health problems
among them. Most of the parents appear to have very little
question about the intellectual and cognitive competence of the
youngsters and are anticipating normal school experiences for
them. In the realm of personality and behavior patterns,
there are more incipient signs of difficulties than in other
areas, but this is true of only 30 percent of the children and
most of these are seen to have moderate rather than serious
problems. The children appear to be well imbedded within
their adoptive families and the relationships appear to be as
close and devoted as one would find in other kinds of adoptive
families or in biological family units.

    The major adjustment measure, a rating of the child's
overall adjustment, suggests that more than 50 percent of the
children are performing extremely well in all spheres of life
and another 25 percent are performing in a way that makes
the outlook for their future adjustment very hopeful. Only
ten percent of the children were showing problems which made
their outlook guarded and only one child was seen as performing at such a low level that the future looked very dim.
This compares well with a study of children who were adopted
when older. On two measures of outcome, Kadushin[1] found
that 82 to 87 percent of the children showed what he considered a successful outcome. Further, the outcome data reported for the Indian adoptions closely approximates what Kadushin found in summarizing the results of a large number of
adoption studies involving 2,236 adoptions. He found that 74
percent of the adoptions were unequivocally successful and another 11 percent were fairly successful. Only 16 percent
were unsatisfactory or poor or low compared to the 11 percent I have found in studying the Indian adoptions.

    One caveat is in order, however. My study has fol-
lowed the children while they are still relatively young and
just about to embark upon their school careers. Many of the
studies cited by Kadushin were of older children. It is to be
expected that as our Indian adoptees get older, the prevalence
of problems will increase. I make this assumption based upon other longitudinal studies which indicate increase in problematic behavior with the passage of years. Nevertheless,
this interim report can be essentially positive. Those who
have promulgated these placements can be well assured that
the overall picture for the children looks quite good.

4. How would you assess your approach to measuring the outcome of the adoptive experience?

Response: It should be recognized that the basic source of data for developing adjustment measures was the interviews with the parents. It is important to note that none of the adjustment measures reported upon involves a direct examination of the child. The outcome measures are thus subject to potential error in that some parents may not have been able to be fully candid with the interviewers. Within the confines of this restriction, however, I have attempted to be as resourceful as possible in developing adjustment measures from several different perspectives. For example, in each of the interviews from the second to the last, items dealing with the adjustment of the child have been included and were later used in the creation of indexes. Thus, adjustment measures have been derived from the adoptive fathers and the adoptive mothers independently as well as from their joint reports (Series Four).

Two approaches to summarizing the adjustment of the children were used: (1) a summation procedure by which symptoms were arbitrarily weighted with respect to their importance and summated for both the Series Four and the Series Five interviews; and (2) a rating procedure in which a professional judgment was used to categorize the overall adjustment of the adoptee by the time of the last interview with the family. The reliability of the professional judgment appears quite high for the Overall Child Adjustment Rating ($r = .82$) although more modest reliabilities were reported for five individual domains subsumed under the overall adjustment. The summated symptom picture developed for Series Four correlated with the Overall Child Adjustment Rating fairly strongly ($r = .53$) and a similar association was found between the Series Five Child Symptom Score and the summary measure ($r = .55$). An index created from the Series Two interviews with the adoptive mothers, called the Index of Child Adjustment, correlated significantly with the Series Four and the Series Five summated scores and the Overall Child Adjustment Rating (the correlations were $.39$, $.37$ and $.40$ respectively). Thus the various measures developed in the study, despite their lack of rigorous definition, appear to be consistent in measuring an overall construct of adjustment. Exclusive of studies which have involved direct assessment of children, these measures appear to be as viable as those that have been used in other adoption studies.

5. How well are you able to predict the adjustment
of the adoptees during the fourth and fifth year of their living
experience with their adoptive families?

Response: The three major outcome variables utilized
in this study are: Series Four Child Symptom Scores, Series
Five Child Symptom Scores and the Overall Child Adjustment
Rating. Using a set of demographic variables which included
the socioeconomic status of the adoptive families, the age of
the adoptive father and mother, the age of the child at placement, the sex of the child, the ordinal position of the adoptee,
the number of Indian children adopted by the family, and the
biological mothers' disability index, I found a multiple correlation of .39 when I analyzed the Series Four Child Symptom Scores and a multiple correlation of .29 when analyzing
the Series Five Child Symptom Scores. Thus, demographic
factors account for only a very modest amount of variance in
the outcome. This is quite similar to the findings on the adjustment of adopted children whose parents were interviewed
twenty to thirty years after their adoption in New York City,
where a series of demographic variables accounted for less
than 20 percent of the explained variance in outcome.[2]

When the attitudinal indexes created from the responses of the adoptive mothers during the Series Two interviews were used as independent variables in a multiple correlation analysis of the Series Four Child Symptom Scores,
the cumulative multiple correlation was .34 with an unimpres-
sive amount of variance in outcome explained by these indexes. A very similar finding was established when these
same index scores were used in a multiple correlation analysis of the Series Five Child Symptom Scores. In similar
fashion, the adoptive fathers Series Three index scores cu-
mulatively produced a multiple correlation of .34 when used
as independent variables in the multiple correlation analysis
of Series Four Child Symptom Scores. Thus, only about 12
percent of the uncorrected variance in outcome was accounted
for. However, these same index scores did show greater
predictive capacity with respect to the Series Five Child
Symptom Scores, producing a multiple correlation of .51 with
about 26 percent of the uncorrected variance accounted for.
Thus, I find some superiority in predictive capacity using the
fathers' attitudes as the independent variables in contrast to
the mothers'.

When I attempted to analyze the Overall Adjustment
Ratings assigned the children by using the interim measures

of adjustment from Series Two through Five, I found relatively superior predictive capacity, with a multiple correlation of
.68 with 47 percent of the variance in this single outcome
measure accounted for.   I am suggesting that a rather simple
procedure of counting symptoms can be very useful as predictive measures of overall adjustment since the Series Five
Child Symptom Score and the Series Four Child Symptom
Score together accounted for 40 percent of the variance in
the Overall Adjustment Rating.   Compared to other studies
of this type, this is a quite good level of predictive capacity.

When a pool was created of all of the demographic
variables, the Series Two adoptive mother attitude indexes,
and the Series Three adoptive father attitude indexes which
could be entered as independent variables in a multiple correlation of the Overall Adjustment Rating, three attitude indexes accounted for the most variance: the Series Three Index of Social Problem Orientation, the Series Two Index of
the Orientation of the Adoptive Mothers to the Adoption of
Negro Children, and the Series Three Index of Strict versus
Permissive Child Rearing.   These indexes accounted for almost 24 percent of the variance in the Overall Adjustment
Rating.   When the socioeconomic status of the adoptive family, the sex of the child, and the biological mother's disability index were also entered into the regression equation, the
cumulative multiple r achieved was .58 with about 34 percent
of the variance explained.   Thus, I have demonstrated the sa-
liency of several attitudinal domains as well as a number of
the demographic factors in the family's situation in understanding outcome measures.   I have speculated about the
meaning of the attitudinal indexes while making quite clear
that they provide only leads to understanding the adjustment
of the children and are by no means conclusive indicators
which can serve as a guide to agencies in the selection of
couples for transracial adoption.

The sifting for predictive indicators of adjustment has
created only a modest yield and such findings are in need of
replication in other studies before they can be employed--in
anything but a very tentative way--in developing screening
procedures for adoption agencies.   I emerge from the research experience very much aware that the task of predicting the outcome of a human experience such as adoption involves many elusive and unmeasurable elements at this stage
of our research competence.   I have the strong conviction
that human beings are relatively unpredictable and much of
adoption practice will continue to be based upon quite sub-

jective judgments on the part of practitioners. Yet I must
say that I obviously do not place too much credence in these
judgments, and see them as highly fallible. Research studies
such as this can only help to sensitize practitioners to important leads in assessing the capacity of couples to undertake transracial adoptions. I do not say this with any sense
of disappointment since my perspective in undertaking this
study was not one which anticipated greater predictability than
the level I have found.

6. What does the study tell us about the relationship
between socioeconomic status and the nature of the adoptive
experience covered by this volume?

Response: In the well known study of independent
adoptions in Florida, Witmer et al.[3] showed small but statistically significant associations between indicators of socioeconomic status and the ratings of the homes and some of
the individual measurements of the children's performance in
school. The differences that were found slightly favored the
children from homes of higher social status as indicated by
the adoptive father's education and occupation. The correlations ranged from .12 to .16. In the follow-up study of
adults who were adopted twenty to thirty years earlier through
four New York agencies, Jaffee and Fanshel[4] found that children raised in higher social class families tended to encounter more personality problems over the years than did their
lower social class counterparts, and study interviewers were
rather clearly predisposed to assign negative rather than positive ratings to higher status families. On a number of other
outcome measures, however, the life adjustment of the adoptee was only weakly related to the socioeconomic status of
the adoptive families.

In my own study of Indian adoptions, I do find among
the subject families a broad range from adoptive parents with
very high status and well paid occupations to fathers who are
blue collar workers, some of them relatively low paid factory
workers. With respect to the Series Four Child Symptom
Scores, the association between socioeconomic status and frequency of symptoms was insignificant ($r = .04$). The picture
does not change much when we look at the Series Five Child
Symptom Scores, although there is some tendency for upper
status families to report more symptoms for their children
($r = .17$). However, when we consider the most important
outcome measure, the Overall Child Adjustment Rating, we
find a significant correlation between the socioeconomic sta-

tus of the adoptive families and the rating of child adjustment.   The high status families had children who were showing poorer adjustment (r = .22).

As a possible source of explanation of this finding, I
can point to the fact that socioeconomic status was linked in
statistically significant fashion to many of my important social attitudinal indexes created from the Series Two and the
Series Three interviews.   For example, there were significant associations between socioeconomic status and the political orientation of the adoptive mothers and fathers, with the
adoptive mothers' traditional versus modern female ideolog-
ical orientation, with the readiness of adoptive mothers and
adoptive fathers to consider the adoption of Negro children,
with the social problem orientation of the adoptive fathers,
with the orientation to adopt children with psychological problems, and with religiosity.

Even when the three attitudinal indexes that were most
closely linked to outcome variables (Index of Social Problem
Orientation, Index of Adoptive Mothers' Orientation to the
Adoption of Negro Children, and Index of Adoptive Fathers'
Strict versus Permissive Child Rearing Orientation) were partialed out, however, there was a significant correlation between socioeconomic status and the Overall Child Adjustment
Rating.   This would indicate that a number of the other attitudinal measures were continuing to play a role in linking socioeconomic status and adjustment.   While no clear delinea-
tion has been made as to how social class status is manifested in specific parental behaviors, I have made a case for
indicating that social class seems to be a rather important
variable in shaping life styles of the adoptive families and I
have demonstrated that class does indeed relate to very different orientations to adoption and to life style.   This is not
surprising in view of the considerable research literature
which links socioeconomic status to a variety of life style orientations.

What is perhaps somewhat surprising is the repetition
of the finding of Jaffee and Fanshel that high socioeconomic
status is linked to more problematic behavior.   This tends to
contradict epidemiological studies which have linked low socioeconomic status with a high frequency of mental disorders. A
summary review of the research literature on this issue by
Dohrenwend and Dohrenwend[5] shows a quite strong linkage in
a variety of studies between socioeconomic status and frequency of symptoms of mental disorder.   Why we should find the

reverse tendency in adoptive families is a matter that requires further investigation. For one thing, the trend among studies is not yet so clearly delineated that we can point to this phenomenon as well established. More studies will have to be undertaken to see whether the tendency noted here will be replicated as a firm finding. Further, we will need to delineate those aspects of life style related to social class which would appear to create more stress for adopted children in upper status families. We would also need to investigate whether the meaning of adoption takes on a different coloration for families according to socioeconomic status. All of this suggests that, rather than the topic being closed out by definitive findings, it is only at the stage where intriguing questions are being raised and where further research would be very useful.

7. How do you view your findings with respect to the relative adjustment of the boys versus the girls in your study population of Indian adoptees?

Response: In the Jaffee and Fanshel retrospective study,[6] it appeared that the sex of the adoptive subjects was only moderately related to their life adjustment over the years. In general, boys fared less well than did girls, particularly in the area of education. The girls also showed some tendency, though not a strong one, to be freer of personality problems over the years. Kadushin,[7] on the other hand, found that sex was not related to his measures of outcome when he studied children who were adopted when older. A contrasting finding is reported by Witmer et al.[8] in their Florida study. They noted that girls were considerably less likely than boys to be regarded as maladjusted and that this is in line with the experience of child guidance clinics and with numerous studies of children's adjustment.

In the present study the findings tend to be somewhat mixed but I emerge with the overall impression that sex is not a major variable in discriminating between those who have shown problems and those who have not. Rather, I point to the fact that the boys and the girls are significantly different on indexes that one would expect would show sex-related differentiation. Thus, the Series Two Index of the Child's Friendliness-Outgoingness shows the boys to be more outgoing. Similarly, on the Series Three index called Child Temperament and the index called Quiet-Shy Child, the boys are obviously much more on the rambunctious, active side.

The interviews have confirmed that, by and large, the adoptive families find the male adoptees quite active children. I have quite clear-cut evidence, however, that the boys and girls do not differ very markedly with respect to the symptom pictures that they show, in that the Series Four Child Symptom Scores and the Series Five Child Symptom Scores show the children to be relatively identical.

However, in terms of the Overall Child Adjustment Rating, there was some tendency to rate the adjustment of the boys as somewhat more problematic, with the significance of the difference almost achieving the standard .05 level (p= .061). Whether this is a transient phenomenon picked up by the rater, which is related to problems parents have in handling rambunctious boys, is not known. It is a lead which might be investigated further in studies of adopted children. At this point, I can only point to the fact that the distinction between the boys' adjustment and the girls' is not very strong, although the girls tend to be somewhat more positively evaluated on one major outcome variable in the study.

8. <u>What is the role of the age of the child as a variable in accounting for the adjustment of the adoptees?</u>

<u>Response</u>: In all child development studies, the age variable is a quite important one. In this study, the reader needs to be aware of the influence of age in several respects. First, a very important variable is the age of the child at the time he was placed in the adoptive home. A second variable is the age of the child at the time of each of the five series of interviews. Finally, a peculiarity of the study, not all of the families completed the fifth series and therefore one needs to be aware of the influence of the age of the child at the time of the last interview with the family. In this connection, a child may be older because the family was interviewed on a fifth occasion or he may be older because he was placed at a later age.

Age at adoptive placement has been of interest to a number of investigators concerned with the adjustment of adopted children. This issue has also concerned those responsible for the administration of adoption services. On the assumption that early adoptions are better for the children involved, agencies throughout the United States have, over the past decade, emphasized the necessity for early placement of children, even to the point of circumventing some of

the traditional procedures that had been built into agency programs. As Reid has noted:

> John Bowlby's brilliant summarization of this re-
> search has had a deep influence upon agencies. As
> conviction developed of the paramount need to the
> child for an early and sustained one-to-one mother-
> ing relationship, other considerations were placed
> in perspective. For example, were a psychological
> test developed tomorrow that could predict when
> the infant was eight months of age what his later
> development would be with accuracy, it is doubtful
> that any good agency would use the test. The reason
> is that we realize how much more important early
> mothering is, and therefore, early placement. Out
> of this conviction the principles of agencies are
> changing rapidly and all progressive agencies in
> the country are doing their utmost to lower the av-
> erage age of placement to its irreducible minimum.
> That minimum still has very different meanings, as
> has been revealed by recent studies. For some
> agencies, it means an average of three weeks of
> age. For others, it is still unfortunately four
> months, but a time will come very soon in which,
> except under unusual circumstances, an agency that
> has not managed to place its children well before
> three months of age will be considered guilty of
> poor practice. [9]

Witmer, et al[10] have reported that adoption outcomes
appear slightly more favorable for children who were placed
early than for the others. They indicate that even when al-
lowance was made for such secondary factors as could be
controlled, a slight but statistically significant relationship
existed between the age at which the child was placed and the
way his adoption seemed to be working out some ten years
later. They caution, however, that there is a vast difference
"between a statistically significant relationship and an invar-
iable or overriding relationship." They further observe,
"the slight and still uncertain association between age at
placement and adoption outcome, for example, may mean
that--other things being equal--the outcome prospects are
slightly more promising if the child is placed before he is
a month old. The fact that the association is relatively low,
however, also means that other important factors, favorable
or unfavorable, are operating simultaneously and could either
reinforce or nullify the effect of this one."

Jaffee and Fanshel, in their follow-up study, found relatively weak relationships between age at adoption and outcome. However, a significant relationship was found between the child's adjustment with respect to his social relations and his age at adoption. The finding was surprising in that it appeared that those children who were adopted older fared better than those who had adopted earlier. This was certainly contrary to the theory by which agencies were operating. However, further analysis revealed that the initial finding could be attributed to the influence of placement through two of the four agencies. Once this influence had been taken into account, the finding was modified and the relationship between age at placement and later adjustment in the sphere of social relationships was weaker.

In the present study I found that age at adoptive placement was significantly correlated with the Series Four Child Symptom Scores (r = .22). That is, the older the adoptee at the time of placement, the more apt was the parent to enumerate symptoms of maladjustment in the Series Four interviews. However, this did not prove to be the case when I analyzed the Series Five Child Symptom Scores, there being a very weak association between age at placement and the symptom picture. However, when I examined the Overall Child Adjustment Rating, the most important outcome measure, a significant association was found between the age variable and the adjustment rating. Here again, I observed that the older the child at the time of placement, the more apt he was to be rated as showing a problematic adjustment. Since the global rating was based upon all information gathered in the series of interviews, it could have been influenced by the artifactual element of whether or not there had been a fifth interview with the parents. However, when this matter was controlled for, this did not serve to modify the finding appreciably. I thus have the overall impression that age is implicated in the adjustment of the adoptees and our data tends to support, albeit in a modest manner, the principle prevailing among adoption agencies that early placements are generally in the best interest of the child.

I have found one potential source of explanation of the difficulties of children who are adopted at a later age: there is a significant correlation between the age at which the adoptees were placed and the index I created to summate the problems shown by the biological mother (r = .22). I have speculated that children who have been placed when older have had more opportunity to encounter deprivations at the hands of sorely troubled and severely maladjusted mothers. In other words, the biological mothers who are beset with the most pernicious problems appear to be those who tended to be less involved in planned surrendering of the children for adoption. More often than not, it was their problematic behavior toward the child that brought into play the legal procedures which resulted in the placement of the child. Thus, the later age of placement is a variable that is also potentially linked to greater exposure to pathological handling on the part of biological parents.

I have also observed that the adoptive mothers of children who were placed at an older age were significantly higher in their manifestations of strictness in which rearing than was true of the adoptive parents who adopted younger children ($r = -.36$). This child rearing index was one of the three most significant variables accounting for variance in the Overall Adjustment Score ($r = -.29$). In this context, when the parents' child rearing orientation and other attitudinal measures are partialed out, the association between age at adoptive placement and overall adjustment gets reduced to the point where the partial correlation is no longer significant.

All in all, I would strongly stress the importance of accounting for the age variable in adoption studies. It is a complex variable and sometimes investigators use analytic approaches which take a simplified view of the causal relationships involved, i.e., they fail to take into account the influence of age and its interaction with other variables.

9. The linkage found between child adjustment measures and the summation of the biological mothers' problems is intriguing. What can be made of it?

Response: This is indeed an interesting finding, although not so clear-cut that one could be sure of one's ground in making assertions about its implications. For one thing, the correlation between the Index of Biological Mothers' Disability and the Series Four and Series Five Child Symptom Scores does not achieve significance. The correlation with the Child Overall Adjustment Rating, however, does achieve statistical significance ($r = .26$). This indicates that the more troubled the biological mother, the more apt is the child to show a less favorable adjustment even after four or five years in the adoptive home.   •

My evaluation of the meaning of this finding has to be

somewhat guarded because I lack a good appraisal of the experience of the adoptees prior to their placements in the adoptive homes. As has been indicated, the basic sources of information about the adoptees' experience were the referral
letters sent to the Indian Adoption Project, and these often
lacked the kind of systematic information required to develop
a good index of child deprivation. Therefore, I can only suggest that the linkage between the biological mothers' problems
and the adoptees' problems suggests that the adoptee was implicated in and exposed to the problems of the biological mother, particularly in her direct handling of him.

The finding might be viewed in the context of Kadushin's
finding that the outcome of the placement of older children
was related to the number of placements experienced.[11] He
also found that the number of pathologies manifested by the
child at the time of placement was related to outcome. In the
absence of any hard data in my own study, I cannot make
more specific the potential importance of the nature of the
mothers' pathology as it affects the course of the adopted
childs' life. Larger philosophical issues are also involved.
While I tend to be environmentalist in my approach to viewing children's adjustment, some investigators would indicate
that the explanation of the linkage between problems shown by
the adoptees and the problems shown by their biological parents might reside in heredity. This is a provocative issue
which would demand further investigation.

10. What is the significance of the religious affiliations of the adoptive parents with respect to the adjustment
of the adoptees?

Response: There are two aspects of this issue: the
religious affiliation of the adoptive parents and their religiosity. From the perspective of religious affiliation, Jewish and
Catholic families were only modestly represented in the study.
However, they are sufficiently represented to draw some perspective on differences among the three groups.

On none of the adjustment measures developed from
Series Two through Series Five have I found any significant
differences among adoptees when compared on the basis of
the religious affiliations of the adoptive parents. The same
holds true for the Overall Child Adjustment Rating and for
the rating of the homes developed after this series of interviews was completed. This contrasts with the finding of Jaf-

fee and Fanshel which showed that Jewish children showed more problematic adjustments than those placed by any of the three other agencies in the study. They showed a greater tendency to have encountered personality problems over the years, to have experienced difficulties in their past and current heterosexual relationships, and to have met with negative experiences in their social relationships. On the other hand, in the same study, the children placed by the Catholic agency showed a strong positive adjustment in the area of social relationships which was decidedly greater than children placed by the other three agencies. This contrasts with the finding of Kadushin[12] that religion is not an important correlate of outcome.

Aside from the matter of outcome, however, there were distinctive differences among the families adopting Indian children based upon religious affiliation. The Jewish families tend to be well differentiated from the Catholic and Protestant families on a number of significant variables. Thus, they are significantly higher in socioeconomic status. They also tended to be more liberal in their political views and less religious. This is a finding which closely approximates other findings reported in the social science literature. Jewish adoptive mothers also indicated a greater readiness to consider the adoption of Negro children, while Jewish adoptive fathers indicated a significantly stronger social problem orientation. The former index was correlated with good adjustment on the part of the adopted children while the latter was correlated with evidence of maladjustment. The implications of the differences among the adoptive families, based on religion, have not emerged as of great significance, but I would not rule out the fact that they may take on importance as the adoptees get older.

The religiosity of the adoptive families was measured on the basis of the Series Two interviews with the adoptive mothers and the Series Three interviews with the adoptive fathers. The association between the two measures was quite firm ($r = -.53$). There was no significant association between the religiosity score developed from the adoptive mother interview and the Series Four Child Symptom Score. The same held true for the religiosity score derived from the adoptive father interview. However, there was a significant relationship between both religiosity measures and the Series Five Child Symptom Scores, with the more religious families showing children with fewer symptoms. The correlation between the mothers' religiosity score and the Series Five Child

Symptom Score was .21; the correlation between the fathers'
religiosity score and the same outcome measure was .25.
However, when I examined the relationship between religiosity
and the major outcome variable, Overall Child Adjustment
Rating, I found almost no association between the religiosity
measure and the child's adjustment. Except for the Series
Five Child Symptom Score, I have not demonstrated a significant link between religiosity and adjustment of children.

> **11.** What have you learned about the implications of
> the adoptive parents' strictness or permissiveness in their
> child rearing and the kind of adjustment scores achieved by
> the adoptees?

Response: Most research studies in adoption have not
looked in any depth at the child rearing practices of adoptive
families. In the research reported here, there is also only
a limited investigation of the phenomenon. Indexes characterizing the degree of permissiveness versus strictness in
the adoptive mothers' and fathers' orientations were created.
The internal reliability of the measures achieved a fairly
high standard. When the association between these measures
and the outcome measures were analyzed, I found almost no
association between them and the Series Four Child Symptom
Scores. A similar lack of significant association between
child rearing practices and the Series Five Child Symptom
Scores was established. However, there was a significant
association between the Mothers' Strict versus Permissive
Child Rearing Index and the Overall Child Adjustment Rating
($r = -.29$). This indicated that permissive orientations were
associated with a better adjustment rating for the adoptees.

This variable proved to be one of the three attitudinal
variables (together with the adoptive fathers' Social Problem
Orientation Index and the adoptive mothers' Orientation to the
Adoption of Negro Children) which best predicted the Overall
Adjustment Rating. I also found a significant association between the adoptive fathers' child rearing orientation and the
outcome measure. This tends to reinforce the belief that
child rearing orientations are important to monitor.

Yet, I must note the failure to show linkage to the
symptom scores. Obviously, the phenomenon of child rearing is more complex than the measures I have created can
illuminate. I can only suggest that the finding of the association between the adoptive parents' permissiveness and the

major outcome variable provides a lead which should encourage more investigation of child rearing tendencies among
adoptive families.

12.   How have the adoptive parents dealt with the In-
dianness of their children?

Response: While most of the parents did not specifically seek out an Indian child for adoption--only one in five
reported doing so--the overall impression is that they not only became quite comfortable with the Indian characteristics
of their children, but for most of the parents this took on a
quite positive quality.   Many adoptive parents reported curiosity on the part of others about where their children had
come from, and almost half reported being stared at when
they went out with their children, but the overall reaction to
this was quite good-natured.   Only an occasional family found
this to be a source of annoyance or concern.

Further, many of the families began to take on a
strong, positive interest in the Indian backgrounds of their
children and planned to encourage their children's interest
in their own backgrounds.   While some families tended to
play down this aspect, they were a distinct minority.   Some
parents went so far as to indicate that they hoped the children would return to the reservations some day and make a
contribution to their people; others hoped to make trips with
the children so that they might someday get related to the
tribes from which they came.   However, because of the young
age of the children, it is still too early to determine how the
children have integrated the information that they are of a
different racial background from their parents.   During the
series of five interviews, there was little evidence that the
children felt uncomfortable about being physically different,
at least as perceived by their adoptive parents.

13.   What is the outlook of the parents with respect
to the kind of future they see for their Indian children?

Response: In the main, the adoptive parents look to
the future with some hope and guarded optimism that their
children will be well integrated within American society, without suffering to any major extent from racist treatment by the
whites with whom they will have contact.   A fairly significant
number are quite realistic that there may be some rough pe-

riods ahead for their children, and they have particularly
identified the late adolescent and young adult years, when
dating and courtship will raise question about the degree to
which their children will be fully accepted by other children
and their families. Some are less than sanguine in their an-
ticipation that their children are bound to experience some
rejection around boy-girl relationships, and plan to protect
them by giving them a strong sense of their own backgrounds
and their own inner worth. An almost equal sized group of
adoptive parents tend to be more optimistic and do not anticipate any appreciable problems in this area. By and large,
they tend to be the parents of the children who are not full-
blooded and hence less strikingly Indian in their appearance.
It does seem critical to follow these families in these later
periods of childhood to determine whether the low-keyed expressions of anxiety increase in intensity over the years.

14. Were there any special disabilities revealed about
the children by the adoptive parents which might stand out as
a characteristic of these particular kinds of adoptions?

Response: In the main, the symptoms revealed by the
children in the Series Four and Series Five interviews do not
seem excessive, although there are categories of disability
which loom somewhat large. Thus, in the Series Four interviews, there were 28 out of 88 children who were said to
have minor eating problems and 22 with relatively mild speech
impairment. There were 40 children who suffered from colds
and, of these, 22 were reported to have chronic symptoms of
colds. There were also some 25 children who suffered allergies or skin disorders and 18 who suffered respiratory
difficulties.

What comes across as perhaps the symptoms most
related to past deprivation are such things as moodiness of
children, the tendency to be under a strain, and sensitivity.
Almost two out of three of the children were reported to be
sometimes or often quite sensitive to the scoldings of the
parents. While the overall character of the children's adjustment is very much on the positive side, respondents often mentioned occasions on which the children would be quite
upset by the expression of parental anger or concerned that
they displeased their parents in some way.

15. Do you feel that the adoption of Indian children

should be continued and perhaps even expanded?

      Response: The question has many policy implications
to which my research was not addressed. I would like,
therefore, to make clear those aspects where I have some
research basis for responding. However, having been im-
mersed in the phenomenon of Indian adoption for some time,
I would also like to offer my impressions about other matters even though this lays me open to the charge of "gener-
alizing beyond the data." These subjective comments are
presented to provoke thought and discussion rather than as
having the authority of "findings."

      First, the results of my research thus far support the
view that the placement of Indian children in white homes appears to represent a low level of risk for the children with
respect to safeguarding their physical and emotional well-being.
The repeated interviews with the adoptive parents left the interviewers with the strong impression that the children were,
by and large, very secure and obviously feeling loved and
wanted in their adoptive homes. Even if the adjustment of
the children proves to be somewhat more problematic as they
get older--particularly during their adolescence when the factor of racial difference may loom larger--the overall prospect for their futures can be termed as "guardedly optimistic." When one contrasts the relative security of their lives
with the horrendous growing up experiences endured by their
mothers--well documented in the summaries Arnold Lyslo received from agencies referring the children--one has to take
the position that adoption has saved many of these children
from lives of utter ruination. In this sense, the research
offers supporting evidence for the continuation and expansion
of these adoptions.

      My research also supports the view that these adop-
tions are quite viable from the perspective of the adoptive
parents themselves. Most of them were highly positive and
even delighted with their adopted children. For them the
adoptions had turned out to be a genuine boon. On the basis
of this benign report and the fact that there has been a growing interest in the adoption of Indian children in the United
States, one could support the expansion of such adoptions.
The fact that there are now apparently fewer white children
available for adoption--due to the availability of the contra-
ceptive pill, the legalization of abortion in some states, and
the decrease in cultural pressure upon unmarried mothers to
give up their babies--makes the availability of Indian children

of even greater interest to prospective adoptive couples.

There is another matter which is not usually mentioned in evaluating adoptions.   From the perspective of society at large, the adoption of children who are destined to
spend all of their childhood years in foster care or in Indian
boarding schools provides a substantial financial saving.   For
example, it has recently been estimated in New York City
that the adoption of an infant who would otherwise stay in
foster care for eighteen years, saves the public close to
$122,500 in payments to agencies offering foster care ser-
vices.[13]   While foster care costs in the areas from which
the Indian children come are less than in New York City, the
savings per child would still come close to $100,000.   For
a group the size of our study population, the savings would
be approximately ten million dollars over an eighteen-year
period.   If one were to apply the approach of cost-benefit
analysis to the adoption phenomenon, such data would be seen
as highly significant.

Given that the children appear to be doing well in their
adoptive homes, that the parents are highly satisfied with
what they have consummated, that the appeal of Indian adoptions to couples applying to agencies is increasing, and that
considerable monies are saved, is there any doubt that the
transracial adoption of Indian children ought be encouraged?
The answer is yes--there is a doubt.

From the perspective of the American Indians--and
not society at large--the promotion of adoption of their children raises very negative emotions.   For example, a fund-
raising letter on behalf of the American Indian Fund several
years ago made the following complaint:

> As a supporter of the American Fund you know the
> sordid history of our nation's treatment of the In-
> dian people.   Incredible as it seems, still another
> squalid chapter has now been added to this sorry
> chronicle.
>
> Irresponsible officials are judging the homes of
> many Indians unfit--by white middle class stand-
> ards--and their young ones are sent off to non-
> Indian foster homes and orphanages ... despite
> protests by Indian leaders.
>
> On some reservations as many as 25 percent of

all children are taken from their parents--50 times
the national rate! And in North and South Dakota
half the children in foster homes are Indians,
though Indians constitute only 3 percent of the Da-
kotas' population .... [14]

Referring to the efforts of Indians to build family life
in the face of the terrible social conditions with which they
are afflicted, Steiner has commented upon what he considers
to be the insidious efforts of those promoting the adoption of
Indian children:

> However, the Bureau of Indian Affairs, together
> with the Child Welfare League of America, re-
> solved the problem of the weakened kinship families
> differently. Those who could no longer care for
> the children of their kin were helped by having
> their children offered to non-Indians to adopt. In
> nine years, 325 of these Indian children were adopt-
> ed.

> Seeing the newspaper advertisement that pleaded,
> 'Adopt an Indian Child,' Deloria, Jr., was remind-
> ed, he said, of the Christmas appeals of the Hu-
> mane Society 'offering puppies for adoption.' The
> young Sioux shook his head sadly. 'It may be hu-
> mane, but it isn't human.'[15]

Obviously, whether Indian children are to be placed
in any significant numbers in white homes in the future will
depend on the attitudes of the Indian tribal organizations.
While approval was given by them for a limited number of
such adoptions when the Indian Adoption Project was launched,
this took place over ten years ago. The climate for transracial adoption has changed in that minority groups tend to
see this as the ultimate indignity that has been inflicted upon
them.

It seems clear that the fate of most Indian children is
tied to the struggle of Indian people in the United States for
survival and social justice. Their ultimate salvation rests
upon the success of that struggle. Whether adoption by white
parents of the children who are in the most extreme jeopardy
in the current period--such as the subjects of our study--can
be tolerated by Indian organizations is a moot question. It
is my belief that only the Indian people have the right to determine whether their children can be placed in white homes.

Reading a report such as this one, Indian leaders may decide that some children may have to be saved through adoption even though the symbolic significance of such placements
is painful for a proud people to bear. On the other hand,
even with the benign outcomes reported here, it may be that
Indian leaders would rather see their children share the fate
of their fellow Indians than lose them in the white world. It
is for the Indian people to decide.

Notes

1. Alfred Kadushin, Adopting Older Children (New York:
    Columbia University Press, 1970), p. 70.

2. Benson Jaffee and David Fanshel, How They Fared in
    Adoption (New York: Columbia University Press,
    1970), pp. 297-299.

3. Helen Witmer, et al., Independent Adoptions: A Follow-
    Up Study (New York: Russell Sage Foundation, 1963),
    pp. 299-303.

4. Jaffee and Fanshel, How They Fared in Adoption, op.
    cit., p. 250.

5. Bruce P. Dohrenwend and Barbara Snell Dohrenwend,
    Social Status and Psychological Disorder (New York:
    Wiley-Interscience, 1969), pp. 9-31.

6. Jaffee and Fanshel, How They Fared in Adoption, op.
    cit., pp. 250-251.

7. Kadushin, Adopting Older Children, op. cit., p. 208.

8. Witmer, et al., Independent Adoptions: A Follow-Up
    Study, op. cit., pp. 280-281.

9. Joseph H. Reid, "Principles, Values and Assumptions
    Underlying Adoption Practice," Social Work, Vol. 2,
    No. 1 (January 1957), pp. 26-27.

10. Witmer, et al., Independent Adoptions: A Follow-Up
    Study, op. cit., p. 344.

11. Kadushin, Adopting Older Children, op. cit., p. 208.

12. Kadushin, <u>Ibid.</u>, p. 209.

13. David Fanshel and Eugene B. Shinn, <u>Dollars and Sense</u>
    <u>in the Foster Care of Children</u>, Child Welfare League
    of America (in press).

14. Undated solicitation letter from the American Indian
    Fund of the Association on American Indian Affairs,
    Inc., New York, N.Y.

15. Stan Steiner, <u>The New Indians</u> (New York: Delta Book,
    Dell Publishing Co., 1968), p. 149.

SELECTED REFERENCES ON TRANSRACIAL ADOPTIONS*

Billingsley, Andrew. "Black Children in White Families,"
Social Work, Vol. 13, No. 4 (October 1968). E. R. Braithwaite's Review of Paid Servant.

Billingsley, Andrew and Jeanne Giovannoni. "Research Perspectives on Interracial Adoptions," in Roger R. Miller,
Editor, Race, Research and Reason: Social Work Perspectives. New York: National Association of Social
Workers, 1969, pp. 57-78.

Boehm, Bernice R. "Adoption," in Encyclopedia of Social
Work. New York: National Association of Social Workers, 1965, p. 66.

Bowman, LeRoy, et al. Children of Tragedy (Report on
Intercountry Orphan Adoption). New York: Church World
Service, National Council of Churches of Christ in the
U.S.A., 1961.

Braithwaite, E. R. Paid Servant. New York: McGraw-Hill,
1968.

Buck, Pearl S. Children For Adoption. New York: Random
House, 1964.

Chambers, Donald E. "Willingness to Adopt Atypical Children," Child Welfare, Vol. XLIX, No. 5 (May 1970), p.
275.

Chakerian, Charles G. Children of Hope. New York: Church
World Service, National Council of Churches of Christ in
the U.S.A., 1968.

Child Welfare League of America. Adoption of Oriental Children by American White Families. New York: Child Wel-

*Prepared by Information Service, Child Welfare League of
America; Rebecca Smith, Director, and Gwen Davis, Librar-
ian.

fare League of America, 1960.

_____. Standards for Adoption (Revised). New York: Child Welfare League of America, 1968.

Davis, Mary J. "One Agency's Approach to the Indian Adoption Project," Child Welfare, Vol. XL, No. 6 (June 1961), pp. 12-15.

Falk, Laurence L. "Identity and the Transracially Adopted Child," Lutheran Social Service, Vol. 9, No. 2 (Summer 1969), pp. 18-25.

_____. "A Comparative Study of Transracial and Interracial Adoption," Child Welfare, Vol. XLIX, No. 2 (February 1970), p. 82.

Fanshel, David. "Indian Adoption Research Project" (News From the Field), Child Welfare, Vol. XLIII, No. 9 (November 1964), pp. 486-488.

Fricke, Harriet. "Interracial Adoption: The Little Revolution," Social Work, Vol. 10, No. 3 (July 1965) pp. 92-97.

Gallagher, Ursula M. "Problems and Progress in Adoption," in Symposium on The Problems in Adoption, January 27-29, 1968, San Francisco, California. (Available from Children's Bureau, Social and Rehabilitation Service, U.S. Department of Health, Education and Welfare, Washington, D.C., 1968.)

Gallay, G. "Interracial Adoptions," Canadian Welfare, Vol. 39, No. 6 (November-December 1963), pp. 248-250.

Graham, Lloyd B. "Children from Japan in American Adoptive Homes," in Casework Papers 1957. New York: Family Service Association of America, 1957, pp. 130-145.

Grossman, Susan J. "A Child of Different Color: Race as a Factor in Adoption and Custody Proceedings," Buffalo Law Review, Vol. 17, No. 2 (Winter 1968), pp. 303-347.

Haight, Frances. "The Development of an Interracial Program (A Board Member Speaks)," Child Welfare, Vol. XXXII, No. 5 (May 1953), pp. 11-12.

Isaac, Rael Jean. Adopting a Child Today. New York:
Harper and Row, 1965.

Jenkins, Alma. "Some Evaluative Factors in the Selection
of Adoptive Homes for Indian Children," Child Welfare,
Vol. XL, No. 6 (June 1961), pp. 16-20.

Lyslo, Arnold. "Adoption for American Indian Children,"
Child Welfare, Vol. XXXIX, No. 6 (June 1960), pp. 32-33.

_____. "Adoptive Placement of American Indian Chil-
dren with Non-Indian Families, Part I - The Indian Project," Child Welfare, Vol. XL, No. 5 (May 1961), pp. 4-6.

_____. "The Indian Adoption Project--An Appeal to
Catholic Agencies to Participate," Catholic Charities Review, Vol. 48, No. 5 (May 1964), pp. 12-16.

_____. "Adoptive Placement of Indian Children," Cath-
olic Charities Review, Vol. 51, No. 2 (February 1967),
pp. 23-25.

Marmor, Judd. "Psychodynamic Aspects of Transracial
Adoptions," Social Work Practice, 1964, Selected Papers,
National Conference on Social Welfare. New York: Co-
lumbia University Press, 1964, pp. 200-209.

McDermott, Robert E. "Oriental Adoptive Placements,"
Catholic Charities Review, Vol. 49, No. 4 (April 1965),
pp. 24-25.

Mitchell, Marion M. "Transracial Adoptions: Philosophy
and Practice," Child Welfare, Vol. XLVIII, No. 10 (December 1969), pp. 613-619.

Nordlie, Esther B. and Sheldon C. Reed. "Follow-Up on
Adoption Counseling for Children of Possible Racial Ad-
mixture," Child Welfare, Vol. XLI, No. 7 (September
1962), pp. 297-304, 327.

PAMY (Parents to Adopt Minority Youngsters). Final Report: PAMY's Progress (1957-1963). St. Paul, Minn.:
Minnesota Department of Public Welfare, June 1963.

Rathbun, Constance and Ralph L. Kolodny. "A Group Work
Approach in Cross-Cultural Adoptions," Children, Vol. 14,
No. 3 (May-June 1967), pp. 117-121.

Raynor, Lois. "Extending Adoption Opportunities for Negro Children," Child Welfare, Vol. XXXII, No. 4 (April 1953), pp. 3-7.

Sarmiento, I. M. "Adoption Week: A Publicity Project in Adoptive Recruitment," Child Welfare, Vol. XLVIII, No. 1 (March 1969), pp. 166-169.

Schapiro, H. L. "Anthropology and Adoption Practice" in Child Welfare League of America, A Study of Adoption Practice, Vol. II (April 1956), pp. 34-38.

Sellers, Martha G. "Transracial Adoption," Child Welfare, Vol. XLVII, No. 6 (June 1969), pp. 355-356, 366.

Turitz, Zitha R. "A New Look at Adoption: Current Developments in the Philosophy and Practice of Adoption" in Source Book of Teaching Materials on the Welfare of Children. New York: Council on Social Work Education, 1969, p. 68.

Valk, Margaret A. Korean-American Children in American Adoptive Homes. New York: Child Welfare League of America, 1957.

_____. "Adoption Service," Children, Vol. 14, No. 5 (September-October 1967), p. 204.

Magazine Articles

"Color and Custody," Time, (November 1, 1968), p. 70.

Dolliver, Barbara. "We're the Lucky Ones!" Good Housekeeping, (December 1969), p. 90.

Feinstein, Phyllis. "A Report on Interracial Adoption," Parents' Magazine (December 1968), p. 48.

Gordon, Stanley. "A Rare Lesson About Love," Look Magazine (March 23, 1965).

King, Helen H. "It's Easier to Adopt Today," Ebony, Vol. XXVI, No. 2 (December 1970), p. 120.

MacDermot, Anne. "We Adopted a Negro," MacLean's Magazine (Canada), (November 19, 1960).

"Mixed Adoptions," Newsweek, (April 24, 1967).

Shepherd, Elizabeth. "Adopting Negro Children: White Families Find it Can Be Done," The New Republic (June 20,
1964).

Silberman, Arlene. "When Noel Came Home," Good Housekeeping, (July 1965).

_____. "My Forty-Five Indian Godchildren," Good
Housekeeping (August 1966).

"Won't Somebody Please Love Me?" Sepia Magazine, (September 1969).

Reports

Frontiers in Adoption: Finding Homes for the Hard to Place.
Joyce Forsythe, editor. Printed by the Michigan Department of Social Services. (Available through COAC Office,
1205 Olivia, Ann Arbor.) (1968) 140 pp.

Mixed Race Adoptions--Report on the First International Conference on Transracial Adoption. The Open Door Society,
5 Weredale Park, Montreal 215, Quebec, Canada (1970).

The Family Planner. Syntex Laboratories, 3401 Hillview
Avenue, Palo Alto, California. Vol. 4, No. 1 (November
1970). (This issue, devoted to adoption, includes several
articles on interracial placements.)

APPENDICES

A. Agencies Placing Children Through the Indian Adoption Project

B. Major Variables Used in This Study

C. Child Progress Scale

D. "Self-Reports of Parents Who Have Adopted Indian Children Compared to Those Who Have Adopted Caucasian Children, " by Edgar F. Borgatta and David Fanshel

Appendix A

AGENCIES PLACING CHILDREN THROUGH
THE INDIAN ADOPTION PROJECT

Prepared by Arnold Lyslo

Voluntary Agencies	No. of Children Placed
The Baby Fold Normal, Illinois	1
Children's Aid and Family Service Northampton, Massachusetts	9
Child and Family Service of Springfield Springfield, Massachusetts	1
Children's Aid Society of Pennsylvania Philadelphia, Pennsylvania	1
Children's Bureau of Delaware Wilmington, Delaware	43
Children's Bureau of Indianapolis Indianapolis, Indiana	20
Children's Friend and Service of Rhode Island Providence, Rhode Island	1
Children's Home of Cincinnati Cincinnati, Ohio	1
Children's Home Society of California San Diego, California	1
Children's Service Bureau of Dade County Miami, Florida	7

Voluntary Agencies (continued)	No. of Children Placed
Children's Services of Connecticut Hartford, Connecticut	1
Family and Child Service of Akron Akron, Ohio	2
Family and Child Service of Washington, D.C. Washington, D.C.	1
Family and Children's Service Pittsburgh, Pennsylvania	2
Family and Children's Service of Schenectady Schenectady, New York	2
Iowa Children's Home Society Des Moines, Iowa	8
Jewish Family Service of Erie County Buffalo, New York	2
Jewish Social Service Washington, D.C.	1
Louise Wise Services New York, New York	46
Lutheran Children's Bureau Philadelphia, Pennsylvania	1
Lutheran Children's Friend Society Minneapolis, Minnesota	3
Massachusetts Society for the Prevention of Cruelty to Children Holyoke, Massachusetts	4
Methodist Children's Home Cincinnati, Ohio	1
New England Home for Little Wanderers Boston, Massachusetts	16

	No. of Children Placed
Voluntary Agencies (continued)	
Child and Family Services of New Hampshire Manchester, New Hampshire	1
Sister Mary Eugene Foundation Teaneck, New Jersey	1
The Spence-Chapin Adoption Service New York, New York	32
Toledo Catholic Charities Toledo, Ohio	2
Vermont Children's Aid Society Burlington, Vermont	4
Welcome House Doylestown, Pennsylvania	3
Woodfield Bridgeport, Connecticut	3
TOTAL	221

Public Agencies	
Arkansas Department of Public Welfare	4
Illinois Department of Children and Family Services	47
Indiana Department of Public Welfare	14
Iowa Department of Social Welfare	16
Louisiana Department of Public Welfare	2
Maine Department of Health and Welfare	2
Maryland Department of Public Welfare	3
Massachusetts Department of Public Welfare	1
Michigan Department of Social Services	2

	No. of Children Placed
Public Agencies (continued)	
Missouri Division of Welfare	39
New Hampshire Department of Health and Welfare, Division of Welfare	2
New York State Department of Social Services	11
Ohio Department of Public Welfare	7
Pennsylvania Department of Public Welfare	8
Puerto Rico Division of Child Welfare	1
Tennessee Department of Public Welfare	1
Vermont Department of Social Welfare	11
Virginia Department of Welfare and Institutions	1
West Virginia Department of Welfare	2
TOTAL	174

Appendix B

MAJOR VARIABLES USED IN THIS STUDY

Name of Variable	Mean and Standard Deviation	Direction	Skewness	Kurtosis
Age of child at place-ment (months)	20.64 (24.56)	--	2.336	6.291
Sex of Child	--	1= boy 2= girl	--	--
Socioeconomic status of the adoptive family	11.58 (3.63)	hi= high status lo= low status	-0.048	-1.255
Adoptive father's age at placement (years)	35.98 (6.20)	--	0.932	2.208

	Mean (SD)	Direction		
Adoptive mother's age at placement (years)	33.33 (5.93)	--	1.4888	5.179
Years adoptive parents married at placement	11.30 (6.98)	--	3.352	20.552
Number of Indian children placed in family	1.45 (0.68)	--	2.003	6.391
Biological mother's disability index	1.97 (1.20)	hi= much disability lo= little disability	0.384	-0.154

Series Two Indexes

Liberal vs. conservative political orientation	24.12 (4.36)	hi= liberal lo= conservative	0.195	-0.6444
Adoptive mothers' life styles	8.43 (1.99)	hi= expanded female role lo= restricted female role	-0.739	-0.3999
Traditional vs. modern female ideology	25.37 (3.42)	hi= modern lo= traditional	0.307	-0.332
Orientation to the adoption of handicapped children	21.07 (4.32)	hi= easily adopted lo= major reservations	-0.532	-0.026

MAJOR VARIABLES USED IN THIS STUDY

Name of Variable	Mean and Standard Deviation	Direction	Skewness	Kurtosis
Orientation to the adoption of children with psychological problems	13.63 (3.49)	hi= easily adopted lo= major reservations	-0.869	-0.701
Orientation to the adoption of Negro children	2.81 (1.63)	hi= easily adopted lo= major reservations	0.866	-0.701
Religiosity of adoptive mothers	2.73 (1.80)	hi= high religiosity lo= low religiosity	1.706	10.271
Strict vs. permissive child rearing	23.42 (4.79)	hi= permissive lo= strict	0.042	-0.736
Security of adoptive mothers' outlook	11.95 (2.73)	hi= cautious lo= optimistic	-0.564	-0.963
Deprivation in adoptive mothers' backgrounds	18.67 (2.42)	hi= high deprivation lo= low deprivation	0.900	1.478
Child's Indian appearance	11.39 (2.80)	hi= looks different lo= does not look different	-0.181	-1.047

	Mean (SD)	Definition		
Child's friendliness-outgoingness	34.558 (4.09)	hi= outgoing lo= retiring or withdrawn	-1.270	0.924
Child activity level	11.12 (2.72)	hi= aggressive lo= passive	-0.101	-0.532
Child adjustment	15.37 (3.04)	hi= low problem lo= high problem	1.063	1.382
Series Three Indexes				
Social problem orientation	20.62 (3.97)	hi= high social concerns lo= low social concerns	-0.135	-1.001
Liberal vs. conservative political orientation	19.35 (2.63)	hi= liberal lo= conservative	-0.124	-0.491
Religiosity of adoptive families	18.66 (5.23)	hi= not religious lo= religious	0.468	-0.452
Lower class-rural background	41.77 (7.12)	hi= lower class-rural lo= middle class-urban	0.100	0.114
Strict vs. permissive child rearing	8.73 (1.84)	hi= permissive lo= strict	0.250	-0.919

MAJOR VARIABLES USED IN THIS STUDY

Name of Variable	Mean and Standard Deviation	Direction	Skewness	Kurtosis
Child's Indian appearance	6.65 (2.19)	hi= looks different lo= does not look different	-0.148	-1.141
Security of parental outlook	11.34 (3.62)	hi= optimistic lo= cautious	-0.340	-0.602
Background support for Indian adoption	10.21 (2.54)	hi= high support lo= low support	0.225	-0.805
Orientation to the adoption of Negro children	3.42 (1.82)	hi= adopted easily lo= major reservations	-0.489	-1.025
Quiet-shy type of child	4.46 (1.57)	hi= quiet-shy lo= noisy-extroverted	0.039	-0.967
Orientation to the adoption of handicapped children	38.20 (6.84)	hi= adopted easily lo= major reservations	-0.823	1.446
Child adjustment	5.17 (1.79)	hi= poorer adjustment lo= better adjustment	0.203	-1.291

Child temperament	11.73 (2.70)	hi= rambunctious lo= quiescent	-0.163	-0.533
Series Four				
Series Four Child Symptom Score	7.99 (5.71)	hi= many symptoms lo= few symptoms	1.496	4.103
Series Five				
Series Five Child Symptom Score	18.02 (8.27)	hi= many symptoms lo= few symptoms	0.376	-0.822
Overall Child Adjustment Rating	2.71 (1.18)	hi= poorer adjustment lo= better adjustment	0.736	-0.146
Home Rating	2.25 (0.93)	hi= poorer home lo= better home	0.752	0.425

APPENDIX C

Indian Adoption Research Project
CHILD PROGRESS SCALE
(Fanshel 1968)

Child's Name:_____   Birthdate:_____

Research Number:_____   Date of
                                Adoptive Placement:_____
Rater:_____
                                Age at Placement:___yrs___mos.
_____
                                Series 1:_____ _____
                                          date   age

                                Series 2:_____ _____
                                          date   age

                                Series 3:_____ _____
                                          date   age

                                Series 4:_____ _____
                                          date   age

                                Series 5:_____ _____
                                          date   age

360

A. PHYSICAL GROWTH AND DEVELOPMENT

This domain covers the child's physical well-being and developmental progress. In the realm of health, focus is upon the presence or absence of disabling health conditions. These include illnesses which may occur episodically as well as conditions of a long standing and chronic nature. The developmental conditions concern such phenomena as physical growth, walking, speech, sleeping, eating and elimination--all related to a perspective of the child as an emerging biological organism.

Problematic Condition (Describe briefly)

Evidenced in Series _____ 1 _____ 2 _____ 3 _____ 4 _____ 5

Problem is rated as:

_____ Serious problem

_____ Moderate problem

_____ Mild problem

Prediction for future course:

_____ Apt to become more serious

_____ Apt to remain stable in present form

_____ Apt to decline in severity or disappear /or has already disappeared

B. INTELLECTUAL AND COGNITIVE COMPETENCE

This domain covers the child's intelligence and intellectual
potential as revealed by the parents' reports of their impressions of his intelligence, his degree of alertness, his reading
readiness, his performance in school (if he is in school).
Include as a problem any condition which may jeopardize the
child's present or subsequent school adjustment (e.g., low
intelligence, thinking disorder, etc.).

Problematic Condition: (Describe briefly)

Evidenced in Series ____ 1 ____ 2 ____ 3 ____ 4 ____ 5

Problem is rated as: Prediction for future course:

____ Serious problem   ____ Apt to become more
                                       serious

____ Moderate problem
                                  ____ Apt to remain stable in
____ Mild problem   present form

                                  ____ Apt to decline in severity
                                       or disappear /or has al-
                                       ready disappeared

C. PERSONALITY CHARACTERISTICS AND BEHAVIORAL PATTERNS

This domain covers pathological elements in the child's personality including psychotic, pre-psychotic and neurotic states, as well as disturbances of character (character disorders). The presence of phobias, deep anxiety states, antisocial behavior, extreme aggressiveness, and like behavior should be noted as problems. Characterological traits are considered problems only if they become dysfunctional for the child in terms of his emotional equilibrium, his sense of well being, and his ability to carry out tasks appropriate for his age and sex.

Problematic Condition (Describe briefly)

Evidenced in Series _____ 1 _____ 2 _____ 3 _____ 4 _____ 5

Problem is rated as: Prediction for future course:

_____ Serious problem   _____ Apt to become more
                                               serious
_____ Moderate problem
                                        _____ Apt to remain stable in
_____ Mild problem   present form

                                        _____ Apt to decline in severity
                                               or disappear /or has al-
                                               ready disappeared

D. SOCIAL RELATIONSHIPS

This domain covers the child's ability to develop satisfying
social ties with other children as well as adults.   The presence of self-isolating tendencies, the selection of inappropriate playmates, insecurity in social situations, excessive
conformity, etc. should be regarded as problems.

Problematic Condition (Describe briefly)

Evidenced in Series _____ 1 _____ 2 _____ 3 _____ 4 _____ 5

Problem is rated as: Prediction for future course:

_____Serious problem   _____Apt to become more
                                         serious
_____Moderate problem
                                    _____Apt to remain stable in
_____Mild problem   present form

                                    _____Apt to decline in severity
                                         or disappear /or has al-
                                         ready disappeared

E. FAMILY RELATIONSHIPS

This domain covers the ability of the adopted child to become integrated within the adoptive family. It refers to tendencies within him rather than the family's attitude towards him (although these are difficult to separate). An adopted child may have problems if he feels the home is not permanently his, if he feels he has a second class status, or he is painfully aware of the contrast in ethnicity between himself and his parents. Problems in relating to either parent or siblings or in accepting parental authority should be noted.

<u>Problematic Condition</u> (Describe briefly)

Evidenced in Series _____1 _____2 _____3 _____4 _____5

Problem is rated as: Prediction for future course:

_____ Serious problem   _____ Apt to become more
                                              serious

_____ Moderate problem
                                        _____ Apt to remain stable in
_____ Mild problem   present form

                                        _____ Apt to decline in severity
                                              or disappear /or has al-
                                              ready disappeared

F. OVERALL ADJUSTMENT RATING

Considering the accumulated information that has been gathered about this child, rate his overall adjustment. An effort should be made to keep this judgment independent of your assessment of the parents.

_____1   Child is making an excellent adjustment in all spheres
           of his life--the outlook for his future adjustment is
           excellent.

_____2

_____3   Child is making an adequate adjustment--his strengths
           outweigh the weaknesses he shows--the outlook for his
           future adjustment is hopeful.

_____4

_____5   Child is making a mixed adjustment--generally the
           problems he faces are serious and the outlook for
           his future adjustment is somewhat guarded.

_____6

_____7   Child is making an extremely poor adjustment--the
           outlook for his future adjustment is unpromising.

G. HOME RATING

Considering the problems the parents have had to face in
caring for this child, make a judgment about the quality of
the home. Try to keep your judgment independent from your
assessment of the child.

A_____   Considering all information secured in the home in-
           terviews, this seems to be the kind of home situation
           one would want a child to have; the kind in which a
           child would have the best opportunity for healthy de-
           velopment.

B_____

C_____   This relates to the kind of home situation in which
           some factors are not as one would like them to be,
           but not the kind that seem likely to be seriously
           harmful to the child.

D_____

E_____   Considering all information secured in the home in-
           terviews, this seems to be the kind of home situation
           from which one would like to protect a child; the kind
           likely to interfere with his happiness and healthy de-
           velopment.

Appendix D

SELF-REPORTS OF PARENTS
WHO HAVE ADOPTED AMERICAN INDIAN CHILDREN
COMPARED TO THOSE
WHO HAVE ADOPTED CAUCASIAN CHILDREN

by

Edgar F. Borgatta
University of Wisconsin

and

David Fanshel
Columbia University School of Social Work and
Child Welfare League of America

dren in a purposive way.   Thus, it may be that such persons
are strongly oriented towards a view that is humanistic and
humanitarian.   They might be firm advocates of a civil liberties and civil rights orientation that is equalitarian.   And,
at a personality level, they might be masochistic, or have
other characteristics which drive them towards this relatively
unusual arrangement for our society.

A third source of hypotheses may be described as the
situational conditions.   For example, it may be that many of
the Indian adoptions occur as relatively incidental and casual
circumstances that arise in communities.   Adoptive parents
may have few peculiarities other than the willingness to take
on a child who is available and has no other home.   Such hypotheses essentially militate against finding differences between the adoptive parents of Indian children and adoptive
parents of other children, suggesting a wide acceptability of
children per se as desirable within the society and a similar
wide variability of tolerance for such "racial" differences
when initial adoption and intimacy within the family is established.

The Current Study

The major study from which these data are drawn is
a longitudinal study of adoptive parents of American Indian
children; the current report emphasizes certain descriptive
aspects of the parents as a group.   In order to make this
description meaningful, however, some standard of comparison is necessary.   The problem here is not to establish that
white adoptive parents of Indian children are different from
the white population at large, or from white parents in general, since to establish such differences begs the question of
whether adoptive parents in general are different from such
populations.   Thus, a comparison group was established for
the adoptive parents of Indian children using the same adoption agencies from which the original sample was drawn.
The agencies were asked to secure the cooperation of adoptive parents of white children to complete a form providing
some data in the areas of values, personality characteristics,
moods, and a minimum of background information.   In theory
such a comparison group would be drawn from the same
sources as the white adoptive parents of Indian children, and
would make a reasonable comparison group.

Adoptive Parents of Indian Children

In the analysis presented here, two basic sets of data are given in parallel. One set is labeled by H and W to indicate matched husband and wife pairs. Not all husbands and not all wives had yet responded to the questionnaire utilized in the data collection, and thus the sample size of 47 husbands and wives is considerably smaller than the 54 males (M) and 72 females (F) who responded from the one hundred project families in which Indian children were adopted. The lesser number of returns from fathers is largely accounted for by the fact that more of them had not yet been seen at the time of this analysis. The father interviews took place in the third year of the placement while the mothers were interviewed during the second. Among the non-project parents, who were the comparison group adopting white children, completion data was much better in the sense that if the family cooperated in providing data, both husbands and wives completed the questionnaires at about the same time. Thus, there were 91 husbands and wives taken as pairs (H and W), and 96 males (M) and 97 females (F) in the comparison group.

Sampling

As is noted above, a limitation is reported in returns from the project parents. Only in half the families had both husband and wife completed the questionnaire. How representative these were of the total group is not easily ascertained, but it will be noted in comparing the W_i and the F_i columns in Tables 1 and 2 that variation of mean response levels is not great.

Examining all of the background data presented in Table 2 reveals that in the families where wives completed questionnaires and husbands did not, the wives were slightly younger and slightly lower on the socioeconomic indicators of education, occupation, and income. These differences, however, would not satisfy ordinary statistical hypothesis testing criteria. The fact that any differences exist, however, leads to a need for cautiousness in interpreting the data. It is not an uncommon phenomenon that those who cooperate in research where questionnaire completion is requested are of higher socioeconomic status and education.

The sample in the non-project families is harder to gauge relative to what it represents. The data were gathered from the same agencies where the Indian adoptions were carried out. However, it is most likely that the cooperating agencies approached the most recent and most available adoptive parents for cooperation in providing the comparison group. Since a number of agencies were involved and detailed records were not kept of who the non-project parents were--completion was anonymous--the sampling biases are not known. Again, however, it may be suspected that some socioeconomic or educational biases may exist with respect to cooperation secured from couples.

With regard to background characteristics which were available from the data, the project parents and the non-project parents differed relatively little. With regard to age, the project parents tended to be slightly older than the non-project parents. The difference for the males is statistically significant both in comparison of the husbands of the project families and the husbands of the non-project families, and in comparing all males of the project families and all males of the non-project families. While in the same direction, the data for the females did not satisfy the arbitrary criteria of significance.[2]

With regard to the socioeconomic indicators of education, occupation, and income, a rather consistent picture is revealed of higher socioeconomic level for the non-project parents, although none of the differences are statistically significant.

Personality Characteristics

In the questionnaire used, three short-form personality inventories were included. The first is the Behavioral Self-Rating Form, and includes five composite scores that are based on self-ratings.[3] No differences occur in the parallel comparisons between project parents and non-project parents. However, some structural differences within the family may exist. Husbands appear to be higher on Assertiveness than wives for both samples, but the difference is greater (and statistically significant) in the non-project families. No differences of substance appear between husbands and wives on the composite score of Likeability. On the self-rating of Intelligence, while no substantial difference is indicated between husbands and wives for the project parents, statistically significant differences occur in the non-project parents, with husbands rating themselves higher on intelligence. With regard to the composite score of Emotionality, the data suggest a possible high Emotionality score for the non-project parents, but the differences do not satisfy the arbitrary criteria of statistical significance used here. In all comparisons, the husband self-ratings are statistically significantly lower on this composite score than the wives. Finally, with regard to the composite score of Responsibility, no statistically significant differences occur. Still, the data are somewhat suggestive in the differences that are noticeable. Namely, for the project parents, the wives tend to be somewhat higher on this composite rating, while the reverse is true for the non-project parents.

As the name implies, the Mood Checklist requests information on the feeling states of the respondents.[4] In the composite score for Affectionate, wives in the project families appear to be somewhat higher than husbands, although the difference is not statistically significant. This appears to be less the case in the non-project families. The additional mood on which some interest may be indicated for future exploration, is in the composite score for Tired. For the project parents the wives appear to be higher than the husbands, while the reverse is true for the non-project parents. Neither of the differences, however, satisfies the arbitrary criteria for statistical significance.

The third short form inventory (S-ident Form) is of a more traditional type, although it uses a relatively small number of items for each composite score.[5] In this more traditional type of personality inventory no differences occur that are interpretable in the comparison of husbands and wives, and it has been previously indicated that no differences existed for the comparison of project parents and non-project parents.

We have not noted the information before, but in Table 1 we also indicate the correlation coefficient between husband and wife scores. The values may be judged, at best, as not being high. The statistically significant values are underlined, and it will be noted that in the self-ratings, there apparently is more consistency for the non-project families, even though it must be emphasized that the consistency is small.

Values

The final set of data presented here are responses to

the segment of the questionnaire which dealt with values.[6] In
our initial expectations about differences that might be found
between the project and non-project families, the main hypotheses we suggested actually dealt with the values these
families would hold. In general, the expectation was that the
project parents, being somewhat "different" in their adoption
of Indian children, would tend to be different in the values
they would hold also. They would be less traditional in orientation, or less conventional with regard to the major institutions of society.

   With regard to the composite score on Adherence to
Authority, that is, acceptance of traditional values of authority, project parents appear to be somewhat lower than non-
project parents. The difference, however, is statistically
significant only for the comparison of the data for wives
(wives considered in parallel or all females considered in
parallel).

   With regard to Need Authority, which is a score com-
posed of two items dealing with the need for more authority
and expectations of obedience from children, no differences
are apparent between the project parents and the non-project
parents. Thus, in the single measure in this form on child-
rearing orientation, no differences occur.

   With regard to Conventional Religiosity, the data appear to indicate lower composite scores for the project parents. Of the four possible comparisons, however, only one
(W_i versus W_w) satisfies the arbitrary criteria for statistical
significance.

   In Adherence to Conventional Sex-Role Structure, differences between project parents and non-project parents are
small, with the non-project parents being somewhat higher.
The difference, however, does not satisfy the arbitrary criteria for statistical significance.

   With regard to Government Laissez-Faire, the project
families are definitely lower on this value than the non-project families, and the differences in all comparisons are statistically significant.

   With regard to Cynical Realism, in each comparison
the project parents appear to be lower than the non-project
parents, but none of the differences achieves a magnitude
large enough to satisfy the arbitrary criteria for statistical

significance. With regard to Fatalism, no interpretable differences occur between the project parents and the non-project parents.

With regard to Civil Liberties Intolerance, project
families are consistently lower on intolerance than non-project families, and all four of the possible comparisons satisfy
the arbitrary criteria for statistical significance. This value
is closely connected with the substantive issue of tolerance
for differences in others which is relevant to the problem of
adopting children of a different race. Thus, the finding is
directly consonant with the expectations. It should be noted,
however, that this is not an indication of causal sequence,
and no implication is made that more tolerance in civil liberties orientation will lead to a higher potential for adoption
of Indian children. To the contrary it is possible that having adopted the Indian children, some additional tolerance enters into the values of the adoptive parents on a post hoc basis.

Four individual items occur in the form which deal
with current issues (rather than values). One of these is an
item which is concerned with the question of separation of
church and state. A second deals with a statement that discrimination is the worst evil of our time. The third deals
with the double standard or traditional standard that women
should not have sexual intercourse before marriage. The
fourth deals with availability of birth control information.
The only differences that were visible in these four items
were in the one dealing with discrimination. Here, as might
be expected, the project parents indicated somewhat higher
belief that discrimination is evil, but the difference satisfied
the arbitrary criteria for statistical significance only for husbands.

Finally, a word needs to be said about the agreement
of husbands and wives on values. Clearly, by examining the
correlation coefficients in Table 2, it will be seen that for
some values there is substantial agreement. The greatest
amount of agreement occurs in those values that may be identified as institutional orientations. The least amount of
agreement occurs on those that might be viewed as life orientations, such as Cynical Realism and Fatalism, which are
sometimes viewed as personality characteristics. Some differences occurred in the amount of agreement for the project
parents when compared to the non-project parents. For example, on Need Authority the project parents appear to have

a substantial amount of agreement, while no correlation is seen for the non-project families. For the project families, there appears to be a high agreement on Civil Liberties Intolerance, while this is less the case for the non-project families. The non-project families appear to be more often in agreement on the birth control issue than is the case with the project families.

General Comments

The nature of this descriptive study must be viewed as exploratory. As we indicated in our introductory remarks, the objective here was to compare white adoptive parents of Indian children with white adoptive parents of white children, the latter representing the more normal situation for society. The expectation was that the white adoptive parents of American Indian children would tend to be less conventional, and possibly more tolerant in orientation. In addition, it was suggested that they might also differ in personality characteristics of a more general nature.

The findings from this descriptive analysis are not entirely clear and consistent. First of all, although the resources required in order to develop the data presented were substantial, the sample sizes are not large. There are sampling deficiencies in the data reported, due in part to the deficiencies in recruitment of respondents. Still, science progresses only by reasonable comparison when full controls are not possible, and this descriptive study moves in the direction of a plausible set of comparisons. With these implicit limitations, it may be judged that the differences that would have been expected are indeed found. The differences, however, are representative of tendencies, and are not to be considered as discrete and dramatic.

Notes

1. Alfred Kadushin, "A Study of Adoptive Parents of Hard-to-Place Children," Social Casework, May 1962.

2. Statistical significance here will indicate that if a symmetric statistical hypothesis were tested at the .05 level, the hypothesis of no difference would be rejected.

3. Edgar F. Borgatta, "A Very Short Test of Personality:
    The Behavioral Self-Rating (BSR) Form, " Psycholog-
    ical Reports, 1964, 14, pp. 275-284.

4. Edgar F. Borgatta, "Mood, Personality, and Interaction, "
    Journal of General Psychology, 1961, 64, pp. 105-137.

5. Edgar F. Borgatta, "A Short Test of Personality: The
    S-ident Form, " Journal of Educational Psychology,
    1965, 63, pp. 309-317.

6. Data on the values of this particular form have never
    been published. Reference should be internal to the
    particular analysis, and otherwise to personal com-
    munication with Dr. Edgar F. Borgatta.

Table 1

PERSONALITY SCORES FOR PROJECT AND NON-PROJECT PARENTS

	Project Parents				Non-Project Parents				r_i	r_w
	H_i	W_i	M_i	F_i	H_w	W_w	M_w	F_w		
Number of Cases	47	47	54	72	91	91	96	97	47	91
Behavioral Self Rating										
Assertiveness	15.1	14.2	14.9	14.4	16.3	14.3	16.3	14.4	-.10	.23
Likeability	20.6	21.1	20.6	20.5	20.5	20.9	20.4	20.6	.11	.24
Intelligence	28.2	28.3	28.5	27.9	29.1	27.7	29.0	27.3	.14	.39
Emotionality	13.4	15.6	13.4	16.1	14.2	17.6	14.4	17.5	.19	.13
Responsibility	29.6	30.2	29.6	30.0	30.3	29.6	30.3	29.3	.09	.33
Mood Checklist										
Insecure	5.5	5.0	5.3	5.0	5.3	5.1	5.3	5.1	.25	.09
Affectionate	12.0	12.8	11.9	12.9	12.5	12.6	12.4	12.6	.25	.20
Tired	6.7	7.4	6.8	7.5	7.7	7.0	7.7	6.9	.04	.14
Concentration	13.0	13.4	13.0	13.5	13.5	13.2	13.5	13.2	.26	.05
Defiant	4.5	4.3	4.5	4.2	4.6	4.0	4.6	4.0	.15	.04
Shocked	3.7	3.7	3.7	3.7	3.7	3.7	3.7	3.7	.26	.31

PERSONALITY SCORES FOR PROJECT AND NON-PROJECT PARENTS

S-ident Personality Scores	Project Parents				Non-Project Parents				r_i	r_w
	H_i	W_i	M_i	F_i	H_w	W_w	M_w	F_w		
Leadership	4.1	3.5	4.1	3.5	3.9	3.8	3.9	3.8	.13	-.12
Impulsivity	15.3	15.5	15.3	15.4	14.9	14.8	15.0	14.8	-.21	.07
Intellectual	7.6	8.0	7.7	8.0	7.5	8.1	7.5	8.1	.16	.16
Aloofness	12.7	12.7	12.7	12.6	12.9	12.1	12.9	12.1	-.06	-.10
Self-Deprecation	23.3	23.3	23.5	23.0	23.4	23.4	23.5	23.4	.17	-.10
Lack of Tension	13.8	14.0	13.9	14.0	13.5	14.3	13.5	14.3	-.10	-.10

H = Husbands
W = Wives
M = Males
F = Females
i = Indian children
w = White children

Table 2

VALUE SCORES AND BACKGROUND INFORMATION FOR PROJECT AND NON-PROJECT PARENTS

	Project Parents				Non-Project Parents					
	H_i	W_i	M_i	F_i	H_w	W_w	M_w	F_w	r_i	r_w
Number of Cases	47	47	54	72	91	91	96	97	47	91
Values										
Adherence to authority	60.6	60.3	60.6	60.6	61.0	61.7	61.0	61.6	.41	.50
Need authority	56.0	56.0	56.0	56.1	56.3	56.4	56.3	56.4	$\overline{.46}$	$\overline{.00}$
Conventional religiosity	55.2	54.7	55.1	55.5	56.1	56.4	56.0	56.4	$\overline{.72}$	.70
Adherence to conventional sex-role structure	60.0	60.0	60.0	60.2	60.7	60.7	60.7	60.7	.50	.52
Government laissez-faire	47.8	47.7	48.0	48.1	49.3	49.2	49.2	49.2	$\overline{.60}$	$\overline{.59}$
Cynical realism	57.2	56.5	57.2	56.7	57.8	57.1	57.8	57.0	$\overline{.16}$	$\overline{.11}$
Fatalism	55.9	56.3	56.0	56.4	56.0	56.2	56.0	56.3	.08	.19
Civil liberties intolerance	59.6	60.2	59.9	60.6	61.2	61.5	61.1	61.5	.60	.25
Non-separation, church-state	46.9	47.0	46.8	47.1	47.0	47.3	47.0	47.3	$\overline{.23}$	$\overline{.38}$
Discrimination is evil	53.3	53.4	53.2	53.3	52.6	53.0	52.6	53.1	.15	$\overline{.14}$
Sexual restriction	52.9	53.0	52.9	53.3	53.2	53.4	53.2	53.4	.39	.40
Birth control	53.7	53.6	53.8	53.5	53.4	53.6	53.6	53.6	$\overline{.01}$	$\overline{.51}$
Background Information										
Age (coded)	5.3	4.7	5.3	4.5	4.7	4.3	4.7	4.4	.71	.69
Education (coded)	5.3	5.0	5.4	4.7	5.6	5.2	5.6	5.2	.78	.49
Occupation (coded)	7.4	7.3	7.4	7.0	7.5	7.3	7.5	7.2	.76	.82
Income (coded)	4.2	4.1	4.3	3.9	4.3	4.2	4.3	4.2	.82	.87